Explainable Machine Learning Models and Architectures

Scrivener Publishing
100 Cummings Center, Suite 541J
Beverly, MA 01915-6106

Engineering Systems Design for Sustainable Development

Series Editor: Suman Lata Tripathi, PhD

Scope: A multidisciplinary approach is the foundation of this series, meant to intensify related research focuses and to achieve the desired goal of sustainability through different techniques and intelligent approaches. This series will cover the information from the ground level of engineering fundamentals leading to smart products related to design and manufacturing technologies including maintenance, reliability, security aspects, and waste management. The series will provide the opportunity for the academician and industry professional alike to share their knowledge and experiences with practitioners and students. This will result in sustainable developments and support to a good and healthy environment.

Publishers at Scrivener
Martin Scrivener (martin@scrivenerpublishing.com)
Phillip Carmical (pcarmical@scrivenerpublishing.com)

Explainable Machine Learning Models and Architectures

Edited by

Suman Lata Tripathi

and

Mufti Mahmud

Scrivener
Publishing

WILEY

This edition first published 2023 by John Wiley & Sons, Inc., 111 River Street, Hoboken, NJ 07030, USA and Scrivener Publishing LLC, 100 Cummings Center, Suite 541J, Beverly, MA 01915, USA
© 2023 Scrivener Publishing LLC
For more information about Scrivener publications please visit www.scrivenerpublishing.com.

Wiley Global Headquarters
111 River Street, Hoboken, NJ 07030, USA

For details of our global editorial offices, customer services, and more information about Wiley products visit us at www.wiley.com.

Limit of Liability/Disclaimer of Warranty

Library of Congress Cataloging-in-Publication Data

ISBN 9781394185849

Front cover images supplied by Pixabay.com
Cover design by Russell Richardson

Set in size of 11pt and Minion Pro by Manila Typesetting Company, Makati, Philippines

Printed in the USA

10 9 8 7 6 5 4 3 2 1

Contents

Preface

Machine learning and deep learning modules are now an integral part of many smart and automated systems where signal processing is performed at different levels. Signal processing in the form of text, image or video needs large data computational operations at the desired data rate and accuracy. Large data requires more use of integrated circuit (IC) area with embedded bulk memories that further lead to more IC area. Trade-offs between power consumption, delay and IC area are always a concern of designers and researchers. New hardware architectures and accelerators are needed to explore with efficient machine learning models. Many real-time applications like processing of biomedical data in healthcare, smart transportation, satellite image analysis, and IoT-enabled systems still have a lot of scope for improvements in terms of accuracy, speed, computational powers and overall power consumption. The current proposal deals with the efficient machine and deep learning models that support high-speed processors with reconfigurable architectures like graphic processing units (GPUs) and Field programmable gate arrays (FPGAs) or any hybrid system.

This book will cover the hardware architecture implementation of the machine algorithm. The software implementation approach and efficient hardware of the machine learning application with FPGA will be the distinctive feature of the book. Security in biomedical signal processing will also be a key focus.

Acknowledgements

Authors would like to thank School of Electronics and Electrical Engineering, Lovely Professional University, Phagwara, India, Department of Computer Science & Information Technology, Nottingham Trent University, Nottingham, UK for providing necessary facilities required for completing this book. Authors would also like to thanks to researchers from different organizations like IIT, NIT, Government and Private Universities and Colleges etc. who are contributing their chapters in this book.

A Comprehensive Review of Various Machine Learning Techniques

Pooja Pathak* and Parul Choudhary†

Dept. of Computer Engineering and Applications, GLA University, Mathura, India

Abstract

The creation of an intelligent system that works like a human is due to Artificial intelligence (AI). It can be broadly classified into four techniques: machine learning, machine vision, automation and Robotics and natural language processing. These domains can learn from data provided, identify the hidden pattern and make decisions with human intervention. There are three types of machine learning: supervised learning, unsupervised learning, and reinforcement learning. Thus, to reduce the risk factor while decision making, machine learning techniques are more beneficial. The benefit of machine learning is that it can do the work automatically, once it learns what to do. Therefore, in this work, we discuss the theory behind machine learning techniques and the tasks they perform such as classification, regression, clustering, etc. We also provide a review of the state of the art of several machine learning algorithms like Naive Bayes, random forest, K-Means, SVM, etc., in detail.

Keywords: Machine learning, classification, regression, recognition, clustering, etc.

1.1 Introduction

Machine learning spans IT, statistics, probability, AI, psychology, neurobiology, and other fields. Machine learning solves problems by creating a model that accurately represents a dataset. Teaching computers to mimic

---

Corresponding author: Pooja.pathak@gla.ac.in
†*Corresponding author*: parul.choudhary_phd.cs20@gla.ac.in

Suman Lata Tripathi and Mufti Mahmud (eds.) Explainable Machine Learning Models and Architectures, (1–10) © 2023 Scrivener Publishing LLC

the human brain has advanced machine learning and expanded the field of statistics to include statistical computational theories of learning processes.

Machine learning is the subdomain of artificial intelligence. There are two subsets of AI – machine learning and deep learning. Machine learning can effectively work on small datasets and it takes less time for training, while deep learning can work on large datasets and it takes more time for training. Machine learning has three types—supervised, unsupervised and reinforcement learning. Supervised learning algorithms such as neural networks are worked with labelled datasets. Unsupervised learning algorithms such as clustering, etc., are worked with unlabeled datasets. Machine learning algorithms are grouped by desired outcome.

Supervised learning: Algorithms map inputs to outputs. The classification problem is a standard supervised learning task. The learner must learn a function that maps a vector into one of several classes by looking at input-output examples. Unsupervised learning models unlabeled inputs. Semi-supervised learning combines labelled and unlabeled examples to create a classifier. Reinforcement learning teaches an algorithm how to act based on data. Every action affects the environment, which guides the learning algorithm. Transduction is similar to supervised learning but does not explicitly construct a function. Instead, it predicts new outputs based on training inputs, training outputs, and new inputs. The algorithm learns its own inductive bias from past experience.

Machine learning algorithms are divided into supervised and unsupervised groups. Classes are predetermined in supervised algorithms. These classes are created as a finite set by humans, which labels a segment of data. Machine learning algorithms find patterns and build math models. These models are evaluated based on their predictive ability and data variance [1].

In this chapter, we review some techniques of machine learning algorithms and elaborate on them.

1.1.1 Random Forest

To realise AI, machine learning is the most powerful technique. There are several algorithms in machine learning, out of which random forest is considered as a group classification technique algorithm known for its effectiveness and simplicity. The Proximities, Out-of-bag error, Variable Importance Measure, etc., are the important features of it. An algorithm based on ensemble learning and belonging to supervised learning can be used for regression and classification. The classifier can be called a "Decision Tree Classifier" from which it chooses the best tree as the final classification tree via voting. Note that as the number of trees increases in a forest, it gives high accuracy and prevents overfitting problems. Random forest algorithm is chosen because it takes less training time, it runs efficiently for a large dataset to predict output with highest accuracy and it maintain accuracy even if a big proportion of data is missing. Figure 1.1 shows a diagram of this algorithm.

Working: It is divided into two phases: first, it combines N-decision trees to create a random forest. And second, it predicts each tree that was created in the first step.

Step 1: First, choose k data points at random from the training dataset.
Step 2: Decision trees are to be built with selected subsets.
Step 3: Then choose any number of trees which we need to build and repeat steps 1 and 2. The random forest algorithm is used in four major sectors: medicine, banking, marketing, and land use. Although it is sometimes mentioned that this algorithm is for regression and classification, that is not true; random forest is good for regression only [2].

1.1.2 Decision Tree

Decision tree [3] represents a classifier expressed as a recursive partition of the instance space. The decision tree is a distributed tree with a root node and no incoming edges.

All of the other nodes have exactly one incoming edge. Internal or test nodes have outgoing edges. The rest are leaves. Each test node in a decision tree divides the instance space into two or more sub-spaces based on input

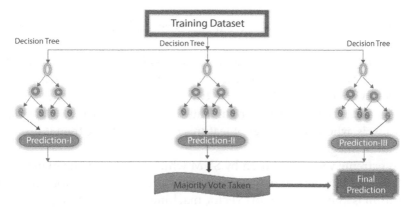

Figure 1.1 Architecture of random forest.

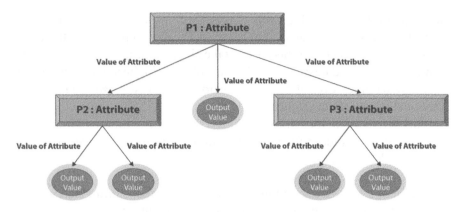

Figure 1.2 Decision tree.

values. In the simplest case, each test considers a single attribute, such that the instance space is portioned according to the attribute's value. In case of numeric attributes, the condition refers to a range. Each leaf is assigned the best target class. The leaf may hold a probability vector that indicates the probability of the target attribute having a certain value. Navigating from the tree's root to the leaf classifies instances based on tests along the way. Figure 1.2 shows a basic decision tree. Each node's branch is labelled with the attribute it tests. Given this classifier, an analyst can predict the customer and understand their behaviour [4].

1.1.3   Support Vector Machine

SVM kernel is the name of a function that transforms low-dimensional space to high-dimensional space. Non-linear separation problems can be solved using this kernel.

The main advantage of SVM is that it is very effective in a high dimension case.

SVM is used for regression as well as classification but primarily it is best for classification purpose; the main purpose is to find distinct input features by hyperplane. If there are two input features then there is only one line and if there are three input features then hyperplane is 2-D plane. The draw is, when the number of features exceeds by three then it becomes difficult to imagine [5].

An extreme vector is chosen by SVM which helps to create hyperplane. Vectors which are nearer to hyperplane are called support vectors; thus, the algorithm is known as support vector machine, illustrated in Figure 1.3.

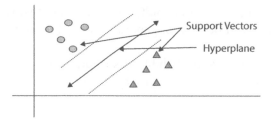

Figure 1.3 Support vector model.

Example: SVM can be understood with an example.

A classification of dog and cat images can be easily done by SVM. In this case, first we train the model and then we apply testing with a creature. Cat and dog are two data points which are distinguished by one hyperplane. If there are extreme cases of cat, then it will classify cat; otherwise dog is to be classified.

There are two types of SVM kernel—linear and non-linear.

In linear SVM, dataset is classified into two classes using one hyperplane; such data is called linearly separable data. While in non-linear, dataset is not classified in one hyperplane; this data is called non-linear data.

1.1.4 Naive Bayes

Naive Bayes is based on Bayes theorem in classification technique. It is one of the methods in supervised learning algorithms and statistical method. But it is used for both clustering and classification depending on conditional probabilities that happen [6].

Let us assume one probabilistic model which allows to capture uncertainty by determining the probabilities of an outcome. The main reason for using Naive Bayes is that it can solve predictive problems; also, it evaluates learning algorithms. It obtains practical algorithms and can merge all observed data [7].

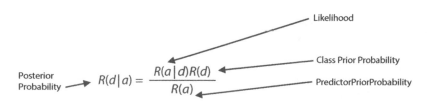

Figure 1.4 Naive Bayes.

Let's consider a general probability distribution of two values R(a1, a2). Using Bayes rule, without loss of generality we get this equation in Figure 1.4.

Considering a general probability distribution of two values R(a1,a2). We obtain without any loss of generality an equation [8].

1.1.5   K-Means Clustering

It is one of the clustering techniques in unsupervised learning algorithm. It classifies number of clusters from given dataset; and for each cluster, k centers are defined [9] as shown in Figure 1.5. This k centers are placed in a calculated way due to various locations which cause different results. Hence the better way is to place each cluster away from the others.

1.1.6   Principal Component Analysis

It is used to convert a set of observation of correlated variables to linearly uncorrelated variable. PCA shown in Figure 1.6 is a statistical process which uses orthogonal transformation. The data dimension is reduced for making the computations faster as well as easier, which is why the process is called "dimensionality-reduction technique". Through the linear combinations, it explains the structure of variance-covariance set of variables [10].

1.1.7   Linear Regression

The linear regression1 algorithm finds relationships and dependencies between variables. It models the relationship between a continuous scalar dependent variable z (also label or target) and one or more (a D-dimensional vector) explanatory variables denoted X using a linear

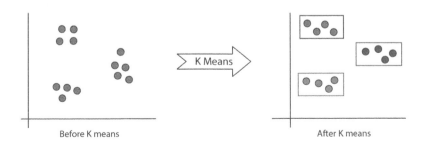

Figure 1.5 Clustering in K-means.

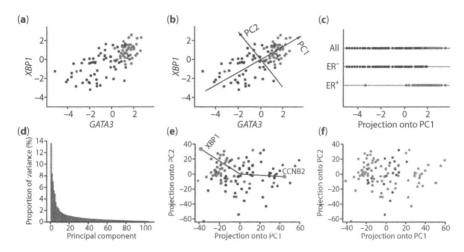

Figure 1.6 Principle component analysis [11].

function. Regression analysis predicts a continuous target variable, while classification predicts a label from a finite set. Multiple regression model with linear input variables is:

$$z = B_0 + B_1 x_1 + B_2 x_2 + \ldots\ldots + e \qquad (1.1)$$

supervised learning algorithms include linear regression [11]. We train the model on labelled data (training data) and use it to predict labels on unlabeled data (testing data).

Figure 1.7 shows how the model (red line) fits training data (blue points) with known labels (z axis) as accurately as possible by minimizing a loss function. We can use the model to predict unknown labels (x value, z value).

1.1.8 Logistic Regression

Like Naive Bayes, logistic regression [12] extracts a set of weighted features from the input, logs them, and adds them linearly. It is a discriminative classifier, while Naive

Bayes is generative. The logistic regression diagram in Figure 1.7 predicts event probability by fitting data to a logistic function. It uses several numerical or categorical predictor variables.

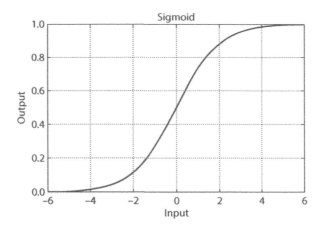

Figure 1.7 Visual representation of the logistic function [14].

Its hypothesis is defined as,

$$A_b\left(y\right)=d\left(b^T\,y\right)$$

Where d is sigmoid function defined as,

$$d(z)=\frac{1}{1+e^{-z}}$$

In machine learning, we use a built-in function called fmin bfgs2 to find the minimum of this cost function given a fixed dataset. Parameters are initial values of parameters to be optimized and a function that, given the training set and a particular, computes the logistic regression cost and gradient with respect to for the x and y dataset. Final value is used to plot training data decision boundary.

1.1.9   Semi-Supervised Learning

Semi-supervised learning combines supervised and unsupervised methods. It can be useful in machine learning and data mining where unlabeled data is present and labelling it is tedious. With supervised machine learning, you train an algorithm on a "labelled" dataset with outcome information [13].

1.1.10 Transductive SVM

TSVM is widely used for semi-supervised learning with partially labelled data. Its generalizations have been a source of mystery. It labels unlabeled data so the margin between them is maximum. TSVM is NP-hard [14].

1.1.11 Generative Models

Data-generating models are generative. It models features and class (complete data). All algorithms modelling P (x, y) are generative because I can use its probability distribution to generate data points. One labelled sample per component confirms mixture distribution.

1.1.12 Self-Training

A classifier self-trains using labelled data. Unlabeled data feeds the classifier. The training set combines unlabeled and predicted labels. It's repeated. The classifier self-trains, hence the name [15].

1.1.13 Relearning

Reinforcement learning focuses on how software agents should act to maximise cumulative reward. Reinforcement learning is one of three basic machine learning paradigms [16, 17].

1.2 Conclusions

In this chapter we survey some algorithms of machine learning. When we have less amount of labelled data then machine learning would be best. In the future we will review

Reinforcement learning. Today, each person uses machine learning algorithm, whether knowingly or unknowingly.

This chapter summarizes supervised learning algorithms and explains machine learning. It also describes machine learning algorithm structures. This area has seen a lot of development in the last decade. The learning methods produced excellent results that were impossible in the past. Due to rapid progress, developers can improve supervised learning methods and algorithms.

References

1. Carbonell, Jaime G., Ryszard S. Michalski, and Tom M. Mitchell. An overview of machine learning. *Machine Learning* (1983): 3-23.
2. Mahesh, Batta. Machine learning algorithms-a review. *International Journal of Science and Research (IJSR)*. [Internet] 9 (2020): 381-386.
3. Ayodele, Taiwo Oladipupo. Types of machine learning algorithms. *New Advances in Machine Learning* 3 (2010): 19-48.
4. Ray, Susmita. A quick review of machine learning algorithms. *2019 International Conference on Machine Learning, Big Data, Cloud and Parallel Computing (COMITCon)*. IEEE, 2019.
5. Vabalas, Andrius, *et al.* Machine learning algorithm validation with a limited sample size. *PloS one* 14.11 (2019): e0224365.
6. Tom Mitchell, McGraw Hill (2015) *Machine Learning.*
7. S. B. Kotsiantis. (2007) Supervised Machine Learning: A Review of Classification Techniques. In *Proceedings of the 2007 Conference on Emerging Artificial Intelligence Applications in Computer Engineering: Real Word AI Systems with Applications in eHealth, HCI, Information Retrieval and Pervasive Technologies, The Netherlands.*
8. Amanpreet Singh, Narina Thakur, Aakanksha Sharma (2016). A review of supervised machine learning algorithms. In *Computing for Sustainable Global Development (INDIACom), 2016 3rd International Conference on.*
9. http://www.slideshare.net/GirishKhanzode/supervised-learning-52218215
10. https://www.researchgate.net/publication/221907660_Types_of_Machine_Learning_Algorithms
11. http://radimrehurek.com/data_science_python/
12. http://www.slideshare.net/cnu/machine-learning-lecture-3 An overview of the supervised machine learning methods
13. http://gerardnico.com/wiki/data_mining/simple_regression
14. http://aimotion.blogspot.mk/2011/11/machine-learning-with-python-logistic.html
15. Dasari L. Prasanna; Suman Lata Tripathi, "Machine and Deep-Learning Techniques for Text and Speech Processing," in *Machine Learning Algorithms for Signal and Image Processing*, IEEE, 2023, pp. 115-128, doi: 10.1002/9781119861850.ch7
16. Kanak Kumar; Kaustav Chaudhury; Suman Lata Tripathi, "Future of Machine Learning (ML) and Deep Learning (DL) in Healthcare Monitoring System," in *Machine Learning Algorithms for Signal and Image Processing* , IEEE, 2023, pp. 293-313, doi:10.1002/9781119861850.ch17.
17. Deepika Ghai, Suman Lata Tripathi, Sobhit Saxena, Manash Chanda, Mamoun Alazab, *Machine Learning Algorithms for Signal and Image Processing*, Wiley IEEE Press-2022, ISBN: 978-1-119-86182-9

Artificial Intelligence and Image Recognition Algorithms

Siddharth[1]*, Anuranjana[1] and Sanmukh Kaur[2]

*[1]Dept. of Information Technology, Amity School of Engineering and Technology,
Amity University Uttar Pradesh, Noida, India
[2]Dept. of Electronics and Communication Engineering, Amity School of Engineering
and Technology, Amity University Uttar Pradesh, Noida, India*

Abstract

Various computer vision tasks, including video object tracking and image detection/classification, have been successfully achieved using feature detectors and descriptors. In various phases of the detection-description pipeline, many techniques use picture gradients to characterize local image structures. In recent times, convolutional neural networks (CNNs) have taken the place of some or all these algorithms that reply and detectors and descriptors. Earlier algorithms, such as the Harris Corner Detector, SIFT, ASIFT and SURF that were once hailed as cutting-edge image recognition algorithms have now been replaced by something more robust. This document highlights the generational improvement in image recognition algorithms and draws a contrast between current CNN-based image recognition techniques and previous state-of-the-art algorithms that don't rely on CNN. The purpose of this study is to emphasize the necessity of using CNN-based algorithms over traditional algorithms which are not as dynamic.

Keywords: Convolution Neural Networks (CNN), Scale Invariant Feature Transform (SIFT), Artificial Intelligence (AI), Speeded Up Robust Features (SURF)

*Corresponding author: siddharthkumar195@gmail.com

Suman Lata Tripathi and Mufti Mahmud (eds.) Explainable Machine Learning Models and Architectures, (11–30) © 2023 Scrivener Publishing LLC

2.1   Introduction

The rising capabilities of artificial intelligence in areas like high-level thinking and sensory handling have made it more revered than human intelligence. Its encounter nature excels in every significant aspect of the supervisory environment. The sole focus of critics since the advent of the fifth computing period has been to pretend that the brain-computer is viable and dynamic [1]. The capacity for computers to decode and identify the contents of the billions of photographs and millions of hours of video that are published on the internet each year is a challenge that has immense importance. However, there has been a lot of study on deriving high-level information from raw pixel data.

Many conventional techniques rely on the discovery and extraction of significant key points. Numerous techniques have been put forth to find and describe characteristics mentioned in [2, 3]. SIFT and ASIFT [4], which are built on and improved upon from Harris Corner Detector [5], are two of the most often used techniques along with SURF [6]. The image matching algorithms usually consist of two parts: detector and descriptor. They first detect points of interest in the compared images and select a region around each point of interest, and then associate an invariant descriptor or feature to each region. Similarities may thus be established by matching the descriptors. Detectors and descriptors should be as invariant as possible [3].

For identifying and categorizing features, researchers have proposed Convolution Neural Network–based algorithms in recent years [7]. CNNs have been effectively employed to tackle challenging issues like speech recognition and image classification. They were first introduced by Fukushimain in 1998. CNNs are made up of neurons, and each one determines the learning's weight and inclination. It also includes an information level, a yield layer, and various hidden layers, where the hidden layer includes standardized layers such as convolutional, pooling, and fully associated layers [10]. The convolutional layer connects two data arrangements using a convolution activity. It pretends to be a certain neuron's input for visual enhancements. The pooling layer is used to reduce the dimensions by partnering the yield of the neuron cluster at a single layer with one neuron [8].

This paper highlights the transition between CNN-based and traditional image detection algorithms. We also draw a contrast between the two methods and why CNNs are preferred over the traditional image recognition/classification methods.

2.2   Traditional Image Recognition Algorithms

Traditional image recognition algorithms consist of a detector and descriptor vector. Before assigning an invariant descriptor or feature to each region, they first identify places of interest in the compared pictures and choose a region surrounding each one. Thus, by matching the descriptors, correspondences can be found. It is best if detectors and descriptors are as invariant as feasible [3].

2.2.1   Harris Corner Detector (1988)

It is a mathematical approach to extracting corners in an image and deducing features in an image. This was first introduced in 1988 and since then it has been used in many algorithms. Determining corners is done by calculating the change in intensity of an image. It is calculated using the eq below which is derived using the Taylor function for the 2D equation.

$$E(u,v) = \sum_{x,y} \underbrace{w(x,y)}_{\text{window function}} \left[\underbrace{I(x+u, y+v)}_{\text{shifted intensity}} - \underbrace{I(x,y)}_{\text{intensity}} \right]^2 \qquad (2.1)$$

Where the term $I\ x + u,\ y + v$ represents the shifted/new intensity and the shift is u and v and $I\ u,\ v$ represents the original intensity.

The above equation can be rewritten in the matrix form as follows,

$$E(u,v) \approx \begin{bmatrix} u & v \end{bmatrix} M \begin{bmatrix} u \\ v \end{bmatrix} \qquad (2.2)$$

Where the M in the above equation is

$$M = \sum_{x,y} w(x,y) \begin{bmatrix} I_x I_x & I_x I_y \\ I_x I_y & I_y I_y \end{bmatrix} \qquad (2.3)$$

We then next calculate the trace and determinant of matrix **M** to find **R**, where **R** is:

$$R = \det(M) - k(\text{trace}(M))^2 \tag{2.4}$$

where,

- $\det(\mathbf{M}) = \lambda 1 \lambda 2$
- $\text{trace}(\mathbf{M}) = \lambda 1 + \lambda 2$
- $\lambda 1$ and $\lambda 2$ are the eigenvalues of **M**

So, the magnitudes of these eigenvalues decide whether a region is a corner, an edge, or flat.

- When |**R**| is small, which happens when $\lambda 1$ and $\lambda 2$ are small, the region is flat.
- When **R**<0, which happens when $\lambda 1 >> \lambda 2$ or vice versa, the region is edge.
- When **R** is large, which happens when $\lambda 1$ and $\lambda 2$ are large and $\lambda 1 \sim \lambda 2$, the region is a corner.

A simple mathematical method for identifying which windows exhibit significant differences when moved in any direction is the Harris Corner Detector. Each window has a score R connected to it. We determine which ones are corners and which ones are not based on this score [5]. The Harris Corner Detector is found to be invariant to translation, rotation, and illumination changes [11], but not scale invariant, as well see some algorithms

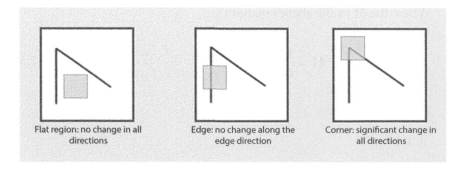

Flat region: no change in all directions   Edge: no change along the edge direction   Corner: significant change in all directions

Figure 2.1 Visualizing corner detection.

that adopted and improved on Harris corner detector (the most famous one being SIFT) [12]. Figure 2.1 above, shows the region variance from flat region to edge and then to a corner region.

2.2.2   SIFT (2004)

In SIFT algorithm (Scale-invariant feature transform) image processing and recognition we try to reduce the image to a set of locally distinct points together with the information of said points. We then look for those points in other images and if the data matches, we can say that the image is similar, even if it is from a different viewpoint [4]. The initial goal of the SIFT method is to compare two images (or two image parts) that can be deduced from each other (or from a common image) by a rotation, a translation, and a scale change. The method turns out to be robust also to rather large changes in viewpoint angle, which explains its success [13].

We take a patch around the key point into account and use intensity values or the changes in intensity values, i.e., the image gradience in this area is used to describe it and turn it into a *Descriptor Vector.*

Now if we have multiple images where we detect the same key points, we can conclude that these are the same images; here, being the same does not necessarily mean being the same as they can be from different angles and with different lighting conditions.

The two images need not be the same, but they are of the same location from varying angles, and by matching the key points in the images we can conclude that they are of the same place [4, 14].

Computation of the SIFT Key Points

The locally distinct points or key points are found using the *Difference of Gaussians Approach*, which means the taken image is blurred using *Gaussian Blur* at different magnitudes. Then all the images are subtracted from each other and then we stack the difference images on top of each other. Then we look for extreme points, so points where the neighbours in the **X-Y** image space are as well as in the space of different levels of smoothing which are locally distinct and which stand out; they are the key points. This is done not only for one image resolution; it is also performed on an image pyramid which means images which are differently scaled in size to find key points that also are distinct concerning scale changes, i.e., if you're closer to an object you'll find the same key point if you're further away [3].

Computation of SIFT Descriptor Vector

This is computed by looking into the local neighbourhood of the key point that we found. We then break the neighbourhood into small areas and find the *Gradients* in these small areas. We use *Gradients* as these are rather strong to elimination changes and some viewpoint changes. The next step is to collect gradients in the local regions into histograms, like how often certain *Gradients* occur, what their magnitude is, etc. Then at the end around the key point, say, in a 4x4 region we have 16 local zones, so we make 16 histograms [13].

Affine Transformations

Depending on variations to the camera and its settings, the illumination, and the object itself, images of even an identical object might differ significantly. For monitoring, searching, and comprehending photos, one option to handle some of these changes is to utilize a description of the object that is unaware of some of the modifications stated above. Commonly employed for this purpose are affine invariants [15].

Affine Invariance

This means that surfaces are considered the same under affine transformations, i.e., linear transformations $x \mapsto Ax + b$, including squeezing and shearing [15].

2.2.3   ASIFT

ASIFT or Affine Scale-invariant Feature Transform is based on SIFT but unlike SIFT, ASIFT can accommodate all the six properties and is capable of simulating with enough accuracy even the distortion caused by the camera's optical axis direction. The ASIFT approach replicates all picture views that may be obtained by altering the two camera axis orientation parameters, namely the latitude and longitude angles. The SIFT approach is then used to cover the remaining four parameters [13].

Advantages of ASIFT over SIFT

- When the number of matches produced by the SIFT algorithm is significant, ASIFT has better accuracy than SIFT [4, 13].

- For the various image types being tested, ASIFT performs better. When visually inspected, the performance is evident in terms of both the number of matches and accuracy [4, 16].
- Even though the computational complexity of ASIFT is more than the SIFT considering the kind of processing power we have today, ASIFT presents a better face for image matching and image registration applications [4].
- ASIFT covers all six affine invariants, unlike SIFT [4, 13].

2.2.4   SURF (2006)

A quick and reliable approach for local, similarity-invariant representation and comparison of pictures is the SURF method (Speeded Up Robust Features). The SURF approach's key appeal is its ability to compute operators quickly using box filters, enabling real-time applications like tracking and object detection [17].

Motivations behind SURF:

- Faster detection of key points
- Less complicated
- Scale and rotation invariant and invariant to photometric changes
- Reduced descriptor dimensions as the feature size directly affects the cost of computation, so we try to maintain a low-size descriptor.

SURF Key Points

The extraction of SURF key points is based on three main methods that reduce the complexity of an image, which makes the SURF algorithm faster than SIFT [17].

- Integral Images
- Hessian Matrix
- Difference of Gaussian

Integral Images

In 1984, the Integral Image or Summed-Area Table was first shown. A rectangular subset of a grid or the sum of values (pixel values) in each image can be quickly and accurately calculated using the Integral Image (the given image). It can be used to determine the average intensity inside a certain image, or this is its primary usage. They allow for fast computation of box-type convolution filters. The entry of an integral image $I\Sigma$ (x) at a location x = (x,y)^T represents the sum of all pixels in the input image I within a rectangular region formed by the origin and x.

$$I\sum(x) = \sum_{i=0}^{i\leq x}\sum_{j=0}^{j\leq y} I(i,j) \tag{2.5}$$

With $I\Sigma$ calculated, it only takes four additions to calculate the sum of the intensities over any upright, rectangular area, independent of its size. The integral images make the Haar features more efficient [19].

For example: Figure 2.2 shows how integral images are calculated for a given set of pixels.

98	110	121	125	122	129
99	110	120	116	116	129
97	109	124	111	123	134
98	112	132	108	123	133
97	113	147	108	125	142
95	111	168	122	130	137
96	104	172	130	126	130

Image 1

98	208	329	454	576	705
197	417	658	896	1137	1395
294	623	988	1340	1701	2093
392	833	1330	1790	2274	2799
489	1043	1687	2255	2864	3531
584	1249	2061	2751	3490	4294
680	1449	2433	3253	4118	5052

Integral Image II

98	110	121	125	122	129
99	110	120	116	116	129
97	109	124	111	123	134
98	112	132	108	123	133
97	113	147	108	125	142
95	111	168	122	130	137
96	104	172	130	126	130

Image 1

98	208	329	454	576	705
197	417	658	896	1137	1395
294	623	988	1340	1701	2093
392	833	1330	1790	2274	2799
489	1043	1687	2255	2864	3531
584	1249	2061	2751	3490	4294
680	1449	2433	3253	4118	5052

Integral Image II

Figure 2.2 Above figures show how integral images are calculated to determine high-intensity key points.

Hessian Matrix

A square matrix of second-order partial derivatives of a scalar-valued function, or scalar field, is known as the Hessian matrix or Hessian. It describes a function with many variables' local curvature. It's a refined way to package all the information of the second derivatives of a function.

Hessian matrix-based interest points: Surf utilizes the Hessian matrix due to its efficiency and precision in computing. Surf depends on the determinant of the Hessian matrix to choose the scale and position rather than employing a separate measure (Hessian-Laplace detector). The Hessian of a given pixel looks something like this:

$$H = \begin{bmatrix} \dfrac{\partial^2 f}{\partial x^2} & \dfrac{\partial^2 f}{\partial x \partial y} \\ \dfrac{\partial^2 f}{\partial y \partial x} & \dfrac{\partial^2 f}{\partial y^2} \end{bmatrix} \tag{2.6}$$

For adapting to any scale, we filtered the image by a Gaussian kernel, so given a point X = (x, y), the Hessian matrix H(x, σ) in x at scale σ is defined as:

$$H(x, \sigma) = \begin{bmatrix} L_{xx}(x, \sigma) & L_{xy}(x, \sigma) \\ L_{xy}(x, \sigma) & L_{yy}(x, \sigma) \end{bmatrix} \tag{2.7}$$

where Lxx(x,) is the convolution of the Gaussian second order derivative with the image I at position x, and Lxy (x,) and Lyy (x,) follow suit. Although Gaussians are the best choice for scale-space analysis, they must be discretized and cropped.

First, convolution with a Gaussian kernel must be used to determine the Hessian matrix's determinant, and then the second-order derivative. Following Lowe's success with DoG approximations (SIFT), SURF uses box filters to enhance the approximation (both convolution and second-order derivative). Due in part to the fact that these approximative second-order Gaussian derivatives can be calculated using integral pictures regardless of size at a very cheap computational cost, SURF is fast.

Table 2.1 Comparative analysis of different algorithms.

Algorithm	Advantages	Gaps	References
Harris Corner Detector	The Harris Corner Detector is invariant to translation, rotation, and illumination change.	Not scale invariant, as we'll see some algorithms that adopted and improved on Harris Corner Detector (the most famous one being SIFT).	[11, 12]
SIFT	The SIFT algorithm is so strong in that it is invariant to both image scale and image orientation. Additionally, it has been found that SIFT performs better when a 3D perspective, different lighting conditions, and the presence of noise are present.	Only four of the six parameters related to affine invariance can be accommodated by SIFT. SIFT descriptor is very large, 128-D. SIFT is considerably slower and less accurate than ASIFT which is based on SIFT but is more robust and covers all six affine invariants.	[4, 13]
ASIFT	ASIFT has better accuracy than SIFT; It presents a better face for image matching and image registration applications and it covers all six affine invariants, unlike SIFT.	Even though ASIFT covers all six affine invariants, it is considerably slower than SURF.	[4, 13, 16]

(Continued)

Table 2.1 Comparative analysis of different algorithms. (*Continued*)

Algorithm	Advantages	Gaps	References
SURF	The main advantage of SURF lies in its speed. SURF uses Hessian matrix, integral images, and DoG to resolve the images and speed up the calculations. It has a small descriptor vector 64-D as compared to SIFT that had 128-D vector, makes it easier to.	The SURF algorithm is not stable to rotation changes, and it does not work properly with illumination.	[17, 19]

The 9x9 box filters approximate Gaussian second-order derivatives with = 1.2. These approximations are represented by Dxx, Dyy, and Dxy. Now, we can approximate the determinant of the Hessian by the following:

$$\det(H_{approx}) = D_{xx}D_{yy} - (wD_{xy})^2 \tag{2.8}$$

By using the above equation, a SURF key point is determined [17, 18].

2.3 Neural Network–Based Algorithms

Deep learning is a powerful artificial intelligence technique that uses multiple informational layers to produce the best results across a variety of classes. Deep learning has demonstrated excellent performance in several fields, particularly in the clustering, dividing, and recognition of images [7]. A very powerful form of a neural network is a convolutional neural network that is used for image recognition, classification and much more. We shall discuss the basic structure of a convolutional neural network, different architectures, generational improvements and why they are superior to traditional methods.

2.4   Convolutional Neural Network Architecture

It is a Deep Learning system that can take in an input image, give various characteristics and objects in the image importance (learnable weights and biases), and be able to tell one from the other. Comparatively speaking, a CNN requires substantially less pre-processing than other classification methods. While filters in older methods are hand-engineered, CNNs can learn these filters/characteristics with adequate training. CNN is crucial in information bases, where there is a need to prepare many hubs and boundaries (e.g., picture handling) [20]. Shown below in Figure 2.3 is the architecture of a CNN.

The architecture of CNN's is divided into different layers and is defined below:

- **Convolutional layer** - The convolutional layer, which determines the output of linked input in an open area, is the fundamental component of the convolutional neural network. A two-dimensional activation guide of the track is created by parts convolved above the data information's height and width, registering the speck item between the input and channel esteems, and performing these operations.
- **Non-linear layer** - The vast potential of non-linear systems must be greater than that of the individual. The info sign will be converted to the yield sign in this layer, and that signal will then be utilized to contribute to the layer below.
- **Pooling layer** - Its main function is to decrease the number of boundaries and counts in the model proportionate to the spatial size of the portrayal. It expedites estimations and avoids the overfitting problem. Maximum pooling is the most well-known variety of pooling layers.

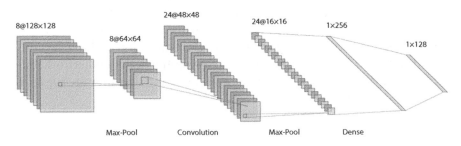

Figure 2.3 General architecture of a CNN.

- **Fully connected layer** - Layers in a neural network that are fully linked have all their inputs connected to every activation unit in the layer above them. The final few layers in most well-liked machine learning models are fully connected layers that combine the data gathered by earlier layers to create the output. The convolution layer takes the greatest time, followed by this layer.

2.5   Various CNN Architectures

2.5.1   LeNet-5 (1998)

Perhaps the most convenient design is LeNet-5. It has three fully associated layers and two convolutional layers [21]. As shown in Figure 2.4, each convolutional layer was followed by an average pool layer. As we undoubtedly already know, the conventional pooling layer included training weights and was referred to as a sub-sampling layer at the time. There are about 60,000 borders in this design. In 1998, LeCuN proposed LeNet [22]. Graphic processing units and even CPUs were not typically used in the early 2000s to speed up training. The main limitation of a classic multi-layered fully connected neural network was that it considered each pixel as a separate input and applied an adjustment to it, which at the time, in 1998, was a significant computational load. LeNet violated the fundamental tenet of an image—that adjacent pixels are connected, and those feature concepts are spread throughout the entire picture—by ignoring this relationship. LeNet was the first convolutional network architecture which condensed the different parameters and could also inadvertently understand features from raw pixels.

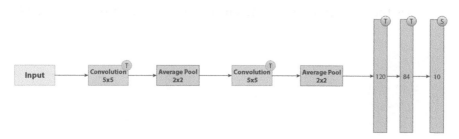

Figure 2.4 Architecture of LeNet, a Convolutional Neural Network for digits recognition. Each plane is a feature map, i.e., a set of units whose weights are constrained to be identical.

2.5.2 AlexNet (2012)

Convolutional neural networks appropriate for various picture classes were created in AlexNet by extending the depth from five (LeNet) to eight layers [23]. Figure 2.5 highlights the structure of AlexNet and the consecutive convolutions it had. The main drawback of an expansion inside and out is overfitting, even though depth generally increases speculation for several photos at once. AlexNet has significant significance in the most recent generation of convolutional neural networks because of its effective learning methodology, and it has also sparked a new wave of study into numerous CNN advancements [24].

2.5.3 VGGNet (2014)

To extend the power of neural structure, the visual geometry group (VGG) applies to a different picture acknowledgement information base in addition to achieving the most cutting-edge accuracy over ILSVRC datasets [26]. Three FC layers are included in the thirteen convolutional layers that make up the VGG-16. Figure 2.6 shows the structure of VGGNet which included 3 fully connected layers at the end; however, three further convolutional layers are included in the VGG-19. They employ 3 x 3 responsive area channels, and each hidden layer is equipped with an amendment non-linearity work. Ren developed a district proposal network employing the recognition organization [27] and convolutional highlights from the entire image. Faster areas with convolutional neural networks and the Region Proposal Network take the top rank for the first time in a long time in the ImageNet Large Scale Visual Recognition Challenge and COCO 2015.

2.5.4 GoogleNet (2015)

On the challenge of ImageNet recognition and characterization, GoogleNet provides the most innovative implementation. The improved use of PC

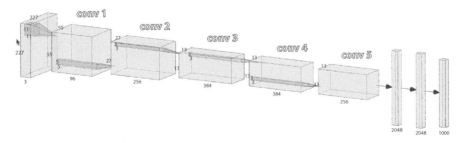

Figure 2.5 Architecture of AlexNet, a convolutional neural network.

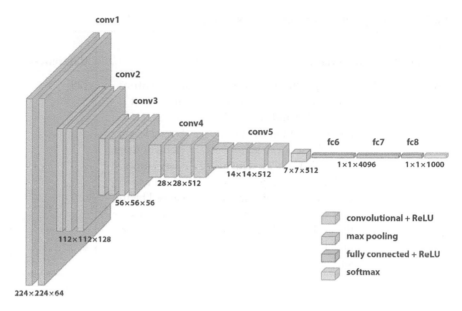

Figure 2.6 Architecture of VGGNet.

assets in the model is the primary indicator of this model [25]. Auxiliary starters were also suggested by GoogleNet to speed up convergence. The main drawback of this architecture was its diverse network topology, which required modifications from segment to segment. Another limitation of GoogleNet was an illustration bottleneck, which greatly reduced the amount of global feature information in the following layer and occasionally can result in the loss of useful data.

Table 2.2 Comparative analysis of CNN models.

CNN model	Advantages	Gaps	References
LeNet-5	It used the spatial relationship to reduce the number of calculations and boundaries, learning progressive component systems with programming; component extraction at a low level.	Vulnerable scaling for various picture classes; channels of enormous size.	[22]

(Continued)

Table 2.2 Comparative analysis of CNN models. (*Continued*)

CNN model	Advantages	Gaps	References
AlexNet	Using large and small size channels on the first (5x5 and 11x11) and last (3x3), low, mid, and undeniable level element extraction; Consider CNN's extensive and in-depth engineering; correction was displayed on CNN; started using the GPU equally as a gas pedal to manage complex structures.	Latent neurons in the first and second layers; learnt element maps' association errors are caused by the enormous channel size.	[28]
VGGNet	It suggested the idea of a productive, responsive field; provided the notion of a simple, uniform geography.	Usage of highly connected layers with high computational cost.	[29]
GoogleNet	Using multiscale channels inside the layers to present; gave a revolutionary idea of separation, transformation, and unity; Using bottleneck layer, standard global pooling finally layer, and weak associations, reduce the number of boundaries. Use of assistant classifiers to increase convergence rate.	Geographic diversity leads to tedious boundary customization; a real bottleneck could cause the loss of important data.	[30]

Conclusion

This paper highlighted the generational improvements in the algorithms used in the field of image recognition/classification, aiming at the shortcomings of each listed algorithm and how it was further improved upon. Through the literature review of multiple research papers, we discovered that algorithms that were once hailed as state-of-the-art algorithms like SIFT [3] had been improved upon. SIFT's derivative ASIFT [13], for example, improved upon a lot of flaws in SIFT [4], and finally SURF [17] was the fastest of them all. The main flaw with these algorithms is that they are hand-engineered and thus do not learn the representation by itself; it is hard coded, and that's why CNNs have an edge over these.

CNN has made great strides in picture processing and vision-based tasks, which has rekindled analysts' interest in ANNs. In this exceptional situation, a few research projects have been conducted to determine the convolutional neural network's performance on these tasks [31]. Convolutional neural networks' progressions can be arranged in several different methods, such as initialization, random work, augmentation, regularization, learning calculations, and design advancements. This study also discusses the historical context of convolutional neural networks, their presentations, challenges, and forthcoming directions concerning the sequence of CNNs in different courses [9]. CNN's square-based engineering supports learning in a measured manner and, subsequently, makes the design less complicated and more reasonable [32].

Therefore, we have examined the shortcomings of many conventional methods and CNN architectures. Moving further, we will examine the application of CNNs to image processing and new innovative CNN architectures and this shall be the future scope of this paper.

References

1. M. Hussain, M.A. Haque, *et al.*, Swishnet: A fast convolutional neural network for speech, music and noise classification and segmentation, 2018, arXiv preprint.
2. Y. Li, S. Wang, Q. Tian, and X. Ding, "A survey of recent advances in visual feature detection," *Neurocomputing*, vol. 149, pp. 736–751, 2015.
3. D. G. Lowe, "Distinctive image features from scale-invariant keypoints," *International Journal of Computer Vision*, vol. 60, no. 2, pp. 91–110.
4. Implementation and Performance Analysis of SIFT and ASIFT Image Matching Algorithms. In: Dash, S., Naidu, P., Bayindir, R., Das, S. (eds.),

Artificial Intelligence and Evolutionary Computations in Engineering Systems. Advances in Intelligent Systems and Computing, vol 668. Springer, Singapore. 2018

5. Harris, Christopher G. and M. J. Stephens. "A Combined Corner and Edge Detector." Alvey Vision Conference (1988).
6. Duan, Hongyan, Zhang, Xiaoyu, and He, Wensi. (2019). Optimization of SURF Algorithm for Image Matching of Parts: Special Issue on Data and Security Engineering. 10.1007/978-981-13-3651-5_11.
7. Shivani Gaba, Ishan Budhiraja, Vimal Kumar, Sahil Garg, Georges Kaddoum, Mohammad Mehedi Hassan, "A federated calibration scheme for convolutional neural networks: Models, applications and challenges", *Computer Communications,* Vol. 192, 2022, 144-162.
8. Xu, Haoyu *et al.* "Foreign object debris material recognition based on convolutional neural networks." *EURASIP Journal on Image and Video Processing* 2018 (2018): 1-10.
9. Hegadi, Ravindra. (2010). "Image Processing: Research Opportunities and Challenges."
10. Li, H. (2015/04). The Research of Intelligent Image Recognition Technology Based on Neural Network. *Proceedings of the 2015 International Conference on Intelligent Systems Research and Mechatronics Engineering,* 1733–1736.
11. Tinne Tuytelaars and Krystian Mikolajczyk, "Local Invariant Feature Detectors: A Survey," *Foundations and Trends Rin Computer Graphics and Vision,* May (2008).
12. Cordelia Schmid, Roger Mohr and Christian Bauckhage, "Evaluation of Interest Point Detectors," *International Journal of Computer Vision,* June (2000).
13. Jean-Michel Morel and Guoshen Yu. 2009. ASIFT: A New Framework for Fully Affine Invariant Image Comparison. *SIAM J. Img.* Sci. 2, 2 (April 2009), 438–469. https://doi.org/10.1137/080732730
14. "SIFT - 5 Minutes with Cyrill" - Youtube
15. Werman M. (2014) Affine Invariants. In: Ikeuchi K. (eds.) *Computer Vision.* Springer, Boston, MA. https://doi.org/10.1007/978-0-387-31439-6_747
16. Wu, Jian; Cui, Zhiming; Sheng, Victor; Zhao, Pengpeng; Su, Dongliang; and Gong, Shengrong. (2013). A Comparative Study of SIFT and its Variants. *Measurement Science Review.* 13. 10.2478/msr-2013-0021.
17. Bay, H., Tuytelaars, T., Van Gool, L. (2006). SURF: Speeded Up Robust Features. In: Leonardis, A., Bischof, H., Pinz, A. (eds.) *Computer Vision – ECCV 2006. ECCV 2006. Lecture Notes in Computer Science,* vol 3951. Springer, Berlin, Heidelberg. https://doi.org/10.1007/11744023_32
18. Oyallon, E., and Rabin, J. (2015). An Analysis of the SURF Method. *Image Processing On Line,* 5, 176–218.
19. Viola, P., Jones, M.: Rapid object detection using a boosted cascade of simple features. In: *CVPR* (1). (2001) 511–518.

20. Q. Zhang, L.T. Yang, Z. Chen, P. Li, A survey on deep learning for big data, *Inf. Fusion* 42 (2018) 146–157.
21. S. Milyaev, I. Laptev, Towards reliable object detection in noisy images, *Pattern Recognit. Image Anal.* 27 (4) (2017) 713–722.
22. Y. LeCun, L. Bottou, Y. Bengio, P. Haffner, Gradient-based learning applied to document recognition, *Proc. IEEE* 86 (11) (1998) 2278–2324.
23. D. Hutchison, LNCS 8588—Intelligent computing theory, 2014.
24. Sharma, S. Gaba, S. Singla, S. Kumar, C. Saxena, R. Srivastava, A genetic improved quantum cryptography model to optimize network communication, in: *Recent Trends in Communication and Intelligent Systems*, Springer, 2020, pp. 47–54.
25. C.-H. Wu, Q. Huang, S. Li, C.-C.J. Kuo, A taught-obesrve-ask (TOA) method for object detection with critical supervision, 2017, arXiv preprint arXiv:1711.01043.
26. X. Xia, C. Xu, B. Nan, Inception-v3 for flower classification, in: *2017 2nd International Conference on Image, Vision and Computing, ICIVC*, IEEE, 2017, pp. 783–787.
27. Dhillon, A., Verma, G.K. Convolutional neural network: a review of models, methodologies and applications to object detection. *Prog Artif Intell* 9, 85–112 (2020).
28. Krizhevsky, A., Sutskever, I., and Hinton, G. (2012). ImageNet Classification with Deep Convolutional Neural Networks. In *Advances in Neural Information Processing Systems*. Curran Associates, Inc.
29. Simonyan, K., and Zisserman, A.. (2014). Very Deep Convolutional Networks for Large-Scale Image Recognition.
30. Szegedy, C., Liu, W., Jia, Y., Sermanet, P., Reed, S., Anguelov, D., Erhan, D., Vanhoucke, V., and Rabinovich, A. (2015). Going Deeper with Convolutions. In *Proceedings of the IEEE Conference on Computer Vision and Pattern Recognition (CVPR)*.
31. Y. Lee, H. Kim, E. Park, X. Cui, H. Kim, Wide-residual-inception networks for real-time object detection, in: *2017 IEEE Intelligent Vehicles Symposium, IV*, IEEE, 2017, pp. 758–764.
32. Liu, C., Cao, Y., Luo, Y., Chen, G., Vokkarane, V., Ma, Y. (2016). DeepFood: Deep Learning-Based Food Image Recognition for Computer-Aided Dietary Assessment. In: Chang, C., Chiari, L., Cao, Y., Jin, H., Mokhtari, M., Aloulou, H. (eds.) Inclusive Smart Cities and Digital Health. ICOST 2016. *Lecture Notes in Computer Science*, vol 9677. Springer, Cham. https://doi.org/10.1007/978-3-319-39601-9_4

3

Efficient Architectures and Trade-Offs for FPGA-Based Real-Time Systems

L.M.I. Leo Joseph*, J. Ajayan, Sandip Bhattacharya and Sreedhar Kollem

Department of Electronics and Communication Engineering, School of Engineering, SR University, Warangal, Telangana, India

Abstract

Real-time monitoring gives accurate timely information, crucial for any production enhancement and decision-making. The most recent technology for field-programmable gate arrays (FPGA) has blurred the gap between hardware and software. By combining measurements from many sensor systems, it is possible to circumvent issues which exist when employing stand-alone systems. This chapter emphasizes the significance of design strategies and algorithm development from several vantage points, as well as their implementation in diverse real-time systems, employing reconfigurable and hybrid approaches. Employing a configurable soft-core processor, on an FPGA will give the adaptability necessary for interfacing with a variety of sensors.

Keywords: FPGA, real-time systems, hybrid architectures, hardware acceleration, SVM, CNN, Zynq, Pynq

3.1 Overview of FPGA-Based Real-Time System

The system whose response seems accurate in a defined time or real time is a real-time system [1]. Flight control mechanisms and real-time monitors are two examples of real-time systems. Real-time systems find applications in different forms pertaining to different application. Real-time systems are classified into two types based on the timing constraints: i) Hard real-time system ii) Soft real-time system.

---

*Corresponding author: leojoseph.lmi@sru.edu.in

Suman Lata Tripathi and Mufti Mahmud (eds.) *Explainable Machine Learning Models and Architectures*, (31–48) © 2023 Scrivener Publishing LLC

Hard real-time system: Hard real-time system performs tasks as expected without any missing deadline [2]. If the performance of the system deviates and violates the deadline, then the entire process suffers with tardiness. Tardiness is a measure of deviation of the system from its expected deadline. Tardiness decreases the overall efficiency of the system abruptly. Flight controllers can be modelled under the category of Hard real-time system.

Soft real-time system: Soft real-time system performs tasks with the exception that it may miss the deadline for certain tasks [2]. If the performance of the system deviates and violates the deadline, then there will be no serious effects, except in rare cases. The system effectiveness is in inverse proportion with tardiness. Tardiness decreases the overall efficiency of the system abruptly. Crossover networks and multiplexing switches are examples of soft real-time systems.

3.1.1 Key Elements of Real-Time System

There are three key elements necessary for the operation of real-time systems:

   i) Work model, ii) Resource Model, iii) Algorithms.

The necessity of the elements is listed below:

   a) Work model explores the system and its application.
   b) Resource model highlights the available resources for any system development for an application.
   c) Algorithms reveals the usage of resources for an application.

3.1.2 Real-Time System and its Computation

Real-time system comprises Real-time clocks to maintain and track the current time, which ensures the completion of a task within a deadline. A reference model architecture along with a real-time Programming Language specifies tasks, which must be completed within a specific time. The revolution in IC technology with add-ons as FPGA, Microcontrollers and processors ascertains the possibility of Real-time digital emulation [3]. CPU-based computing bases are imposed with sequential design, which limits the extension of these platforms in the real-time environments. In this aspect a flexible computing platform is essential that handshakes the CPU-based platforms with real-time systems. The preceding point can be realized through a flexible reconfigurable digital computing platform called a field-programmable gate array (FPGA). FPGA can be used as a base for the design, and computation of a low-power CMOS chips. These chips have a flexible programmable logic, which enables its usages in bench-top systems.

3.1.3   FPGA Functionality and Applications

Field Programmable Gate Arrays (FPGAs) comprise the grid of programmable interconnects, which establish connection among reconfigurable logic blocks (CLBs). FPGAs can be customized from the user end as per the user's requirements and application needs. Application Specific Integrated Circuits (ASICs) are dedicated FPGAs made specifically for a specified design purpose that are non-customizable in nature [3]. (OTP) FPGAs (programmed once at a time) are design specific but it has limited outreach, in comparison with general purpose FPGA, due to its limitation and non-customizable nature.

FPGAs provide an effective alteration for any type of design. In the same aspect ASIC also place a vital role in terms of competing technology. The two technologies ASIC and FPGAs are compared by means of information. The proposition between these two technologies should be considered before choosing either of them for the design purpose. In earlier days, FPGAs were used in design that required high operating speed, high design complexity, and higher volume designs. The advancement in the IC technologies enables the FPGA to offer better frequency in the range of MHz.

3.1.4   FPGA Applications

The previous section reveals that FPGAs seem preferable for the development of real-time applications. The programming approach of FPGAs acts as a challenging platform for many vendors like Xilinx and Altera to offer comprehensive solutions to many designs, which requires reconfigurable hardware, software and predefined IP cores, for utilizing third-party applications. The utilization of FPGAs in different domains are as summarized below:

Automotive – The FPGA-based interior design of an automotive ensures driver safety and comfort, and inclusion of entertainment systems make the design commercially viable.
Consumer Electronics – Common household electronics are tailored nowadays with embedded chips that find applications in the Digital Television displays, Wearable gadgets display, set-top boxes [3].

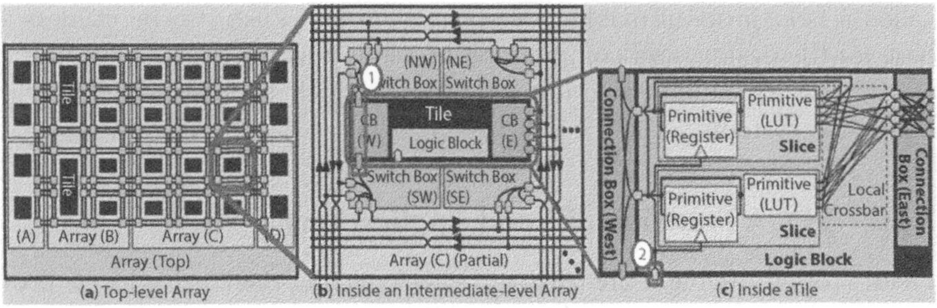

Figure 3.1 FPGA architecture [4] (open access).

Data Center – Increases the potential of high-bandwidth cloud computing circuitry, which includes high-storage low-latency Servers. It also supports the higher-end operations of Storage Area Network (SAN) [3].

FPGAs are sustainable for a variety of applications like image processing, medical imaging, and industrial monitoring and automation. FPGAs are flexible, faster to design and quicker in prototyping with reduction in non-recurring engineering costs (NRE) [3].

Medical – FPGA families can be used in the display of several medical equipments, associated with monitoring and diagnosing applications. It also acts as an interface between sensing and monitoring applications [3].

Security – FPGAs provide support in the development of domestic and industrial surveillance systems; FPGA provides solution to trending applications, emerging in frequent manner with its reconfigurable architecture. The adaptable nature of FPGA allows the user to sustain both hardware and software design protocols [3].

3.1.5   FPGA Architecture

A core FPGA architecture shown in Figure 3.1 is a composition of several customizable logic blocks [CLBs], which are linked to one another by a fabric, a network of programmable interconnects (round cited in section 3.1.3). "Input/output (I/O) blocks" connect the core FPGA with external devices.

The logic operation delegated to the module is carried out by CLB. I/O blocks and CLBs are connected using Programmable Multiplexers, horizontal and vertical routing channels. The complexity of the FPGA is proportionate to its number of CLBs. Hardware descriptive language is used to design the functionality of CLBs and Programmable Structured

Multiplexer (PSM) [5]. Advanced FPGA has about 1,100 input output blocks and 3,30,000 logic blocks.

The CLB referred to is the composition of i) Logic Block, ii) Interconnect, iii) Input-output blocks.

Logic Block: The programmable logic block is responsible for providing digital systems with the fundamental elements necessary for computation and storage. A fundamental logic element includes programmable logic, a flip-flop, and fast carry logic [5], to reduce the amount of space and the time it takes to process information.

Modern FPGAs are comprised of a variety of distinct blocks, such as memory blocks and multiplexers. Memory used for configuration is utilized across all logic blocks, to regulate the function of each individual element.

Interconnect: To finish off a user-defined design unit, the programmable routing creates a connection between "logic blocks and input/output blocks" [5], so that they can communicate with one another.

Input-Output Blocks: The input-output blocks serve as a programmable interface between the routing architecture and the logic blocks, allowing these two layers to communicate with components, which are external to the system.

Recent advances in hybrid devices facilitates extensible processing features in reconfigurable device technology, where FPGA is housed with an embedded core through an AXI bus interface. This hybrid platform design leads to achieve low-latency communication between user logic in the FPGA, with low power concentric workloads on the CPU, by putting the FPGA and CPU on the same chip. By combining measurements from many sensor systems, it is possible to circumvent the issues that exist when employing stand-alone systems. The idea of implementing the FPGA, along with CPU and its functionalities, will be discussed in the next section.

3.1.6   Reconfigurable Architectures

Gerald Estrin proposed the idea of building a computer with a conventional CPU. The reconfigurable hardware triggers the idea of developing a reconfigurable computing. The main processor acts equivalent to that of a reconfigurable hardware. The hardware intends to perform another task, once the prior task got completed. This approach initiates the base for developing a hybrid computer architecture that combines speed of hardware and flexibility of software [6]. Field-programmable gate arrays (FPGAs) are reconfigurable devices with several computational units, whose functioning is controlled by a cluster of programmable configuration bits. The spatial orientation of the device changes relative to time and application, to apply the best computing strategy, to speed up a particular or specific application. The device structure will be reoriented once again, to accommodate a new application in a sequential manner. The structure of reconfigurable devices can be modified by changing the entire hardware or a part of the hardware at the time of compilation. Downloading a logic in the modified device structure provides flexibility that functions in contrast with Von Neumann computers, which consist of a set of instructions to be carried out sequentially during run time. The program should be adaptable to the hardware, to perform in association with the flexibility of the reconfigurable systems. This makes the system perform better, for any application, which are adaptive to a reconfigurable environment. In short, General-Purpose Computers are well known for their performance and Application Specific Integrated Circuits (ASIC) for their flexibility; the performance and flexibility are the two important aspects for any reconfigurable structure. Reconfigurable computing bridges the performance leverage between hardware and software by intending an excellent flexibility than hardware, while potentially attaining higher efficiency than software [4]. Designing a single device with both the GPC's flexibility and the ASIC's performance is preferable and possible through the reconfiguration approach. ASIC implementation strategy often results in a quicker, more compact, and lower power design than an FPGA implementation. However, the demand for hybrid (ASIC-FPGA) devices is being driven by the rising market demands for design flexibility. To accommodate numerous design alternatives with a single mask set, designers must combine ASIC circuits having high density with intrinsic flexibility of FPGA circuits [4]. To shorten design time and promote standardization, it is possible to construct a "base design" that may be used by succeeding devices in repetition with remarkable modifications. Since most consumer and workplace goods come in a variety of low- to high-end configurations, it is possible to use this underlying design approach, by adding new features to each model. This idea can be used in a variety of devices, such as computers, printers, fax machines, and scanning equipment. FPGA's multiply, accumulate and processing capability enables the collaboration with DSP applications. When designing a DSP system, parallel structures and arithmetic algorithms can be used to maximize efficiency and outperform single or multipurpose DSP devices. By combining the capabilities of ASICs and FPGAs in a single design, it is possible to improve the performance of a system in ways that are not possible with just one of these circuit technologies alone.

Other designs that support various standards over a single device like camera, LED, transceivers confine themselves with hybrid ASIC/FPGA structure [4]. The hybrid designer without programmable base is forced to choose FCI (Forced Carry Input) logic at the chip level, which changes from time to time. The programmers usually bypass the design requirements, finalization strategy that potentially delay the release of the finished device. ASIC and programmable logic can work together on a single device to satisfy circumstances. In addition to other challenges of a comparable nature, various regional standards might also be implemented into the PGA cores. This would be a challenge to overcome. It is highly improbable that the design team will make use of this new capability, until it is commercially feasible. For design teams to enjoy the advantages in terms of performance and density features of an ASIC, they will have to consider NREs and TA% that sound higher than they would with FPGAs. The feasibility of the ASIC design seems uncertain due to the term "unique mask".

Every design that relates to ASIC requires a unique mask set during chip production, unlike customized FPGAs. By tailoring the circuits and connectors to the requirements of each individual application, it is possible to achieve high levels of performance and density. Nonetheless, there is a rapid increase in the cost of the mask sets that is increasing successively. As a direct consequence of this, the cost of the perdie is increasingly made up of the cost of the mask in many instances. In addition to the issue of partitioning, designers working with embedded FPGAs will have to deal with several other challenges. How many FPGA gates to incorporate is a fundamentally important question. In addition to having sufficient space for the initial application, the FPGA must also have sufficient unused FPGA resources to make room for any future logic designs. This is a crucial consideration during the planning stage of the design process because, once the hybrid device has been fabricated out of silicon, it is possible that a second, more expensive mask set will be required if the capacity of the FPGA is not sufficient to manage the anticipated configurations. The design team is responsible for considering any potential increases in the amount of logic that will be programmed into the FPGA and accurately predict the achievable embedded FPGA use to avoid this undesirable circumstance. During the beginning stages of the ASIC design process, interconnect requirements need to be carefully considered. The interface between the Application specific FPGA and the ASIC is fixed in the mask set. To assist in the design of the reconfigurable SOCs, it will be necessary to use improved CAD tools to address these challenging architectural and design planning issues. The power, area, and performance parameters of both ASIC and FPGA associated architectures need to be accurately predicted by optimization tools, to categorize hybrid designs. In order to provide assistance to the designers in selecting the most appropriate logic level partition, and specific circuitry options, for each component of the hybrid design, tools that can efficiently and swiftly evaluate these tradeoffs will be required to analyze how differently the architectures differ in these aspects [4, 6]. With the aid of digital signal processors (DSPs), microcontrollers, or microprocessors, SVM control mode can now be implemented digitally. The preceding statement can be evidenced by considering a three-phase system with direct matrix converter (DMC) for digital implementation. DMC is a power converter that converts one form of electrical energy to another form, by changing its voltage or frequency. DMC uses transistors as switches in its design. The transistor switching losses affect the performance of the DMC to a great extent, which requires highly complicated compensation techniques. Several hybrid algorithms and configurations are proposed to compensate transistor switching losses. The example demonstrates how important it is to utilize hybrid configurations and algorithms when developing an effective system design. The following section will discuss the specifics of various FPGA configurations and algorithms, as well as their associated trade-offs.

3.2 Hybrid FPGA Configurations and its Algorithms

3.2.1 Hybrid FPGA

A normal integrated circuit (IC) that has been pre-programmed for a specific application, or to carry out certain tasks after production, is referred as a hybrid Field-Programmable Gate Array (FPGA) [7]. FPGAs are distinguished by several important characteristics, including increased speed, programmable functionalities, increased design volume, and decreased complexity. As a result of the ongoing development of technology, FPGAs have become a practical choice for all designs and markets. The growing application of hybrid FPGAs across a wide range of industries, which allows for the creation of products featuring distinctive qualities at cost-effective prices, is the primary factor propelling the growth of this market. The increase in demand for the manufacturing of electronic components in different aspects is the primary factor, driving growth in the field programmable gate array market [7]. Existing devices like ASIC, DSP and other multiprocessors may hamper the expansion of the hybrid market. The market for hybrid FPGAs is anticipated to expand rapidly during the coming years. This section provides important information on the market status of the leading participant in the hybrid FPGA market and highlights the major trends and opportunities that are currently present in the industry. The global market for hybrid FPGAs is broken down into numerous submarkets that are categorized according to configuration, technology, nodal size, and vertical application. Many businesses are making efforts to promote organic growth initiatives, which include new product launch, refined product approvals, patenting their innovations and ideations. Acquisitions, as well as partnerships and collaborations, are examples of inorganic growth strategies. Because of these actions, participants and collaborative bodies can expand their customer bases and their business operations. As a result of the increasing demand in the market for hybrid FPGAs, market participants can anticipate future opportunities for growth that will be both lucrative and advantageous.

3.2.2   Hybrid FPGA Architecture

The hybrid FPGA architecture shown in Figure 3.2 is comprised of different technologies in terms of its dependency level. In the figure, different memory units are combined together to sustain parallel processing. This analysis served as the foundation for the methodology that was used to develop the new architecture, which is referred to as the Hybrid FPGA. This analysis was performed on a large collection of memory circuits to determine which types of logic resources will best match the requirements of the circuits, in terms of chip space.

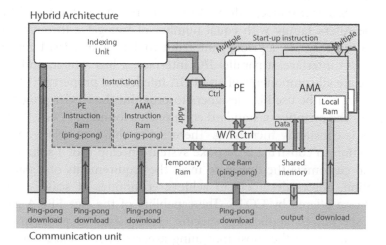

Figure 3.2 Hybrid FPGA architecture [8] (open access).

3.2.3   Hybrid FPGA Configuration

Designers of embedded and real-time systems are always faced with the issue of incorporating more computational power, in addition to maintaining ever-tighter system requirements. Components that are available commercially off the shelf (also known as COTS) are recommended as best practices for lowering designing costs, and leveraging the constraints, in the lag of time to market. Establishing a balance between two opposing design forces—generalization and specialization—is still a challenging task to develop COTS components, which can be reused in a variety of applications that utilize real-time embedded applications. Thus, it is still important to keep this in mind. When system designers attempt to strike a balance between the two competing forces of cost and performance, they are all too familiar with the tension that is created as a result of the competition between the two. When designing a system, it is in everyone's best interest to make use of COTS components whenever possible. This will help keep costs down and reduce the amount of time needed to bring the product to market (round cited section 3.1.2), but these components may not be adequate to meet stringent performance requirements. When compared to COTS components, custom components can reach much higher performance, but they come with much higher development costs and longer time to market. The recent development of hybrid chips, which combine central processing unit (CPU) and field-programmable gate array (FPGA) components, is an intriguing example of cutting-edge technological progress. These hybrid chips offer the potential for significant hardware customization, in addition to the economies of scale that come with COTS. For instance, Xilinx's Virtex II Pro can combine its IP cores with the Altera family with equal number of free gates through inheritance. As an example, a priority interrupt controller, a DRAM controller, a serial I/O interface, a parallel I/O interface, a bus arbiter, and an I/O interface are all components of an FPGA intellectual property (IP) system library that can be used by designers to program the FPGA programmable gates. The quantity of standard components found in FPGA IP system libraries is constantly increasing. There is the ability to select an FPGA IP collection to construct a bespoke system-on-chip (SoC) solution. The ability to customize the design to meet the requirements of a particular application, allows designers to achieve economies of scale, comparable to those offered by COTS. The capability of the free FPGA gates to permit specialized application-specific components to perform-critical functions is one of the most intriguing aspects of specialization. This is one of the reasons why specialization is becoming increasingly popular.

The performance of an FPGA-based implementation is still less than that of a comparable application-specific IC, but it is frequently acceptable and has a far better price/performance ratio. For system developers, maximizing the potential of these hybrids is an intriguing challenge. Replacing existing COTS design with a single chip and programming them with a common set of FPGAs Ip's is time-consuming and device-specific, which goes against the intended goals of modularity, portability, and reuse. Most system programmers will not be able to utilize these hybrids' full potential without knowledge of hardware design techniques and tools. New capabilities that make it possible to synthesize hardware designs from a higher-level language syntax that is easier to understand make it possible for the programmers to take an important step toward being able to create components that are stored within the FPGA. A comprehensive programming model is required to completely abstract away hardware-specific details, eliminating the need for the designer to differentiate between the use of CPU hardware and FPGA hardware components. It is possible to develop a transparent platform for system implementation. Programming languages typically provide high-level syntax for this purpose. This will give programmers access to the hybrid system's full potential and let them use true componentization and reuse best practices to cut down costs and speed up time to market. Hybrid computational model and runtime services must be defined and designed by hardware and software to realize this potential. To address system-level design for embedded systems, researchers are examining flexible design languages, hardware software specifications, and system design tools [9]. System-level specification capabilities, which can be used to drive software synthesis and hardware synthesis, are being sought after by projects such as System-C, Ptolemy, and Rosetta [9]. Software synthesis can be driven by these capabilities. Increasing the level of abstraction used in FPGA programming is how this objective can be met. This will make it possible for FPGA designers to have more leeway in their work. A newly evolving VHDL standard and System Verilog are also currently being developed that eliminate the distinction between the hardware-software interface and system-level perspective. The objective of these approaches differ, but they all aim to increase the level of abstraction necessary for designing and integrating hardware and software components. It is essential to conduct research into the high-level programming language capabilities of FPGAs, to determine whether these capabilities enable the skills of the software engineers to put forth their abilities to work across the hybrid boundaries. The current hybrid computational models typically treat FPGAs as computational accelerators that passively act as subroutines during the computation of data flow [9]. Any higher-end programming model that abstracts the bus architecture, memory, and low-level peripheral protocols will transfer hybrid components into a transparent computing platform. These computing platforms are necessary to program against FPGA-CPU barrier. Software components and its interactions are defined by programming models. Messaging and shared memory protocols are component interfacing mechanisms, which are consistently utilized in modern technology. Both mechanisms allow components to communicate with one another. Both mechanisms are implemented efficiently in embedded systems that provoke the aspirants to explore the merits of the technologies they favor [9].

3.3   Hybrid FPGA Algorithms

The goal of heterogeneous multi-core processors is to increase the overall performance of computations for computing-related applications. To achieve high-performance computation, it uses cores with different capabilities. To effectively use the hybrid processor as a platform for software, which demands high-speed and performance metrics, some of the algorithms used in hybrid platforms are highlighted and listed below:

1. Hybrid ANN – PSO algorithm
2. Hybrid chaos-AES Encryption algorithm
3. Hybrid Artificial bee colony algorithm
4. Bandwidth limited optimized routing algorithm
5. Technology mapping algorithm.

Design solutions frequently make use of rapid prototyping, and diagnostic systems include pre-built control functions as well as a specialized real-time hardware simulator. These types of systems are built on a development environment. The FPGA is only utilized to execute the operations related to commutation problems and supplement the DSPs' responsibilities. The hybrid algorithms are typically integrated in the DSP. The DSP can only execute a certain number of instructions per sampling cycle. The number of PWM that can be controlled, and the time required for algorithmic calculations, affects the computation time. The modulation and commutation algorithms required to function must be carried out. SVM-based approaches require more effort to implement than carrier PWM-based methods [10]. With reference from section 3.1.4 switching transistors at a high frequency in the range of kHz is now achievable, because of the development of new power semiconductor devices. Transistor use in matrix converters also presents excellent prospects for lowering commutation losses and boosting power density (round cited from section 3.1.4). In traditional DSP systems, it can be challenging to apply a sophisticated strategy for transistors with very short durations, caused due to high switching frequencies. The special characteristics of programmable logic devices and their hardware implementations have recently gained popularity. Field programmable gate arrays (FPGAs) are appealing. They are used in a variety of scientific and industrial domains due to their speed of processing, parallel operation, configurability, and flexibility. Hardware SVM methods can often be classified into two categories. The first group uses a hybrid DSP-FPGA strategy, while the second simply uses an FPGA. Due to the parallelism of the proposed solution, there is even another significant benefit. Even though these factors are rigidly limited, taking concurrency into account increases the usefulness significantly. On the other hand, the FPGA with algorithmic realization is not used for the complete implementation of the algorithm. SVM hardware implementations relies on the "pure" FPGA, with no DSP integration. This indicates that a programmable logic device is used to run the entire method. Due to the stringent limitations of the synthesis tools, this strategy is significantly more challenging to apply. Advanced mathematical procedures and functions, such as exponential functions, are particularly challenging to describe. However, the use of the FPGA yields advantages over conventional microprocessors due to its processing speed, and the capacity for parallel computing of a limited number of tasks. The benefits of using a System-on-a-Chip (SoC) to construct an SVM algorithm on hardware as opposed to conventional DSPs. Due to FPGAs' primary advantages—extremely fast processing speeds and the capacity for concurrent task execution—their application in SVM algorithms is becoming more and more common. However, current techniques typically use external tools, necessitating the need of hardware description languages [10, 11]. In addition, most of the solutions are built on a hybrid structure, which still uses the conventional DSP to carry out (typically) mathematical operations. The algorithms and their successful implementation are realized by using appropriate hardware. The software that is realizable on the hardware insists on the orientation of design and the performance of the hardware. When it comes to maintaining the consistency of their designs, the designers will find that the hardware accelerated architecture is an essential solution. The following section will concentrate on the topic of hardware-accelerated architecture in relation to FPGA synthesis.

3.3.1 Relevance of Hardware-Accelerated Architecture to FPGA Software Implementation

In many contemporary applications of artificial intelligence, machine learning is widely used. Such applications are supported by a variety of hardware platforms. The graphics processing unit, also known as the GPU, is the one that is used most frequently, because it can carry out computations quickly and can be adapted to work with a wide variety of different approaches. In comparison to graphics processing units, FPGAs exhibit a better efficiency, even though their processing speed is significantly slower than GPU. It is suitable for different kinds of machine learning–based algorithms. Application specific integrated circuit architectures have been suggested with the goal of achieving the highest possible level of energy efficiency, at the expense of lessening the system's ability to be reconfigured. Analog computing cannot be used for high-resolution computations because it requires an analog-to-digital converter (ADC). For this reason, analogue computing is not appropriate for most applications that involve artificial intelligence (AI). However, analog computation is a promising methodology for computing complex machine learning algorithms due to its low design cost and better computing speed.

Machine learning is currently being utilized in a significant number of modern applications of artificial intelligence. Real-time human computer interfacing systems like advanced driver assistance systems, face detection for video surveillance, and early cancer detection using image recognition, are just a few examples of the kinds of interactions that have been made possible due to the breakthrough in computation capability that this system possesses. When it comes to all these applications, having a high detection accuracy requires extensive machine learning calculations that require a higher level of computations. As a direct consequence of this, the hardware-accelerated platform must adhere to stringent requirements. Most applications today use general-purpose computing engines, particularly graphics processing units (GPUs). But recent research from the academic community and industry reveals development of ASICs for machine learning, particularly in deep neural networks (DNN). The many types of ML acceleration, the hardware accelerator architecture, and the method for increasing ML computation's hardware computing efficiency are highlighted in this section.

Accelerator using GPU/FPGA in the datacenter is taken for analysis. GPUs provide a large array of hardware options and better computing power with reliable ecosystem. Several miniature graphics processors are often used to implement the GPU architecture. The local cache and independent computing units included in each graphics processor make them suitable for matrix multiplication. Numerous mini processors have a shared high-speed bus, which enables quick data transfer between mini processors. For example, NVIDIA's DGX-1 supercomputer has eight Tesla GPUs that use the Pascal graphical processing architecture. Every graphics processing unit (GPU) has multiple processors, and each of those processors has several CUDA cores. Both the graphics processing unit (GPU) and the random-access memory (RAM) have respective clock rates of 700 MHz and 1.3 GHz. The GPU includes a 16 GB global memory, a 4096-bit memory bus, and a 4 MB L2 cache [12]. Figure 3.3 depicts the DGX-1 system's structure. With the assistance of the NV Link interconnect network, any two GPUs can be physically separated from each other by fewer than one GPU. The GPU cluster is connected to the duplex switch through PCI cable.

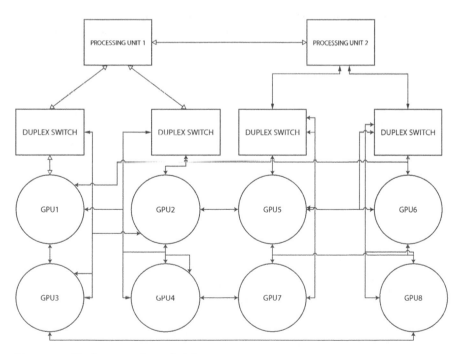

Figure 3.3 Hardware accelerated architecture.

3.4 CNN Hardware Accelerator Architecture Overview

The CNN hardware accelerator architecture can be broadly divided into two groups. The two types of computing architectures are central and sparse. A sample central computing architecture is shown in Figure 3.4. Nodal arrays are part of the main computer architecture. The nodal array comprises many gateways to support parallel processing. The output of each filter will be collected at the database and fed back into the memory for the computation of the subsequent sequences. When calculating the large kernel-sized CNN, the central processing architecture's massive nodal array is advantageous. A sparse computational architecture, on the other hand, is composed of small convolution units that are suitable for small-sized kernels. Sixteen convolution units with a kernel size of 3 by 3 make up the computational Array.

Computing convolution operations have the advantage of streamlining the data flow. However, only 3 by 3 convolution is supported by the computing unit.

To support specific types of machine learning algorithms to enhance hardware performance, ASIC-based architectures are proposed. To support types of machine learning–based algorithms, such as a deep convolutional

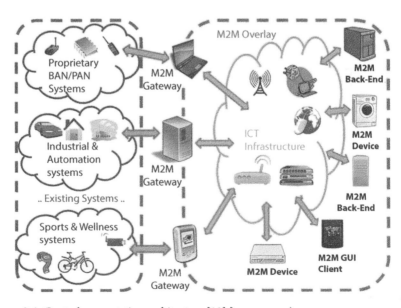

Figure 3.4 Central computation architecture [13] [open access).

network with model compression approach, ASIC architectures offers enhancement in hardware efficiency. ASIC displays the best energy economy and computing performance when compared to the GPU and FPGA [14–16], but at the expense of reconfigurability to different machine learning–based algorithms. The designers should choose the most suitable computation hardware platform based on the individual applications.

3.5   Summary

This chapter provides a quick overview of the most recent design techniques that are gravitating toward field-programmable gate arrays (FPGA), which help to blur the line between hardware and software. Real-time benchmarks are used to highlight the significance of design methods and algorithms in the process of developing real-time systems, and a variety of hybrid configurations and architectures are dissected and examined in great detail. This chapter was written with the intention of showcasing various architectures, configurations, and design techniques in a single flow. This will allow readers to grasp and realize the real-time system, which will help construct an investigative benchmark in the system design-related domains.

References

1. Stankovic, J.A., Son, S.H., Hansson, J., "Misconceptions about Real-time Databases.," Springer, vol. 593, doi: https://doi.org/10.1007/0-306-46988-X_2.
2. G. Bernat, A. Burns and A. Liamosi, "Weakly hard real-time systems," *IEEE Trans. Comput.*, vol. 50, no. 4, pp. 308–321, Apr. 2001, doi: 10.1109/12.919277.
3. J. Luo, G. Coapes, T. Mak, T. Yamazaki, C. Tin, and P. Degenaar, "Real-Time Simulation of Passage-of-Time Encoding in Cerebellum Using a Scalable FPGA-Based System., 2016," *IEEE Trans Biomed Circuits Syst*, vol. 10, no. 3, pp. 742–753, 2016, doi: 10.1109/TBCAS.2015.2460232.
4. Omar Diouri, Ahmed Gaga, Hamid Ouanan, Saloua Senhaji, Sanaa Faquir, Mohammed Ouazzani Jamil, "Comparison study of hardware architectures performance between FPGA and DSP processors for implementing digital signal processing algorithms;," *Appl. FIR Digit. FilterResults Eng.*, vol. 16, 2022.
5. "Basic FPGA Architecture and its Applications." [Online]. Available: https://www.watelectronics.com/components/

6. Bhandarkar, S. M., Arabnia, H. R., & Smith, J. W., "A Reconfigurable Architecture for Image Processing and Computer Vision," *VLSI Parallel Comput. Pattern Recognit. Artif. Intell.*, pp. 29–57, 1995.

7. Kaviani, A., & Brown, S., "Hybrid FPGA Architecture.," *Fourth Int. ACM Symp. Field-Program. Gate Arrays*, 1996, doi: doi:10.1109/fpga.1996.242249.

8. Cheng R, Yao L, Yan X, Zhang B, Jin Z., "High Flexibility Hybrid Architecture Real-Time Simulation Platform Based on Field-Programmable Gate Array (FPGA).," *Energies*, vol. 14, no. 19, p. 6041, 2021, doi: https://doi.org/10.3390/en14196041.

9. Waza, Abida & Mir, Roohie & Hakim, Najeeb-Ud-Din., "Reconfigurable Architectures.," *J. Adv. Comput. Sci. Technol.*, 2012, doi: 1. 10.14419/jacst. v1i4.518.

10. Wiśniewski, R., Bazydło, G., & Szcześniak, P., "SVM algorithm oriented for implementation in a low-cost Xilinx FPGA. Integration.," 2018, doi: doi:10.1016/j.vlsi.2018.10.002].

11. P. S. Zuchowski, C. B. Reynolds, R. J. Grupp, S. G. Davis, B. Cremen and B. Troxel, "A hybrid ASIC and FPGA architecture," pp. 187-194," *IEEEACM Int. Conf. Comput. Aided Des. 2002 ICCAD 2002*, pp. 187–194, doi: 10.1109/ICCAD.2002.1167533.

12. Du, Li, and Yuan Du., "Hardware accelerator design for machine learning.," *Mach. Learn.-Adv. Tech. Emerg. Appl.*, pp. 1–14, 2017.

13. J. Latvakoski *et al.*, "Towards Horizontal Architecture for Autonomic M2M Service Networks," *Future Internet*, vol. 6, no. 2, pp. 261–301, 2014, doi: 10.3390/fi6020261.

14. S. L. Tripathi, S. Saxena, S. K. Sinha and G. S. Patel (2021) Digital VLSI Design Problems and Solution with Verilog, John Wiley & Sons, Ltd. DOI:10.1002/9781119778097

15. Dasari L. Prasanna; Suman Lata Tripathi, "Machine and Deep-Learning Techniques for Text and Speech Processing," in *Machine Learning Algorithms for Signal and Image Processing*, IEEE, 2023, pp. 115-128, doi: 10.1002/9781119861850.ch7

16. Badiganti P.K., Peddirsi S., Rupesh A.T.J., Tripathi S.L. (2022) Design and Implementation of Smart Healthcare Monitoring System Using FPGA. In: Rawat S., Kumar A., Kumar P., Anguera J. (eds.) *Proceedings of First International Conference on Computational Electronics for Wireless Communications. Lecture Notes in Networks and Systems*, vol 329. Springer, Singapore. https://doi.org/10.1007/978-981-16-6246-1_18

4

A Low-Power Audio Processing Using Machine Learning Module on FPGA and Applications

Suman Lata Tripathi[1,2]*, Dasari Lakshmi Prasanna[1] and Mufti Mahmud[2]

[1]VLSI Design Lab, Lovely Professional University, Punjab, India
[2]Department of Computer Science, Nottingham Trent University, Nottingham, UK

Abstract

Increasing demand for smart devices lead to the extensive use of machine learning techniques focused on large data processing in the form of text, audio, or image signals. The validity of such machine learning modules is based on their performance optimisation and accuracy in real-time systems. Also, low power consumption is another major challenge for any smart portable device to maintain the load on the battery and battery backup for a longer time. As such, the analysis must be performed before finalising any application-specific chip or board for such signal processing modules that can be implemented with reconfigurable architectures like field programable gate arrays (FPGA) boards. FPGA facilitates to development of real-time systems corresponding to the prototype of ML modules for different types of signals or data. This chapter gives details about the machine learning classifiers (MLC) that are frequently used for audio signal processing along with the development of real-time systems with FPGA for these modules.

Keywords: MLC, audio signal processing, FPGA, Xilinx Vivado, biomedical data

4.1 Introduction

Machine Learning Classifiers (MLC) are used in many areas; the applications of MLC are biometric identification, document classification, email spam classification, handwritten recognition, image classification, speech

---

*Corresponding author: tri.suman78@gmail.com

Suman Lata Tripathi and Mufti Mahmud (eds.) Explainable Machine Learning Models and Architectures, (49–64) © 2023 Scrivener Publishing LLC

recognition, text categorization, etc. For TDS assistive technology MLC is used to classify the command from the voice signal of the user. Audio signal processing modules include speech detection, instrument retrieval, glitch detection, etc. MLC are used to distinguish the audio data from the mixed sound signal followed by class-based segmenting of the audio clips [1].

Audio data like an animal, humans, surroundings, noise, music, speech sounds and various non-vocal audio signals are frequently appearing in the form of digital audio data in many computer-based applications. Different audio classifiers are used to make an effective audio system that automatically recognizes the specific sound, and is processed for certain applications [2].

4.2   Existing Machine Learning Modules and Audio Classifiers

Several methodologies are available to extract certain audio data from the input audio data. A binary classification consists of two classes and multi-label consists of multiple class labels where each sample is mapped to a set of target labels [3]. There are different methods to recognize or classify the data according to the classifying method, which are Logistic Regression, K-Nearest Neighbors (KNN), Naive Bayes (NB) algorithm, Stochastic Gradient Descent (SGD), Support Vector Machine (SVM), Decision Tree (DT), and Random Forest (RF).

Unlike image processing, retrieving audio data processing from large files is very difficult. The author [4], proposed a novel for classifying the audio using general sounds and audio scenes as a dataset. The audio module contains audio frames, clips, shots, and high-level semantic units for feature extraction. The audio data is segmented into shots, clips, and frames as 20-30 ms. The SVM learning module is used to classify the general sounds and calculate the accuracy of the learning module.

There is much research on audio classification mainly on speech and music retrieving data. The authors [5] developed and evaluated a classifier for a combination of speech and music. They focused on the development of two features SMR (speech-to-signal ratio) and SIMPL (stereo-input mix-to-peripheral level) to get better accuracy. Although SMR is a hidden characteristic of audio mixtures, it is highly correlated with the features of the signals that can be measured. In contrast to most instruments, vocals are typically situated at the stereo center in broadcast mixing techniques. SIMPL is an objective measure of signal quality.

Using textual information as the class labels instead of audio samples from target classes, the authors [6] proposed a zero-shot method for audio classification. A semantic class label embedding was generated from the textual labels of audio classes using Word2Vec (vector representation of words), after audio features embeddings were extracted from audio recordings using VGG (visual geographical group). A bilinear model is used to classify audio. The classification output is a class with the maximum compatibility with the given audio feature embedding. The input includes audio feature embeddings and semantic class label embeddings, and the output is a binary class that contains the most compatible audio feature embeddings.

The audio recognition is done using different approaches like regression, classification and other approaches and the analysis of identifications is discussed in [7]. In this, the authors extracted the dataset documents from web resources and stored in the local disk. MATLAB library was used for initializing and data processing. The feature extraction is done using neural networks. The system execution is performed in MATLAB 2018 and calculated the efficiency of the system.

Audio classification is not only used in multimedia classification for recognition or classifying the data files, it is also helpful in ATs. Using speech as a base to control multiple devices for assisting the able and unable bodies is the main focusing area in biomedical application. The tongue is the least effective organ in the whole body; it is easy to access speech as input for devices to control. In the paper [8], the authors designed a TDS for accessing the computer and PWC (power wheelchair). In addition to the navigation of a 50-m obstacle course, three control strategies were utilized to drive the PWC. Additionally, the two Likert scale questionnaires used to evaluate the qualitative aspects of its use – one short (eight questions) and one longer (46 questions) – were used to evaluate some of the qualitative aspects of using the TDS.

The authors [9], discuss customized TDS circuitry. Computers can be controlled independently by moving the tongue, and directing commands to them. Tracers such as neodymium magnets placed on the tongue are used to track tongue movements. As the tongue moves, the magnetic field inside and around the mouth varies. Inductive magneto-inductive sensors on a headset are mounted bilaterally to detect the variations. A portable screen is connected wirelessly to the raspberry-pi to transmit the information. A wireless TDS is designed [10] to control the smartphones. By using permanent magnetic traces pierced on tongue, the commands are detected. This TDS is linked to iPhone using wireless customized module for accessing the wheelchair, light, computer, television, and telephone.

In paper [11], the authors designed an intraoral-TDS (iTDS) to control smartphone, PWS and computer. A dual-band antenna is shared between band 915 MHz and 433 MHz and a coil is shared with the lower band 27 MHz, in order to minimize external RF interference effects. Battery charging is also shared to reduce overall size and weight of the Transmitter (Tx). To maintain the wireless link robustness in mouth environment dynamically, the Tx incorporates two adaptive matching networks at 433 MHz and 915 MHz, respectively.

There are different modules involved to implement the audio classifying module [12–14] as shown in Figure 4.1. For processing the audio, we need to consider amplitude, duration, frequency, sampling rate, etc. The modules included in the development of an audio classifier using learning techniques are a microphone or audio sensor to collect the raw audio data, filters for removing the noise, MLC to classify the data according to the training dataset, and Bluetooth module for processing the classified data to a device.

In [15], an audio-visual fusion was developed for obtaining both audio and visual paths to identify the emotions of a user using video. VAD (voice activity detector) is used as a pre-processing stage to eliminate the background noise and segment out the noise not related to speech. It uses short-time energy and zero crossing rate (STE and STZCR) as the features. The audio analyser and feature-level fusion are developed for speech classification. The multiple outputs are produced from the audio path because the speech signal is divided into multiple sub-portions with particular lengths.

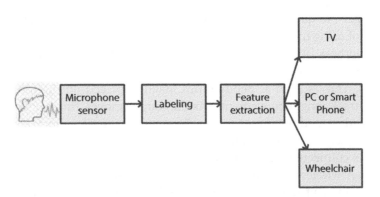

Figure 4.1 Block diagram of audio processing unit.

A modest intentional alteration to an audio source that is imperceptible to human ears, and which causes a machine-learning model to malfunction, is known as an adversarial audio assault. Since adversarial attacks have the potential to lead such models to make inaccurate predictions, this raises security concerns regarding the machine learning algorithms. In [16], the authors presented some adversarial attack, which has a high impact on audio signals and evaluated the resistance of learning modules. They proposed an approach to secure the audio signals from adversarial attacks by representing the audio signal as DWT (discrete wavelet transform) and SVM. Various pre-processing units are included for enhancing spectrogram, generating, reducing dimension, and smoothing. Features are extracted from patches of spectrogram using SURF (speed-up robust feature) algorithm. K-means is used for further clustering. SVM is used to train the dataset.

In [17], features are extracted in both domains time and frequency. In time domain short-time energy and ZCR are calculated and the centroid of audio frequency spectrum, sub-band energy ratio and mel-frequency cepstral coefficients were calculated in frequency domain extraction. The SVM technique is used to classify the audio signal. The design classifies the audio signal effectively and has an accuracy of 90%.

Classifying the audio takes multiple stages, like labelling, extracting, and classifying using training set from audio base. Figure 4.2 shows the block diagram of audio classification. The audio will collect using audio/magnetic sensors, or microphone. The audio will undergo filtration to remove noise from the raw audio signal. The filter signal then divides into frames or labels for further process. Features will extract for classification. Using learning module and training dataset the audio will be classified and send to devices using Bluetooth.

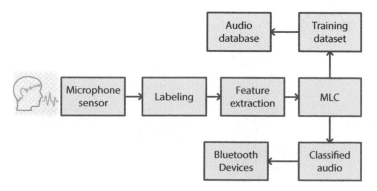

Figure 4.2 Block diagram of audio classification using ML.

The flow chart shown in Figure 4.3 classifies the data according to training data. After noise removal EMI kernel sends the data to ML classifier. The steps are as follows:

1. Start.
2. Data is send by EMI attenuator which is task from the user.
3. If the task==1, it means the instruction given by the user is movement of the wheelchair, otherwise it moves to accessing the computer or smartphone.
4. Yes: moves to next block and compares the data by training data. No: Moves to the next decision step.
5. If the data matches the training data, then the command is given and flow will end. Otherwise, moves to the 2nd block and again collects the data.
6. Steps 4 and 5 will repeat for accessing computer and smartphone.
7. End.

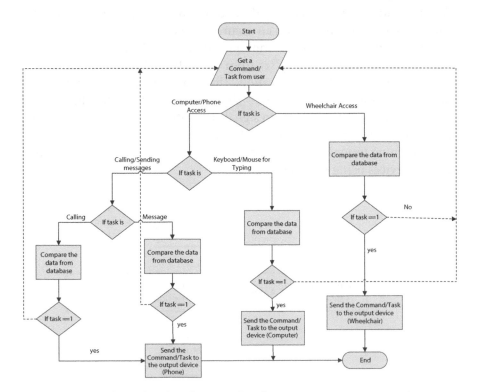

Figure 4.3 Flow chart of machine learning classifier.

Now, after the classification final command is given to the electronic devices through Bluetooth and the task will be performed accordingly. The circuit will implement on FPGA.

Steps involved in implementing the MATLAB code as shown in Figure 4.4:

1. Circuit is designed using MATLAB algorithm or Simulink.
2. Next step is to simulate and debug the MATLAB code.
3. HDL code is generated using HDL app.
4. After verifying the design, synthesis and analysis take place. Here we have to create the project and synthesis and implementation takes place.

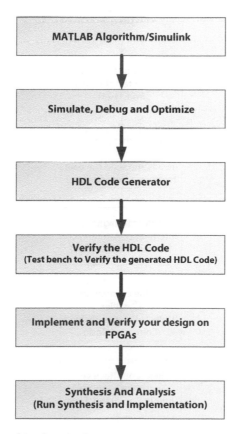

Figure 4.4 FPGA-based implementation.

4.3 Audio Processing Module Using Machine Learning

Reconfigurable FPGA board is useful in implementing and prototyping different design modules for any kind of signal processing. Here, all the algorithms are implemented through programming in Verilog HDL or VHDL using Xilinx Vivado. Through HDL, we can generate RTL level design block, synthesise and generate a bitstream for implementation on FPGA.

A basic model of audio signal processing is shown through the block diagram in Figure 4.1. The proposed model consists of three major parts/ blocks which help the device to transfer the data/instruction and decides

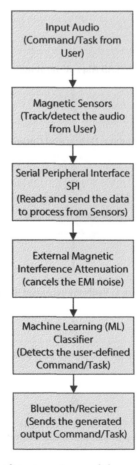

Figure 4.5 Flow diagram of audio processing module.

the performance of the system. Those are Serial Peripheral Interface, external magnetic interference attenuation and classifier. The block diagram of the local processor is given in Figure 4.3.

The flow diagram (Figure 4.5) shows the raw data transmitted to perform an action/command given by the user using audio processing module.

The design steps are:

i)   the user gives the command as audio/voice instruction.
ii) the raw data will track by magnetic sensors.
iii) these magnetic sensors send the data to the processor; SPI will collect the data and processes it to EMI kernel.
iv) In the EMI kernel the data noise will attenuate and noise-free data is send to ML classifier.
v)   ML classifier compares the data which is processed by dataset which was already given to the device as training data. The final instruction/command is detected by using classification algorithms.
vi) The ML classifier sends the output as command to the devices.

The magnetic sensors are attached to the user tongue, which collects the raw data from the user and sends the data to the processor through magnetic fields generated by sensors. The processor should be within the surroundings because the magnetic field does not cover up the maximum area. A lot of sensors are available, and the sensors are selected by their accuracy performance. The hall effect sensors can acquire 1% output error, which is very low. Hall effect sensors are particularly suitable for high-current or low-voltage applications.

4.4   Application of Proposed FPGA-Based ML Models

One of the applications of a machine learning module in the biomedical field is Assistive technology (AT). There are a number of ATs available in the market that help individuals to independently communicate with the environment through their body movements and senses. They are able to send commands through various sensor modalities, such as eye movements, facial expressions, head motion, voice recognition systems, electro-myography switches, electroencephalogram (EEG) and electrooculogram (EOG).

One AT is TDS, in which all the devices that are operated by tongue/voice are included. People who are suffering from paralysis and damaged spinal cord can use these devices without stressing out, because tongue nerves are the least effective nerves in the whole body. Using TDS is easy for SCI (spinal cord injury) and paralyzed patients. The authors in [18] designed a tongue-operated system. Force sensitive resistors are used to send data to the controller, which controls the surrounding of the users in four different modes: communication with caretaker, emergency contact, home automation, and controlling the wheelchair. This methodology does not require any installation or piercing of magnetic sensors or ICs.

In paper [19], a neuromorphic binaural auditory sensor designed completely in spike domain is analyzed in terms of its architecture, design flow, and FPGA implementation. The paper presented a model of the digital cochlea that decomposes audio signals using pulse frequency modulation rather than classical digital signal processing techniques. By using an address-event representation interface, it provides a set of frequency-decomposed audio information based on spike information encoded directly as spikes. The experiment implemented a 64-channel auditory system on a Virtex-5 FPGA board. Various audio signals were used to stimulate the system to characterize its response.

In [20], the authors developed and implemented a processor for stress detection using two learning algorithms SVM and KNN, considering the different physiological sensors used to collect features to monitor stress detection. Heart rate, heart rate variability, galvanic skin response, and accelerometer are the physiological sensors that are considered to collect the input data for detecting stress. The data is collected by performing shooting tasks, and by manipulating the performance feedback. Three levels of stress were stimulated: no feedback (low-stress), medium and high. The experiment was conducted considering 16 features and resulting in a 35-second window to elaborate on the stress. The design is implemented on Artix-7 FPGA board and ASIC post-layout in 65 nm CMOS technology.

In [21], the authors designed and implemented an image quality assessment (IQA). This is useful to identify the visual quality automatically without others' judgment. IQA is classified into three depending on the availability of reference images. References: full reference (FR), reduced reference (RR) and no reference (NR); this means complete reference, partial availably and no reference needed. ML algorithms – SVM, RT (regression tree), non-linear regression (NLR), artificial neural networks (ANN) and fuzzy logic (FL) are used to estimate the IQA Implemented using C code on VIVADO HLS and the design tested on Virtex-7 FPGA board. TDS is implemented on IGLOO nano FPGA board [22], which is ultra-low-power onboard intraoral TDS. The blocks which are included for developing the iTDS are SPI, EMF (electromagnetic field) attenuation and classifiers.

4.5   Implementation of a Microphone on FPGA

For sending a real-time raw audio signal, an onboard microphone is used. Ethernet is used to access the microphone and CIC (Cascaded Integrator Comb) compiler IP is used, which reduces the filter implementation time while providing the ability to make trade-offs between differing hardware implementations of their CIC Filter specification. Clocking wizard and FIFO (first-in-first-out) generator (13.2) IPs are used. Native interface type FIFO is selected for data storage and retrieval. Clocking wizard (6.0) IP

Table 4.1 Utilisation summary.

Module	LUTs	Registers	Block RAM	Slices	DSP	FFs	I/O
Microphone	414	716	0.5	201	2	716	14
EMI Filter	98	716	112	41	4	12	32

Table 4.2 Summary of design timing summary.

Setup	Time (ns)	Hold	Time (ns)	Pulse width	Time (ns)
Worst Negative Slack (WNS)	0.796	Worst Hold Slack (WHS)	0.087	Worst Pulse Width Slack (WPWS)	3.000
Total Number of Negative slack	0.000	Total Number of Hold slack	0.000	Total Number of Negative slack	0.000
Number of failing end points	0	Number of failing end points	0	Number of failing end points	0
Total number of end points	2043	Total number of end points	2043	Total number of end points	877

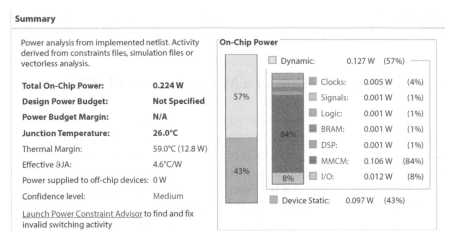

Summary

Power analysis from implemented netlist. Activity derived from constraints files, simulation files or vectorless analysis.

Total On-Chip Power:	**0.224 W**
Design Power Budget:	**Not Specified**
Power Budget Margin:	**N/A**
Junction Temperature:	**26.0°C**
Thermal Margin:	59.0°C (12.8 W)
Effective ϑJA:	4.6°C/W
Power supplied to off-chip devices:	0 W
Confidence level:	Medium

Launch Power Constraint Advisor to find and fix invalid switching activity

On-Chip Power

Dynamic:	0.127 W	(57%)
Clocks:	0.005 W	(4%)
Signals:	0.001 W	(1%)
Logic:	0.001 W	(1%)
BRAM:	0.001 W	(1%)
DSP:	0.001 W	(1%)
MMCM:	0.106 W	(84%)
I/O:	0.012 W	(8%)
Device Static:	0.097 W	(43%)

Figure 4.6 Power analysis of audio module on FPGA.

simplifies the configuring process of clocks in FPGA. According to user requirement the clocking wizard generates HDL code for configuring the clock circuits. Table 4.1 and Table 4.2 show, respectively, device utilisation and timing summary observed on FPGA. The total on chip power obtained on FPGA is 0.224W, out of which 57% dynamic and 43% static power consumption are shown in Figure 4.6.

4.6   Conclusion

Reconfigurable architectures like FPGA can be used for the implementation of machine learning model to observe a real-time response with improvement in accuracy, speed and power consumption. This process of implementation is followed by identifying the suitable machine learning algorithm for any specific task and implementing it through HDL code, synthesis and bitstream generation using simulation software like Xilinx Vivado. The generated bitstream is used to implement the same on FPGA board or prototyping before proceeding to the layout and fabrication of ASIC.

4.7   Future Scope

Biomedical data processing is another key area of research to make efficient and accurate biomedical devices and sensors [23–25]. A situation like

COVID-19 [26, 27] also attracts designer focus on improvising biomedical devices in terms of performance [28] with the addition of advanced techniques. Machine learning helps [29, 30] in optimising data that need to be evaluated through hardware and must be explainable. Also, the interfacing of sensors for large biomedical data is a major concern of designers which is possible with FPGA boards.

References

1. Lata Tripathi, S., Dhir, K., Ghai, D., & Patil, S. (Eds.). (2021). *Health Informatics and Technological Solutions for Coronavirus (COVID-19)* (1st ed.). CRC Press. https://doi.org/10.1201/9781003161066

2. D. L. Prasanna and S. L. Tripathi, "Machine Learning Classifiers for Speech Detection," *2022 IEEE VLSI Device Circuit and System (VLSI DCS)*, 2022, pp. 143-147, doi: 10.1109/VLSIDCS53788.2022.9811452.

3. Prasanna, Dasari L., Tripathi, Suman Lata (2022) Machine and Deep-Learning Techniques for Text and Speech Processing, pp. 115-128 https://doi.org/10.1002/9781119861850.ch7

4. F. Rong, "Audio Classification Method Based on Machine Learning," *2016 International Conference on Intelligent Transportation, Big Data & Smart City (ICITBS)*, 2016, pp. 81-84, doi: 10.1109/ICITBS.2016.98.

5. A. Chen and M. A. Hasegawa-Johnson, "Mixed Stereo Audio Classification Using a Stereo-Input Mixed-to-Panned Level Feature," in *IEEE/ACM Transactions on Audio, Speech, and Language Processing*, vol. 22, no. 12, pp. 2025-2033, Dec. 2014, doi: 10.1109/TASLP.2014.2359628.

6. H. Xie and T. Virtanen, "Zero-Shot Audio Classification Based On Class Label Embeddings," *2019 IEEE Workshop on Applications of Signal Processing to Audio and Acoustics (WASPAA)*, 2019, pp. 264-267, doi: 10.1109/WASPAA.2019.8937283.

7. K. Kumar and K. Chaturvedi, "An Audio Classification Approach using Feature extraction neural network classification Approach," *2nd International Conference on Data, Engineering and Applications (IDEA)*, 2020, pp. 1-6, doi: 10.1109/IDEA49133.2020.9170702.

8. B. Yousefi, X. Huo, J. Kim, E. Veledar and M. Ghovanloo, "Quantitative and Comparative Assessment of Learning in a Tongue-Operated Computer Input Device--Part II: Navigation Tasks," in *IEEE Transactions on Information Technology in Biomedicine*, vol. 16, no. 4, pp. 633-643, July 2012, doi: 10.1109/TITB.2012.2191793.

9. C. B. Pratap, Godviya and G. S. Let, "Smart Reading Aid using Tongue Drive System for Disabled patients," *2018 International Conference on Control, Power, Communication and Computing Technologies (ICCPCCT)*, 2018, pp. 563-566, doi: 10.1109/ICCPCCT.2018.8574313.

10. J. Kim, X. Huo and M. Ghovanloo, "Wireless control of smartphones with tongue motion using tongue drive assistive technology," *2010 Annual International Conference of the IEEE Engineering in Medicine and Biology*, 2010, pp. 5250-5253, doi: 10.1109/IEMBS.2010.5626294.

11. F. Kong, M. Zada, H. Yoo and M. Ghovanloo, "Triple-Band Transmitter with a Shared Dual-Band Antenna and Adaptive Matching for an Intraoral Tongue Drive System," *2018 IEEE International Symposium on Circuits and Systems (ISCAS)*, 2018, pp. 1-5, doi: 10.1109/ISCAS.2018.8351709.

12. Rong, Feng. (2016). Audio Classification Method Based on Machine Learning. 81-84. 10.1109/ICITBS.2016.98.

13. H. Phan, L. Hertel, M. Maass, R. Mazur and A. Mertins, "Learning Representations for Nonspeech Audio Events Through Their Similarities to Speech Patterns," in *IEEE/ACM Transactions on Audio, Speech, and Language Processing*, vol. 24, no. 4, pp. 807-822, April 2016, doi: 10.1109/ TASLP.2016.2530401.

14. D. Barchiesi, D. Giannoulis, D. Stowell and M. Plumbley, "Acoustic scene classification: Classifying environments from the sounds they produce", *IEEE Signal Process. Mag.*, vol. 32, no. 3, pp. 16-34, May 2015.

15. K. P. Seng, L. -M. Ang and C. S. Ooi, "A Combined Rule-Based & Machine Learning Audio-Visual Emotion Recognition Approach," in *IEEE Transactions on Affective Computing*, vol. 9, no. 1, pp. 3-13, 1 Jan.-March 2018, doi: 10.1109/TAFFC.2016.2588488.

16. M. Esmaeilpour, P. Cardinal and A. Lameiras Koerich, "A Robust Approach for Securing Audio Classification Against Adversarial Attacks," in *IEEE Transactions on Information Forensics and Security*, vol. 15, pp. 2147-2159, 2020, doi: 10.1109/TIFS.2019.2956591.

17. Shuiping, Wang and Zhenming, Tang and Shiqiang, Li, "Design and Implementation of an Audio Classification System Based on SVM," *Procedia Engineering*, 2011, vol. 15, pp. 4031-4035, doi: 10.1016/j.proeng.2011.08.756.

18. J. Johri, J. Pillai and M. Shakya, "Tongue Operated Integrated System," *2017 14th IEEE India Council International Conference (INDICON)*, 2017, pp. 1-6, doi: 10.1109/INDICON.2017.8488082.

19. A. Jiménez-Fernández *et al.*, "A Binaural Neuromorphic Auditory Sensor for FPGA: A Spike Signal Processing Approach," in *IEEE Transactions on Neural Networks and Learning Systems*, vol. 28, no. 4, pp. 804-818, April 2017, doi: 10.1109/TNNLS.2016.2583223.

20. N. Attaran, A. Puranik, J. Brooks and T. Mohsenin, "Embedded Low-Power Processor for Personalized Stress Detection," in *IEEE Transactions on Circuits and Systems II: Express Briefs*, vol. 65, no. 12, pp. 2032-2036, Dec. 2018, doi: 10.1109/TCSII.2018.2799821.

21. G. T. Tchendjou, E. Simeu and F. Lebowsky, "FPGA implementation of machine learning based image quality assessment," *2017 29th International Conference on Microelectronics (ICM)*, 2017, pp. 1-4, doi: 10.1109/ ICM.2017.8268848.

22. S. Viseh, M. Ghovanloo and T. Mohsenin, "Toward an Ultralow-Power Onboard Processor for Tongue Drive System," in *IEEE Transactions on Circuits and Systems II: Express Briefs*, vol. 62, no. 2, pp. 174-178, Feb. 2015, doi: 10.1109/TCSII.2014.2387683.

23. Badiganti P.K., Peddirsi S., Rupesh A.T.J., Tripathi S.L. (2022) Design and Implementation of Smart Healthcare Monitoring System Using FPGA. In: Rawat S., Kumar A., Kumar P., Anguera J. (eds.) *Proceedings of First International Conference on Computational Electronics for Wireless Communications. Lecture Notes in Networks and Systems*, vol. 329. Springer, Singapore. https://doi.org/10.1007/978-981-16-6246-1_18

24. Kanak Kumar, Soumyadeepa Bhaumik Suman Lata Tripathi, "Health Monitoring System", in *Electronic Device and Circuits Design Challenges to Implement Biomedical Applications*, Elsevier, 2021. Doi: https://doi.org/10.1016/B978-0-323-85172-5.00021-6

25. Kanak Kumar, Anchal Sharma, Suman Lata Tripathi, "Sensors and Their Application", in *Electronic Device and Circuits Design Challenges to Implement Biomedical Applications*, Elsevier, 2021. https://doi.org/10.1016/B978-0-323-85172-5.00021-6

26. V Dhinakaran, M Varsha Shree, Suman Lata Tripathi, P M Bupathi Ram, "An Overview of Evolution, Transmission, Detection and Diagnosis for the Way Out of Corona Virus", in *Health Informatics and Technological Solutions for Coronavirus (COVID-19)*, CRC Taylor & Francis, 2021. https://doi.org/10.1201/9781003161066

27. Suman Lata Tripathi Kolla Prakash, Valentina Balas, Sushanta Mohapatra, Janmenjoy Nayak, *Electronic Device and Circuit Design Challenges for Biomedical Applications*, Elsevier, 2021. https://doi.org/10.1016/C2020-0-02289-9

28. Kanak Kumar; Kaustav Chaudhury; Suman Lata Tripathi, "Future of Machine Learning (ML) and Deep Learning (DL) in Healthcare Monitoring System," in *Machine Learning Algorithms for Signal and Image Processing*, IEEE, 2023, pp. 293-313, doi: 10.1002/9781119861850.ch17.

29. Deepika Ghai, Suman Lata Tripathi, Sobhit Saxena, Manash Chanda, Mamoun Alazab, *Machine Learning Algorithms for Signal and Image Processing*, Wiley IEEE Press, 2022.

30. Sandhya Awasthi, Ritu Chauhan, Suman Lata Tripathi, Tanushree Datta, "COVID-19 research: open data resources and challenges", in *Biomedical Engineering Applications for People with Disabilities and Elderly in a New COVID-19 Pandemic and Beyond*, Elsevier, 2021. https://doi.org/10.1016/B978-0-323-85174-9.00008-X

5

Synthesis and Time Analysis of FPGA-Based DIT-FFT Module for Efficient VLSI Signal Processing Applications

Siba Kumar Panda[1]*, Konasagar Achyut[2] and Dhruba Charan Panda[3]

[1]Xeedo Technologies Pvt Ltd, Bangalore, India
[2]J.B. Institute of Engineering & Technology, Hyderabad, India
[3]Department of Electronics Science, Berhampur University, Odisha, India

Abstract

Now is the era of high-speed processors with reconfigurable architectures. The dedicated architectures have a wide variety of applications in signal processing, image processing, and audio/video processing provinces. Further implementation of those dedicated architectures in FPGA/ASIC level plays an important role. Synthesis and static timing analysis of FPGA-based Decimation in Time Fast Fourier Transform (DIT-FFT) architecture for VLSI signal processing application is presented in this chapter. This work presents a continuous flow such as RTL design, simulation, synthesis, and implementations as well as timing investigation of the designed module. The architecture is designed and verified for different values of N and converted to corresponding gate level netlist using synthesis. Post-synthesis, utilization and power report are recorded. The post-implementation and timing confirm that the design for N=8 consumes 780 LUTs (logic), 257 registers (BRAMs), 0.163W on-chip power, set up slack 3.258ns, hold slack 0.430ns with timing cohesively meeting at 24ns. Post-timing analysis, physical layout of the designed circuit with proper routing is also obtained. The implementations were carried out using vivado IDE tool with Artix7 FPGA board in 28nm technology.

Keywords: Critical path delay, DIT-FFT, data path delay (DPD), FPGA, LUT, static timing analysis (STA), slack

*Corresponding author: panda.sibakumar08vssut@gmail.com

Suman Lata Tripathi and Mufti Mahmud (eds.) *Explainable Machine Learning Models and Architectures,* (65–80) © 2023 Scrivener Publishing LLC

5.1   Introduction

In wireless network systems, ICs have to process signal to extract the original information. This processing takes place after the data pass through several analog components such as ADCs, Op amps, etc. To make them work accordingly a solemn course of action is brought up right from RTL till the GDSII [1]. Likewise in billion transistor one such bunch of digital signal processing core uses a dedicated section in which to process complex signal [2–21]. Many algorithms have been implemented to process the composite data associated with complex signals. The FFT is an integral part of DSP. This algorithm allows the processor to convert the information from one domain to other. Many works have been done to reduce the complexity of this algorithm, such as Prime Factor FFT algorithm, Bruun's FFT algorithm, Rader's FFT algorithm, Bluestein's FFT algorithm, Cooley-Tukey FFT algorithm and Hexagonal FFT algorithm. In this paper, we have considered Cooley-Tukey algorithm, also known as Decimation in Time – Fast Fourier Transform (DIT-FFT). To improve its performance for VLSI implementation, Rauf *et al.* in [4], have proposed a design based on split radix with user-defined input resolution. Also, Radix 4 butterfly structured DIT FFT algorithm, using floating point calculations as in [7] by Prabhu *et al.* In [8], Nuenfeld *et al.* have come up with improvised radix 2 and radix 4 butterfly architectures concentrating on low power consumption. Paul *et al.* have proposed floating point FFT algorithm considering energy efficient butterfly units in [11]. Ma *et al.* in [12] have implemented pipelined architecture for radix 2 FFT algorithm on FPGA. A use of ganged butterfly engine enabled the design to compute in 11 μs at 200MHz frequency. XOR gate topology with adder compressors in the butterfly structures of radix 2 DIT FFT has shown to use 5.69mW of power in an optimized single pipelined structure. Design of FFT architecture given by Cooley-Tukey is used for SOC telecom-based applications as classified by Saponara *et al.* in [14]. They used the architecture for OFDM and MIMO schemes at 12.375MHz. In [15], Huang *et al.* have used the concept of offset binary coding (OBC) mechanism along with sliding block distributed arithmetic (SDBA). This considerably reduced the usage of available LUT slices, RAMs, etc., in FPGA. Table 5.1 summarizes the state-of-art on VLSI implementation of DIT-FFT module. However, the synthesis and timing analysis of the DIT-FFT module is rarely reported in open literature [16]. This work makes an attempt to provide a step-by-step process to achieve this. This is necessary for digital signal processor and cryptographic applications.

Table 5.1 Performance comparison of various state-of-the-art designs.

References	Technology	Area	Delay	Power (Total on chip)	PDP	LUT	Flipflops	ADP
[1]	---------	---------	7 ns	---------	--------	954	336	--------
[3]	45 nm	0.61mm²	---------	404.39mW	--------	21,603	4,142	--------
[6]	---------	---------	--------	5.377 W	--------	437	--------	--------
[7]	---------	3345 μm²	2381 ps	583.4mW	--------	--------	-------	7964.4
[9]	--------	---------	--------	--------	1651.6	--------	1406	---------
[10]	45 nm	0.973mm²	7 μs	68 mW	--------	--------	---------	6.811
[13]	--------	--------	---------	--------	---------	8614	---------	---------

The above discussion motivates us to develop a synthesized and time analyzed DIT-FFT architecture for efficient VLSI Signal Processing applications. Considering digital signal processor and cryptographic applications, in every stage various multiplication algorithms are required. These computations require designing of efficient architecture at system level and specifically at chip level. That's why a dedication towards the Simulation-Synthesis-Timing analysis is the central focus of this work, which is presented neatly here. The offered work is designed also with FPGA. We have summarized the obtained results in tabular manner for purposes of clear understanding. Finally, it is believed that the presented architecture may establish a new route for imminent research.

5.2   Implementation of DIT-FFT Algorithm

5.2.1   A Quick Overview of DIT-FFT

The basic element of DSP block is signal. A signal carries information between two terminals. All the continuous time varying signals, after being converted to quantized discrete signal (digital), are sent to DSP cores. A DFT is a method to convert a time domain signal to frequency domain which holds amplitude, frequency and phase values. These values are later used for high-speed computational process. The basic equation of DFT is,

$$X(K) = \sum_{n=0}^{N-1} x(n) w_N^{kn} \tag{5.1}$$

where $K = 0,1,2,3.....N-1$, $x(n)$ is input signal amplitude at time n and $w_N^{kn} = e^{-j2\pi/N}$ called a twiddle factor representing complex information.

In this, N-Point DFTs are partitioned recursively into N/2 DFTs in butterfly structure. This form of dividing DFT blocks is the simplest form of FFT algorithms, known as Radix-based DFT. A DFT of N-length sequence can be calculated by using N/2 DFT blocks repeatedly until we are left with only one DFT block for all input samples, providing the final output value. Figure 5.1 shows the DIT-FFT algorithm.

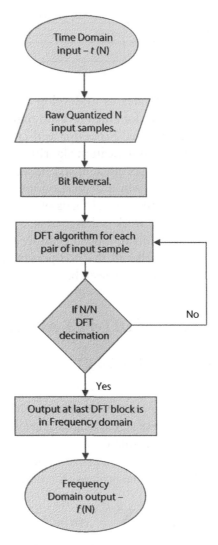

Figure 5.1 Representation of DIT-FFT algorithm flow.

5.2.2   Algorithmic Representation with Example

The examples shown below are considered only for two samples for ease of understanding Twiddle factors cause variation according to the number of input samples. Considerably an emphasized procedural view of this algorithm with an example is presented in Figure 5.2 while Figure 5.3 shows a simplified working nature of DIT-FFT algorithm.

5.2.3   Simulated Output Waveform

A single clock and reset ports have been used synchronous to all DFT blocks to extract the output. The values processed are in offset representation; also, the output received is in offset binary format (Excess 16). With respect to acquired output, we can add/subtract input value to the offset value. For more clarity, we can see the output wave forms attained while

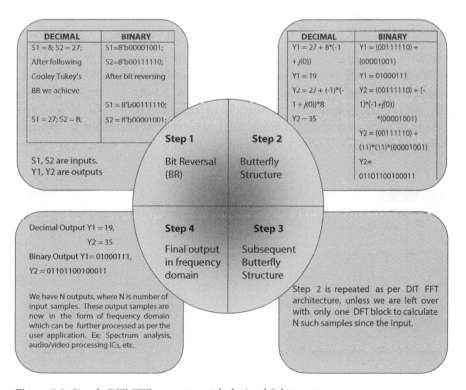

Figure 5.2 Simple DIT-FFT execution with decimal & binary inputs.

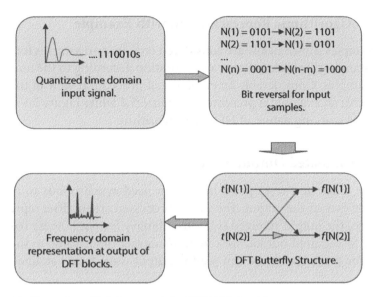

Figure 5.3 Illustration of brief approach for DIT-FFT algorithm.

verifying the design by giving inputs manually for samples N = 2, 4 and 8. Wave forms for N = 4 and 8 can be seen in Figure 5.4 and Figure 5.5, respectively. Here lower case s1, s2, s3....s8 are inputs and upper case S1, S2....S8 are the outputs in the waveform representation. For N = 2, the design depicts only a single block DFT structure as the input length has only two inputs.

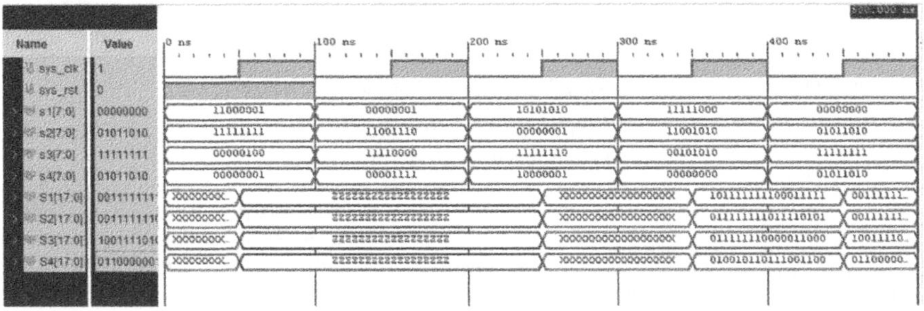

Figure 5.4 Output waveform for samples N = 4.

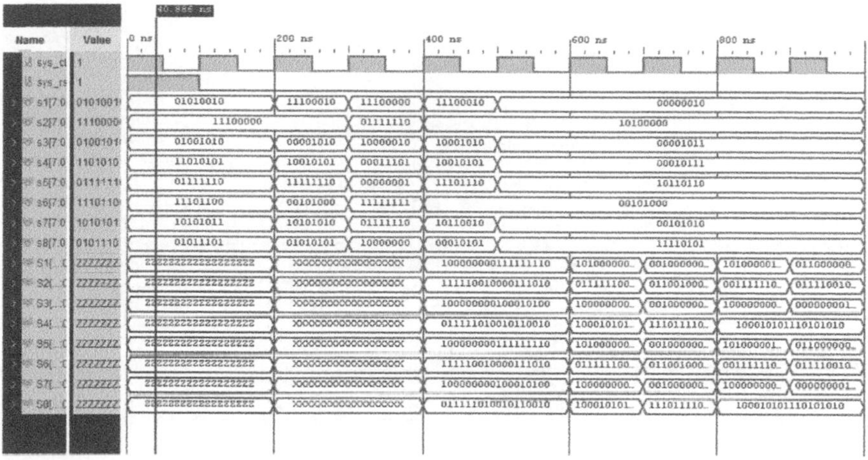

Figure 5.5 Output waveform for samples N = 8.

5.3   Synthesis of Designed Circuit

In this work, synthesis of DIT-FFT architecture is performed using vivado Design Suite in Verilog HDL environment, considering radix 2 butterfly structure. The Xilinx Synthesis Technology (XST) allows users to synthesize any design written in Verilog/VHDL. The device used is xc7a200tffV1156 with speed grade -1. Synthesized representation or RTL schematic or gate level schematic for N = 4 length input samples can be seen in Figure 5.6. The design is written with respect to the architecture of radix 2 butterfly DIT-FFT structure proposed by Cooley and Tukey. Single clock and reset pin is synchronous to whole design from the top module of the RTL abstraction. Similarly, Figure 5.7 shows RTL schematic for N = 8 length input samples, where usage of logic elements varies as the input size differs. After design has been synthesized in gate level, we can observe the performance of the FPGA for the samples N = 2, 4 and 8. Values include power consumption of fabric and utilization of cells, slices, FFs, etc., which is briefly termed as area. These individually related values are depicted in Table 5.2, which helps us to realize the synthesized design utilization over FPGA.

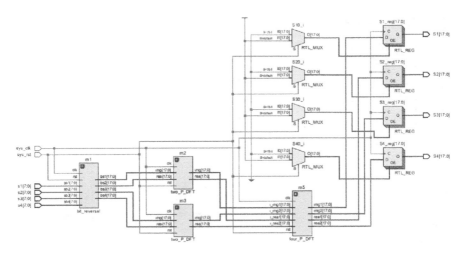

Figure 5.6 RTL schematic for N = 4 DIT-FFT.

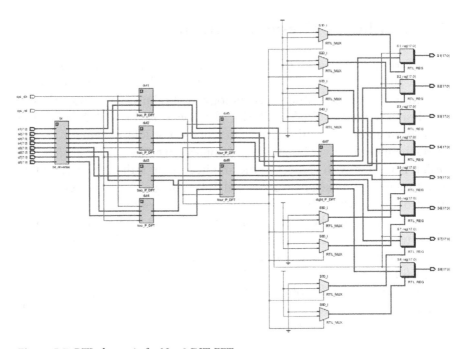

Figure 5.7 RTL shematic for N = 8 DIT-FFT.

Table 5.2 Post-synthesis performance parameters.

Value of N	FPGA board used	Report_utilization (area)	Report_power (on chip power)
N=8	Artix7	Slice LUT = 826 Slice register = 185 DSP = 22	Total on Chip Power (W) = 71.3 Static power (W) = 1.684 Dynamic power (W) = 69.71
N=4	Artix7	Slice LUT = 164 Slice register = 93 DSP = 11	Total on Chip Power (W) = 31.6 Static power (W) = 0.336 Dynamic power (W) = 31.30
N=2	Artix7	Slice LUT = 40 Slice register = 37 DSP = 3	Total on Chip Power (W) = 12.7 Static power (W) = 0.135 Dynamic power (W) = 12.59

5.4   Static Timing Analysis of Designed Circuit

We performed the STA for our design, helping us to perform timing checks such as setup and hold timing checks for the entire design in four possible paths: All registers pins to all registers, all input pins to all registers, all registers to all output pins and all input pins to all output pins. The proposed approach for STA could be observed from Figure 5.8. This helped the design to meet the specific operable clock frequency so that the original data isn't lost at any micro architectural block of a design. Setup timing check allows the data to arrive at a flip flop/register before a clock signal can arrive, and hold timing check ensures that the data is stable until the clock signal has gone low. After getting timing summary, the frequency at which the design has met the setup slack as well as hold slack for four paths mentioned above, are included in Table 5.3. Based on the specified clock period/clock frequency the power consumed and area utilization has also been brought into the consideration. As we are performing STA after RTL generated netlist, we do not have any crosstalk or clock tree paths for

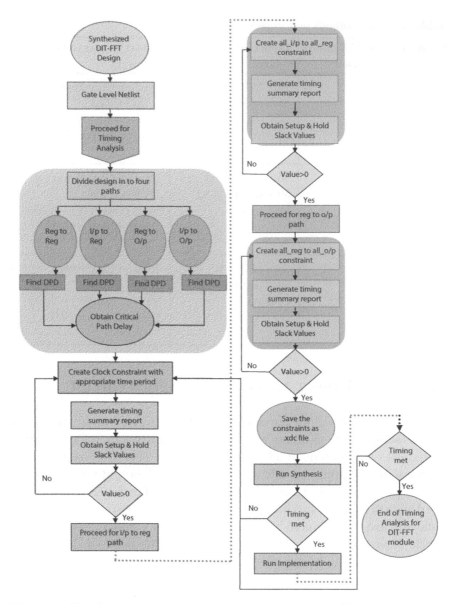

Figure 5.8 Flowchart representing static timing analysis of DIT FFT design.

Table 5.3 Post-timing analysis performance parameters.

Value of N	Report_utilization (Post-Implementation & timing)	Report_Power (Post-Implementation & timing)	Report_timing_ summary	Timing meet at
N = 8	Slice LUT = 780 Slice Registers = 257 LUT as logic = 780 BRAM Tile = 257	Total on chip Power (W) = 0.163	Setup Slack = 3.258ns Hold Slack = 0.430ns	24ns
N = 4	Slice LUT = 158 Slice Registers = 93 LUT as logic = 158 BRAM Tile = 93	Total on chip Power (W) = 0.148	Setup Slack = 1.574ns Hold Slack = 0.321ns	20ns
N = 2	Slice LUT = 38 Slice Registers = 37 LUT as logic = 38 BRAM Tile = 37	Total on chip Power (W) = 0.118	Setup Slack = 1.506ns Hold Slack = 0.062ns	15ns

timing analysis, thus making it a more elementary approach for fixing the timing issue for any design. Following as per the flowchart steps, we have come across several timing issues for three different samples. These are fixed by considering closest time period to the highest Data Path Delay

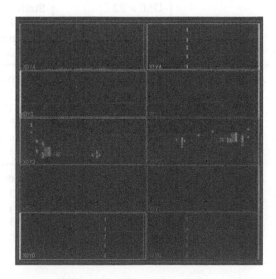

Figure 5.9 Post-timing analysis layout for N = 4 DIT-FFT.

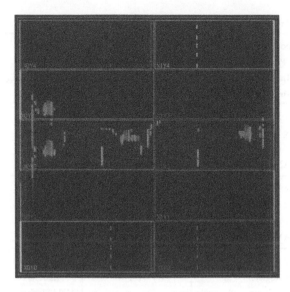

Figure 5.10 Post-timing analysis layout for N = 8 DIT-FFT.

Table 5.4 Post Synthesis-post timing performance parameters.

Value of N	Using FPGA board	Report_ utilization (area)	Report_power (on chip power)
N=8	Artix7	Slice LUT = 775 Slice register = 257 DSP = 22	Total on Chip Power (W) = 73.89 Static Power (W) = 1.674 Dynamic Power (W) = 72.2
N=4	Artix7	Slice LUT = 157 Slice register = 93 DSP = 11	Total on Chip Power (W) = 32.69 Static Power (W) = 0.352 Dynamic Power (W) = 32.34
N=2	Artix7	Slice LUT = 38 Slice register = 37 DSP = 3	Total on Chip Power (W) = 12.72 Static power (W) = 0.135 Dynamic Power (W) = 12.58

(DPD). The DPD is obtained from the three paths: all registers to all registers, all inputs to all registers and all registers to all outputs.

If the time period which has been set meets the setup slack and hold slack requirements, then that time period/constraint is saved for the further implementation of the design for layout post timing analysis. Figure 5.9 shows DIT-FFT design layout routed over the chosen FPGA for N=4. From this we can say that timing fixture plays a greater role for the routing when we compare DIT-FFT for N=4 post timing layout with N = 8. Here cells or nets are placed according to delay constraints. Timing fixture also provides information about exact path connections, buffer/inverters connection, etc. This way we can also say that DIT-FFT for N=8 routing does differ from N = 2 and N = 4, as seen in Figure 5.10. Once the design has been routed, we can have the utilization of different cell, slices, BRAMs, FFs, etc., from the fabric, as displayed in Table 5.4. This helps the user to visualize if the RTL design written is favorable with the availability of BRAMs, FFs, etc., from the chosen fabric/FPGA.

5.5   Result and Discussion

The values related to timing are the parameters obtained by the design for several input sampling sizes (N = 2, 4, & 8). After synthesis of the design, the utilization parameters for FPGA are shown in Table 4.3. From the available 134600 LUTs, 365 BRAM Tiles, and 740 DSP blocks, 0.7% of LUT, 75% of BRAM tiles and 2.97% of DSP has been utilized for N = 8 sample inputs. Similarly, for N = 4, 0.18% of LUTs, 25% of BRAM tiles, and 1.49% of DSP blocks have been utilized; for N = 2, 0.05% of LUTs, 10% of BRAM tiles, and 0.41% of DSP blocks have been utilized. Post timing fixation values in Table 4.4 confirm that the proposed DIT-FFT architecture designed with offset binary representation for complex twiddle factors justifies the synthesis and the time period required for four different paths subsequently divided to meet the overall design. With this, we can ensure that the design is error free with respect to pin to pin time stipulation.

5.6   Conclusion

Timing analysis is an important pathway towards signing off any chip because engineers must be aware how fast the chip/task is going to run, how fast the data is reaching the output from input ports of design. This work shows a practice towards the synthesis and timing analysis of DIT-FFT architecture for VLSI Signal Processing modules. With strict adherence to the Simulation-Synthesis guidelines and by following the Static timing analysis procedure rules, the designed modules met timing at 24ns, 20ns and 15ns for different values of N such as 8, 4 and 2, respectively. It is also found that the proposed design after timing works efficiently with consumable resources of 780 LUTs as logic and 257 BRAM as tile. The Power report confirms that the design consuming 0.163w of on chip power after implementation and timing closure is a notable efficient power value. The high-speed and low-power performances of the proposed architecture make it suitable for wide-ranging on-chip signal processing applications.

References

1. Siba Kumar Panda; Konasagar Achyut and Swati K. Kulkarni. "Industry 4.0: A Road Map to Custom Register Transfer Level Design". In *Advances in Industry 4.0: Concepts and Applications*, edited by M. Niranjanamurthy, Sheng-Lung Peng, E. Naresh, S. R. Jayasimha and Valentina Emilia Balas, Berlin, Boston: De Gruyter, 2022, pp. 21-50.
2. Changela Ankur; Zaveri Mazad and Verma Deepak, FPGA implementation of high-performance, resource efficient Radix-16 CORDIC rotator based FFT algorithm, *Integration, the VLSI Journal*; 2020; 1-12.
3. Ganjikunta Ganesh Kumar and Sahoo Subhendu Kumar, An area-efficient and low-power 64-point pipeline Fast Fourier Transform for OFDM applications, *Integration, the VLSI Journal*, 57, 2017; 125-131.
4. Rauf Adnan; Pasha Mohammed Adeel and Masud Shahid, Towards Design and automation of scalable split-radix FFT Processor for High Throughput Applications. *Microprocessors and Microsystems*, Elsevier. 65, 2017; 148-157.
5. Kar Subhajit; Ganguly Madhabi and Das Saptarshi, Using DIT FFT Algorithm for Identification of Protein Coding Region in Eukaryotic Gene. *Biomedical Engineering: Applications, Basis and Communications*, 31(1), 2018; 1-10.
6. Panda S.K. and Panda D.C, Developing High-Performance AVM Based VLSI Computing Systems: A Study. In: Pattnaik P., Rautary S., Das H., Nayak J. (eds.) *Progress in Computing, Analytics and Networking. Advances in Intelligent Systems and Computing*, 2017;710.
7. Prabhu E.; Mangalam H. and Karthick S., Design of area and power efficient Radix-4 DIT FFT butterfly unit using floating point fused arithmetic. *Journal of Central South University*, Springer, 23, 2016;1669-1681.
8. Neuenfeld Renato; Fonseca Mateus and Costa Eduardo, Design of Optimized Radix – 2 and Radix – 4 Butterflies from FFT with Decimation in Time. In: *VII Latin American Symposium on Circuits and Systems (LASCAS)*, 2016; 171-174.

9. Blake Anthony and Hunter Matt, Dynamically Generating FFT Code. *Journal of Signal Processing Systems*, Springer. 76, 2014; 275-281.

10. Qadeer Shaik; Khan Mohammed Zafar Ali; Sattar Syed Abdul and Ahmed, A, Radix – 2 DIT FFT with Reduced Arithmetic Complexity. In: *International Conference on Advances in Computing, Communications and Informatics (ICACCI)*, 2014; 1892-1896.

11. Paul Augusta Sophy Beulet; Raju Srinivasan and Janaki Raman Raja, Low power reconfigurable FP-FFT core with an array of folded DA butterflies. *EURASIP Journal on Advances in Signal Processing*, 2014; 144: 1-17.

12. Ma Zhen-guo, Yu Feng; Ge Rui-feng and Wang Ze-ke, An efficient radix-2 fast Fourier transform processor with ganged butterfly engines on field programmable gate arrays. *Journal of Zhejiang University SCIENCE C*, 12(4); 2011; 323-329.

13. Fonseca Mateus Beck; A Eduardo; Costa Da Cesar and Martins Joao B. S, Design of power efficient butterflies from Radix-2 DIT FFT using adder compressors with a new XOR gate topology. *Analog Integr Circ Sig Process*, Springer Science Business Media, LLC. 73(3);2012;945-954.

14. Saponara Sergio; Rovini Massimo; Fanucci Luca; Karachalios Athanasios; Lentaris George and Reisis Dionysios, Design and Comparison of FFT VLSI Architectures for SoC Telecom Applications with Different Flexibility, *Speed and Complexity Trade-Offs. Circuits, Systems and Signal Processing*, Springer, 31;2011;627-649.

15. Huang Walter; V David and Anderson, Modified Sliding-Block Distributed Arithmetic with Offset Binary Coding for Adaptive Filters. *Journal of Signal Processing System*, Springer Science Business Media, LLC. 63;2010; 153-163.

16. Parhami B., *Computer Arithmetic: Algorithms and Hardware Designs*. 2nd Edition, Oxford University Press, New York, 2010. ISBN No. 978-0-19-532848-6.

17. Chadha Rakesh and Bhasker J., *Static Timing Analysis for Nanometer Designs: A Practical Approach*. Springer-Verlag US, 2009; ISBN No. 978-0-387-93819-6.

18. Mano M. Morris and Ciletti Michael D., *Digital Design*. Fourth Edition. Pearson Education, Inc. 2008; ISBN No. 978-8131714508.

19. Parhi Keshab K., *VLSI Digital Signal Processing Systems Design and Implementation*. A Wiley-Interscience Publication, 1999; ISBN No. 978-0471241867.

20. Deepika Ghai, Suman Lata Tripathi, Sobhit Saxena, Manash Chanda, Mamoun Alazab, *Machine Learning Algorithms for Signal and Image Processing*, Wiley IEEE Press, 2022, ISBN: 978-1-119-86182-9

21. Dasari L. Prasanna; Suman Lata Tripathi, "Machine and Deep-Learning Techniques for Text and Speech Processing," in *Machine Learning Algorithms for Signal and Image Processing*, IEEE, 2023, pp. 115-128, doi: 10.1002/9781119861850.ch7

6

Artificial Intelligence–Based Active Virtual Voice Assistant

Swathi Gowroju*, G. Mounika, D. Bhavana, Shaik Abdul Latheef
and A. Abhilash

*¹CCSE, Sreyas Institute of Engineering and Technology, Hyderabad,
Telangana, India*

Abstract

As we all know, there are many voice assistants which determine the user's intent which can be identified by the user input in spoken or textual form. Unlike the other voice assistants, here we can open multiple tabs or apps concurrently. Though the input is taken, the voice assistant will be activated till the user says to exit the app. It is a very useful tool for reminders, searching, opening, and saving applications as the user needs. The proposed virtual-based voice assistant helps people to communicate with the computer, which indeed saves time. The processes which are to be implemented will work under AI modules like speech recognition, pyttsx3, and operating system. This new version has added three features. They are movie recommender, book recommender, and some Covid protection features. The movie recommender and the book recommender work on the users' interests. For example, the movie recommender helps users to find the best movie according to their interest in different genres and displays it based on the IMDB ratings and the number of users watching. This also includes series recommenders too, like web series. The same process is applied to book recommender. The books are displayed according to user interests based on author and genres (romcoms, thrillers, etc.). Because of the rapid spread of Covid-19, precautions should be taken mandatorily. All the Covid symptoms are stored in our database, through which users can receive information and advice based on their symptoms. All these processes work under AI modules like speech recognition, pyttsx3, and operation system.

Keywords: Speech recognition, pyttsx3, operation system

Corresponding author: swathigowroju@sreyas.ac.in

Suman Lata Tripathi and Mufti Mahmud (eds.) Explainable Machine Learning Models and Architectures, (81–104) © 2023 Scrivener Publishing LLC

6.1   Introduction

This voice assistant works just like other voice assistances such as Siri and Google Assistant. In this project, artificial intelligence modules are used. It will detect the speech and save it in the database and then retrieve it from the database and execute the command given by the user and delete it from the database. To do this process, AI modules are used, such as, to recognize speech, speech recognition module is used, to detect the voice of the user and respond to it correctly, pyttsx3 module is used, and also for searching files in the folders, OS (operating system) modules are implemented. To open other applications and websites like Google, Firefox, YouTube, Wikipedia, and web browser modules are used. As the interactions between the user and your window assistant skills are in free form, the assistant will understand the language naturally without any interruptions and also in the view of context. It consists of a special feature, i.e., we can open multiple tabs or apps concurrently. Although the input is taken, the voice assistant will be in activate mode until the user says to exit the app. If not, the assistant keeps on taking the commands given by the user.

Aside from the lack of research in the field, many of these efforts face difficulties in retrieving BIM data using speech recognition systems. Keyword-based search engines are one of the most common pitfalls. Autodesk's Voice 360 plugin, for example, is used to accomplish Forge Viewer instructions. The user can use voice recognition to give instructions instead of mouse and keyboard inputs. Moreover, the Voice 360 plugin uses rule key phrases and is limited to a list of eligible items [1]. The small handful of keywords in lexicon search engines is a significant limitation.

Moreover, finding accurate results is difficult when the recall and precision attributes used during the search are limited [2]. Words that have different meanings or phrases that serve the same purpose produce irrelevant search results [2]. Motawa [9] created another search approach for searching BIM data, this time using the IFC database to create an NLP-based repository for scanning BIM data. This technique is indeed limited because the IFC pattern focuses on object relationships. It signifies that all of an element's detailed data is not transferred to the IFC template [3].

With the foregoing in mind, there is a need to develop a manageable information source proficient in fetching fractal data in BIM models by multiple users with varying levels of experience in voice assistant software applications, thereby reinforcing the paper's purpose.

However, there is a significant knowledge gap in the building projects for this. It is frightening to research the subject. Few attempts have been made to use AI voice commands to socialize with BIM models. Shin *et al.* [7] created a framework for BIMASR (building information modeling automatic speech recognition) to allow BIM people to engage with the BIM model using natural language (NL)-based questions. The developed solution, however, is extensive and contains multiple tasks. The solution was built around the Google Cloud API for speech recognition and the Oracle database with the Eclipse platform for interacting with Dynamo.

Furthermore, the originality of a study in the building construction discipline concerns the development of understanding and its effects on practice [3–5]. With all that in mind, the current study offers novel insights into the dynamics of using talk as a new method of communication with BIM platform via "contingency approaches." Contingency approaches bring to light "what processes and practices apply where in circumstances, what connections retain but do not retain in whose situations, or where do approach method and do not collaborate, etc."

6.2   Literature Survey

It is a process to learn from previous research and elaborate the extension of the previous study in our thought process and research performed. The goal of every research is to obtain new solutions and inventions. In general, we use five main steps in the literature survey as mentioned in Table 6.1.

As we all know, there are many voice assistants which determine the user's intent which can be identified by the user input in spoken or textual form. Unlike the other voice assistants, here we can open multiple tabs or apps concurrently. Though the input is taken, the voice assistant will be activated till the user says to exit the app. It is a very useful tool for reminders, searching, opening, and saving applications as the user needs. This virtual-based voice assistant helps people to communicate with the computer, which indeed saves time.

The movie recommender and the book recommender work on the users' interests. For example, the movie recommender helps users to find the best movie according to their interest in different genres and displays it based on the IMDB ratings, several users watched.

Table 6.1 Literature survey of virtual voice assistants from the past decade.

S. no.	Author	Year	Methodology	Data set used	Algorithm	Eval-Param
1.	David et al. [2]	2018	By 2018, voice assistance had been the milestone discovered in a battle between the leaders of the technology.	Cleveland heart disease dataset	Logistic regression (LR), Artificial neural network (ANN), K-Nearest Neighbor (KNN), naïve bays (NB), and decision tree (DT).	LR-84% ANN-60% KNN-69% NB-75% DT-70%
2.	Amrita et al. [3]	2020	A virtual assistant is a gift for people of the 21st century. Even though many problems are being faced and yet to be solved in voice assistants like voice recognition, human interaction, etc., to solve those challenges faced by voice assistance the present voice assistance project is taken up.	Electronic health records (EHRs)	Co-clustering and supervised learning methods, data-driven	

(*Continued*)

Table 6.1 Literature survey of virtual voice assistants from the past decade. (*Continued*)

S. no.	Author	Year	Methodology	Data set used	Algorithm	Eval-Param
3.	George et al. [4]	2019	By growing its potential. This voice assistant technology uses AI through cloud computing by which it can communicate to users in natural language.	Catalog and Cleveland	Logistic regression, multilayer perceptron, support vector machine, decision tree, random forest, naïve Bayes	S-95% C-98%
4.	Peter et al. [5]	2013	Virtual personal assistant focuses on user-based data. It determines various programs through natural language processing that are available and examines the best software as VPA. It helps in the holding and analysis of data within the context of the user.	Cleveland, long beach, Switzer-land, Hungarian stat log	Random forest bagging method, AdaBoost boosting method, Gradient boosting method, Decision tree bagging method, K- Nearest Neighbor bagging method.	99.05%

(Continued)

Table 6.1 Literature survey of virtual voice assistants from the past decade. (*Continued*)

S. no.	Author	Year	Methodology	Data set used	Algorithm	Eval-Param
5.	Deepak et al. [6]	2019	One of the inventions in this concept was to discover a way of human-computer cooperation, by which the machine will understand the language and adjust it to provide accurate results.	Kaggle	Modified salp swarm optimization (MSSO) and adaptive neuro-fuzzy inference system (ANFIS), Levy flight algorithm	99.45%
6.	Kshama et al. [7]	2017	Voice recognition has a history with several major inventions. Voice assistants had become a major feature of mobiles and wearable devices.	Quantized deep neural networks (DNNs)	Quantized deep neural networks (DNNs)	96.6%
7.	Gowroju et al. [8]	2018	The devices act as each company's entry point into the market of the connected home. All three companies have their style and specialties in the market.	Cleveland dataset	Random forest with linear mode	88.7%

6.3   System Functions

All the applications that are related to the computer are worked with the help of user voice commands, i.e., the user will give the voice command so that the assistant will take the voice command by using a speech recognition module that internally converts speech form to text form and responds accordingly to the user's interest command. Because of this, the main advantage is it saves time and energy for the user.

For example, if the user wants to write any document or do any activity, he can use a voice assistant by giving a voice command. It converts the user's speech into text form [8–11]. During the whole process, the voice assistant will be in the activated mode and does not close unless the user

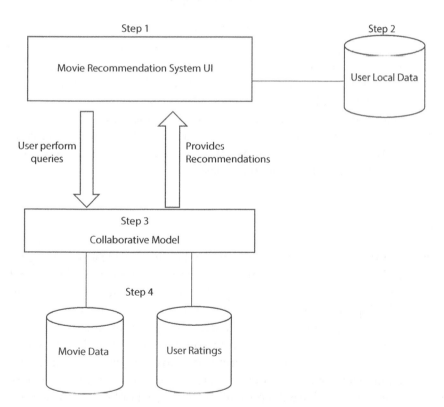

Figure 6.1 Architecture diagram of virtual-based voice assistant using artificial intelligence.

says to exit. The user work will be completed without any other interruptions. It also has high security regarding the data. That is, when the user wants to log in to his system using his voice, the voice assistant will detect the user's voice by calculating the user's frequency as shown in Figure 6.1. This means that only the owner can login to his system.

$$v_\omega = f\lambda$$

v_ω is the speed of sound

f is its frequency

λ is its wavelength

The user finds it easy to locate his file and need not follow up all the folders; the command open file name is given, and the file will be opened. And whatever is required by us for specific functions can be done through voice commands, through which the voice assistant gathers whole information, classifies it, and displays the information that is appropriate to the human command. Even though mail functions are performed through voice assistance, we can log in to our mail account and send mail through voice commands. We can perform functions like saving a file and launching various types of applications through voice assistance.

6.4   Model Training

The proposed system analyses all the prediction classifications using the proposed model. The graphical representation is shown in Figure 6.2. Figure 6.2.a depicts a graph of the age distribution of users to recommend the books. Figure 6.2.b depicts a graph of the year of publication of books to recommend to users. Figure 6.2.c depicts a graph of ratings regarding books. Figure 6.2.d depicts a graph to count the ratings of books. Figure 6.2.e depicts a graph of average ratings of books. Figure 6.2.f depicts the correlation matrix of user-id, movie-id, rating, and timestamp for the book recommendation. Table 6.2 represents the rating of books from the dataset, and Table 6.3 represents average rating calculated from the dataset along with the predicted value of total number of ratings.

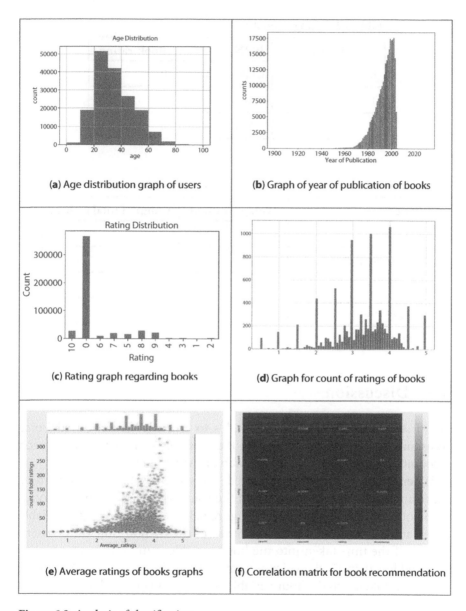

(a) Age distribution graph of users

(b) Graph of year of publication of books

(c) Rating graph regarding books

(d) Graph for count of ratings of books

(e) Average ratings of books graphs

(f) Correlation matrix for book recommendation

Figure 6.2 Analysis of classification.

Table 6.2 Rating of books.

	User-ID	ISBN	Book-rating
0	276725	03454104X	0
1	276726	1.6E+08	5
2	276727	4.5E+08	0

Table 6.3 Average rating of books with count of total ratings.

Title	Average_ratings	Count of total ratings
'71' 1014	4	1
'burbi the 1986	4	17
'helloboy' 2007	3.17647	1
'might mummy' 1985	3.5	1
'right mid' 1987	3	2

6.5   Discussion

The first step is to import the modules to create a Virtual-Based Voice Assistance. So we will be importing the modules such as pyttsx3, speech recognition, DateTime, Wikipedia, web browser, and OS.

When the process has been started, the voice assistant greets the user according to the time mentioned on the user's system. The simple modulation of human voice is shown in Figure 6.3. We will be taking a variable called an hour and the hour variable stores the current time of the user's system. If the time taken into the hour variable is more than or equal to zero and less than 12, the voice assistant wishes the user "Good Morning". If the time taken into the hour variable is more than or equal to 12 and less

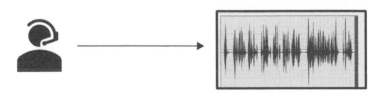

Figure 6.3 Frequency modulation of a human voice.

than 18, then the voice assistant wishes the user "Good Afternoon". And if the time is different from either of these times, then the voice assistant wishes the user "Good Evening". Here we will be using the voice () function to read the commands. We have given the name of our voice assistant as John.

The voice assistant of our system should be able to take the inputs given by the user and process the user's commands. Here we will be creating a function called to take command (). The function does not have any parameters. Here we will be taking a variable and it creates an object for the speech recognizer using the recognizer class. Using features the recognizer listens to the audio for seconds from the start of the audio. We will be using the microphone method to access the inbuilt microphone in the system. The microphone acts as a source to give the input command by the user and it takes the audio as input. The voice assistant waits for 5 seconds to recognize the voice; if the user says nothing, then the voice assistant asks for the user to say the command again. If the user says something, then the input is recognized. The voice assistant thus performs speech recognition on the input audio data. It is used to transcribe audio files. Here we even print the command spoken by the user.

6.5.1   Furnishing Movie Recommendations

Then we will be writing the function for the movie recommendations. The Recommend Movie function is the same as the function for book recommendations and it takes the book name as the parameter of the function. The variable RTG stores the information related to the particular movie name which is given as the parameter to the function. It retrieves the data from the table that consists of information on all the movies. Then the rating of that particular movie is correlated with all the other movie ratings and the list of movies is stored in the mov variable, which will then further move or go forward. Thereby it will correlate the respected column which is already given in the DataFrame with all other columns. After correlating columns, it computes the scores of correlations and gives the result back to us. So, with this process, we are using "core with" and applying it to the entire/whole movie_matrix DataFrame which includes all the matrices of the user's movie ratings. By correlating with the user- selected movie name and ratings, it just gives us the items that correlated. Throughout this process, it drops all the missing results by using the action called "dropna". Then we will sort the movies in descending order so that the highest-rated movies appear first and the lowest-rated movie appears last. We will be taking only the top five movies from the list of movies retrieved after correlation. We will be using a for loop to retrieve and print the movie data. There is another function for movie recommendations called Recommend_MOVIET(). This function just retrieves the top five rated movies. The overall ratings are based on the IMDB ratings.

Now we will be writing a function called Movie_Recommenders with a variable named id as its parameter. if the value of id is 0, then the voice assistant asks for the user to provide any user interest such as a search for a similar movie. Now let's take a variable q and call the takeCommand() function which takes the commands from the user. Then we will set a temporary variable to a value of 0. If the command given by the user is "go back", then the voice assistant goes out of the movie's recommendations. If the user says yes as the command, then the voice assistant asks the user to tell the name of the movie so that the voice assistant could recommend the user similar kinds of movies. Now the temporary variable is set to 1 and the function Recommend_MOVIE() is called to list out the similar kind of top five movies. If the user gives the command as no or does not say any command, the control goes to Recommend_MOVIET() command and prints the top five rated movies. If the value of the temporary variable is zero, then the voice assistant asks the user to speak the command again so that it can recognize the command given by the user correctly.

6.5.2   KNN Algorithm Book Recommendation

We write a function named Recommend_Book() to handle book recommendations. This function filters the books present in CSV files based on the user ratings. The filtering is done by using the well-known algorithm

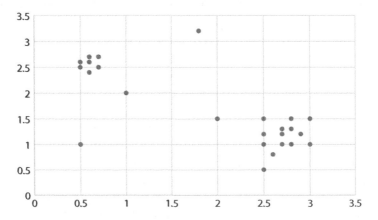

Figure 6.4 KNN - algorithm for book recommendation.

called the K-Nearest Neighbor algorithm. This algorithm generally creates an imaginary/virtual boundary to classify the data. Whenever new or fresh data comes in, the KNN algorithm's job is to predict whether the respected data matches the nearest point of the boundary line as shown in Figure 6.4. Now we will be checking this particular book name with the overall data frame that consists of the book ISBN, author name, book name, and the ratings of the book. We will be storing its data in a variable called book_id. Here we have used NumPy, and to check for that particular book the function 'NumPy.where()' will return the element's indices in the form of an input array where the respected given condition is satisfied. So, here we used one of the most used essential classification algorithms called the K-Nearest Neighbor algorithm. It generally belongs to the domain of supervised learning. It does its job by performing pattern recognition, intrusion detection, data mining, etc.

We will give data called training data which will divide the coordinates into respective groups. The KNN algorithm will store the whole available data and predict the data which matches the nearest point of the boundary line as shown in Figure 6.4. This algorithm can also be applicable for "Regression" problems but it is mostly used for classification problems. So, in this process, we are using the KNN algorithm to take similar kinds of books. The function reshapes (1, -1) is used to retrieve a single columnar row from the entire data frame. Then we will store the similar top five rated books into an array and print the array. There are other function book recommendations named Recommend_BookT() to retrieve the top five rated books from the data frame.

6.6   Results

When the user runs the program, the voice assistant gets enabled, and the voice assistant starts to speak. The speak () function is used for retrieving the voice of the voice assistant. It wishes the user based on the time, if the time is less than 12, the voice assistant wishes the user Good Morning, if the time is less than 18 hours then the voice assistant wishes the user Good Afternoon, if the time is greater than 18 hours then the voice assistant wishes Good Evening to the user and tells the voice assistant.

After the voice assistant wishes the user, the voice assistant starts taking the user's commands. It shows as 'Listening' as shown in Figure 6.5, which means that the voice assistant has already been enabled and it can take commands from the user. This is present till the user completes to say the command to a voice assistant. The commands can be playing music,

Figure 6.5 Layout of testing platform.

recommending a book, recommending the movie, covid symptoms, covid precautions, and opening the files present on the system. The below screenshot shows us the output that will be displayed when the user asks for the voice assistant to open the files present on the system. When the user says the command 'open power point', the voice assistant listens to what the user has said and starts recognizing the command. If the voice assistant could be able to recognize it, it executes the command. If the voice could not understand the command said by the user, it asks for the user to say the command again and if that particular application or the local file is not present on the system, then the voice assistant tells the user that the particular application or the local file is not present on the system.

Here the 'open power point' command is valid and it would be recognized by the voice assistant. The PowerPoint application gets opened. And now the user could be able to work with the PowerPoint application. Though the application has been opened, the voice assistant will not get disabled. The voice assistant is still enabled and could open any other files or applications simultaneously when this application is already present in the background. The voice assistant gets disabled and stops taking the commands when the user says to exit for the voice assistant as shown in Figure 6.6. Then the voice assistant terminates the process.

Figure 6.6 Accessing local files available on the system.

Initially, the voice assistant wishes the user, the voice assistant starts taking the user's commands. It shows as 'Listening' which means that the voice assistant has already been enabled and it can take commands from the user. This is present till the user completes to say the command to a voice assistant. The commands can be playing music, recommending a book, recommending the movie, covid symptoms, covid precautions, and opening the files present on the system. The screenshot shows us the output that will be displayed when the user asks the voice assistant for getting web access a applications through the browser.

When the user says the command 'open Facebook', the voice assistant listens to what the user has said and starts recognizing the command. If the voice assistant could be able to recognize it, it executes the command. If the voice could not understand the command said by the user, it asks for the user to say the command again. When the command uttered by the user is invalid, the voice assistant asks the user to tell the command again. It asks for the command until it gets a valid command. Whenever it gets a valid command, immediately it starts executing the command i.e., through the browser opening the web application. Here the 'open Facebook' command is valid and it would be recognized by the voice assistant as shown in

Figure 6.7 To access the web browser.

Figure 6.7. Hence, the Facebook web application gets opened. And now the user could be able to work with the Facebook web application by logging into the user's account. Though the application has been opened, the voice assistant will not get disabled. The voice assistant is still enabled and could open any other files or applications simultaneously when this web application is already present in the background. The voice assistant gets disabled and stops taking the commands when the user says to exit for the voice assistant. Then the voice assistant terminates the process.

The voice assistant wishes the user at the beginning of the process, the voice assistant starts taking the user commands. It shows as 'Listening' which means that the voice assistant has already been enabled and it can take commands from the user. This is present till the user completes to say the command to a voice assistant. Until the user says any command, the voice assistant will continuously listen and recognizes for user's voice. The commands can be playing music, recommending a book, recommending a movie, covid symptoms, covid precautions, and opening the files present on the system. The screenshot shows us the output that will be displayed when the user asks the voice assistant for recommending books based on ratings. When the user utters a command as 'recommend the movie', voice assistant gets enabled. The Voice assistant checks whether the command is valid or not. If it is a valid command, accordingly voice assistant will execute the command.

If the command given by the user is invalid, it speaks out the command 'please tell again'. This command will be repeatedly executed till the user says a valid command. When user utter valid command, voice assistant verifies and executes the command. The Command for getting

Book Recommendations based on ratings is 'recommend book'. After user giving 'recommend book' command, voice assistant gets enabled and checks whether it is a valid command or not. Here 'recommend book' is a valid command for the voice assistant. When voice assistant finds the command regarding book recommendations as a valid command, it accepts the command and asks the user for any similar books. This means voice assistant is asking the user whether he/she is interested in getting or reading similar kind of books. When user answers the voice assistant by using 'yes' command, voice assistant verifies the command is valid or not. Here the command is valid and the command is 'yes' as shown in Figure 6.8.

Figure 6.8 To acquire book recommendations.

Now the voice assistant will ask the user to tell the book name. Here after asking the book name, voice assistant starts listening. It shows as 'Listening' which means that the voice assistant has already enabled and it is able to take the commands from the user. This is present till the user completes to say the command to voice assistant. If it could recognize the valid book name uttered by the user, it provides the top five rated books that are similar to the book name given by the user. Voice assistant wishes the user at the beginning of the process, the voice assistant starts taking the user commands. It shows as 'Listening' which means that the voice assistant has already enabled and it is able to take the commands from the user. This is present till the user completes to say the command to voice assistant. Until user says any command, voice assistant will continuously listen and recognizes for user's voice. The commands can be play music, recommend book, recommend movie, covid symptoms, covid precautions and opening the files present on the system. The below screenshot Figure 6.4, shows us the output that will be displayed when the user asks the voice assistant for recommending books based on ratings. When the user utters a command as 'recommend book', voice assistant gets enabled. Firstly, voice assistant checks whether the command is valid or not. If it is a valid command, accordingly voice assistant will execute the command. If the command given by the user is invalid, it speaks out the command 'please tell again'. This command will be repeatedly executed till the user says a valid command. When user utter valid command, voice assistant verifies and executes the command. Here the command is valid and the command is 'no'. The voice assistant will ask the user to tell the book name. Here after asking the book name, voice assistant starts listening. It shows as 'Listening' which means that the voice assistant has already enabled and it is able to take the commands from the user. This is present till the user completes to say the command to voice assistant. If it could recognize the valid book name uttered by the user, it provides the top five rated books. If user says the command 'yes' command when the voice assistant asks for similar books, then it provides the top five rated books similar to the book name that was given by the user. That means the books similar to the user given book name are provided the other. If the user gives 'no' as the command for the query 'Search for any similar book?', now here voice assistant furnishes the top five rated books. Whenever user says no for the similar books query, voice assistant will not ask the book name rather provides the top five rated books.

Primarily the voice assistant wishes the user at the beginning of the process, the voice assistant starts taking the user commands. It shows as 'Listening' which means that the voice assistant has already enabled and it is able to take the commands from the user. This is present till the user completes to say the command to voice assistant. Until user says any command, voice assistant will continuously listen and recognizes for user's voice. The commands can be play music, recommend book, recommend movie, covid symptoms, covid precautions and opening the files present on the system. The screenshot shows us the output that will be displayed when the user asks the voice assistant for recommending books based on ratings. When the user utters a command as 'recommend movie', voice assistant gets enabled. Firstly, voice assistant checks whether the command is valid or not. If it is a valid command, accordingly voice assistant will execute the command. If the command given by the user is invalid, it speaks out the command 'please tell again'. This command will be repeatedly executed till the user says a valid command. When user utter valid command, voice assistant verifies and executes the command. The Command for getting Movie Recommendations based on ratings is 'recommend movie'. After user giving 'recommend movie' command, voice assistant gets enabled and checks whether it is a valid command or not. Here 'recommend movie' is a valid command for the voice assistant. When voice assistant finds the command regarding book recommendations as a valid command, it accepts the command and asks the user for any similar movies. This means voice assistant is asking the user whether he/she is interested in getting or reading similar kind of movies. When user answers the voice assistant by using 'yes' command, voice assistant verifies the command is valid or not. Here the command is valid and the command is 'yes'.

The voice assistant now will ask the user to tell the movie name. Here after asking the movie name, voice assistant starts listening. It shows as 'Listening' which means that the voice assistant has already enabled and it is able to take the commands from the user. This is present till the user completes to say the command to voice assistant. If it could recognize the valid book name uttered by the user, it provides the top five rated IMDB ratings that are similar to the book name given by the user. Firstly, voice assistant wishes the user at the beginning of the process, the voice assistant starts taking the user commands. It shows as 'Listening' which means that the voice assistant has already enabled and it is able to take the commands from the user. This is present till the user completes to say the command to voice assistant. Until user says any command, voice assistant will continuously listen and recognizes for user's voice. The commands can be play music, recommend book, recommend movie, covid symptoms, covid precautions and opening the files present on the system. The below screenshot shows us the output that will be displayed when the user asks the voice assistant for recommending movies based on IMDB ratings. When the user utters a command as 'recommend movie', voice assistant gets enabled. Initially voice assistant checks whether the command is valid or not. If it is a valid command, accordingly voice assistant will execute the command. If the command given by the user is invalid, it speaks out the command 'please tell again'. This command will be repeatedly executed till the user says a valid command. When user utter valid command, voice assistant verifies and executes the command.

The Command for getting Movie Recommendations based on ratings is 'recommend movie'. After the user giving 'recommend movie' command, voice assistant gets enabled and checks whether it is a valid command or not. Here 'recommend movie' is a valid command for the voice assistant. When voice assistant finds the command regarding movie recommendations as a valid command, it accepts the command and asks the user for any similar books. This means voice assistant is asking the user whether he/she is interested in getting or reading similar kind of movies. When user answers the voice assistant by using 'no' command, voice assistant verifies the command is valid or not.

Here the command is valid and the command is 'no'. Now the voice assistant will ask the user to tell the movie name. Here after asking the book name, voice assistant starts listening. It shows as 'Listening' which means that the voice assistant has already enabled and it is able to take the commands from the user. This is present till the user completes to say the command to voice assistant. If it could recognize the valid movie name uttered by the user, it provides the top five rated movies based on IMDB ratings. If user says the command 'yes' command when the voice assistant asks for similar movies, then it provides the top five rated movies similar to the movie name that was given by the user. That means the movies similar to the user given movie name are provided the other. If the user gives 'no' as the command for the query 'Search for any similar movie?', now here voice assistant furnishes the top five IMDB rated movies. Whenever user says no for the similar movies query, voice assistant will not ask the movie name rather provides the top five rated movies as shown in Figure 6.9.

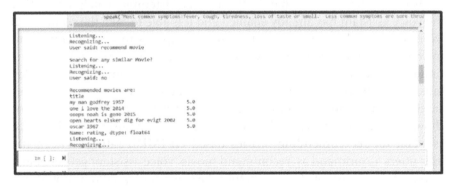

Figure 6.9 To obtain movie recommendations (…).

After the voice assistant wishes the user, the voice assistant starts taking the user commands. It shows as 'Listening' which means that the voice assistant has already enabled and it is able to take the commands from the user. This is present till the user completes to say the command to voice assistant. The commands can be play music, recommend book, recommend movie, covid symptoms, covid precautions and opening the files present on the system. The Figure 6.9 also shows us the output that will be displayed when the user asks to the voice assistant for the covid symptoms and precautions. When the user says the command 'covid symptoms', the voice assistant listens to what user has said and starts recognizing the command. If the voice assistant could be able to recognize, it executes the command. If the voice could not understand the command said by the user, it asks for the user to say the command again and if that particular command could not be able to process or retrieved, then the voice assistant tells the user that the particular could not be able to recognize by the voice assistant.

Table 6.4 Descriptions of ratings for movies.

	User_Id	Movie_Id	Movie_rating	Time_stamp
Count no.	1008361268.00	100836972.0000	100836462.00	1.008364290e+05
Average	326.127527864	194335.295794718	3.50169357	1.205946443e+09
Stdn	1236.61849031	3553280.98719589	1.042525279	2.1669226310e+08
Minimum	1.0100000	1.0000100	0.50011000	8.284971246e+08
25 percent	177823.0000	1199285.0000	3.01930000	1.021915824e+09
50 percent	325147.0000	295163.0000	3.518000	1.186024487e+09
75 percent	477389.0000	8123782.0000	4.1380000	1.435994563e+09
Maximum	61035900.000	19360142389.000	5.049900000	1.537282799e+09

Here the 'covid symptoms' command is a valid command and it would be recognized by voice assistant. So as the command is recognized by the voice assistant and the command gets executed by the application. The voice assistant displays the covid symptoms and it also utters out the covid symptoms. The same way, the covid precautions command will also be working. When the user says the command 'covid precautions', the voice assistant listens to what user has said and starts recognizing the command. If the voice assistant could be able to recognize, it executes the command. If the voice could not understand the command said by the user, it asks for the user to say the command again and if that particular command could not be able to process or retrieved, then the voice assistant tells the user that the particular could not be able to recognize by the voice assistant. The comparison is made using its rating and time stamp as shown in Table 6.4 to take decision on recommendation.

Here the 'covid precautions' command is a valid command and it would be recognized by voice assistant. So as the command is recognized by the voice assistant and the command gets executed by the application. The voice assistant displays the covid precautions and it also utters out the pre-cautions to be taken to does not get affected by covid. Though the appli-cation has been opened, the voice assistant will not get disabled. The voice assistant is still enabled and could open any other files or applications simultaneously when this application is already present in the background. The voice assistant gets disabled and stops taking the commands when the user says to exit for the voice assistant. Then the voice assistant terminates from the process.

6.7   Conclusion

The main purpose of this project to provide a voice assistant that identifies and displays the answers to the user questions and provides accurate information that is required by the user. A desktop voice assistant which is already in use provides excellent service. But the system that is developed now is made on Python language (Python 3.8). Different types of libraries from Python are used for speech recognition, text, short mail transfer protocols (SMTP). It gives information regarding news and weather, it can play music, it performs search; we can set up an alarm and can display the time and date. The user can get information through this application tool. It reduces both human power and time. With the use of Natural Language Processing the user can ask questions in a formal way. There is no specific predefined format to ask queries.

It is designed to reduce human effort and control applications and devices with the human voice. We can use this device to interact with other intelligent voice-controlled devices like a weather report of a city via internet, IOT applications, sending an email, and setting alarm events to calendar. The accuracy of the devices is increased with use of machine learning. This device can also be designed to accept commands in more than one language, and respond in the same language that the user employs. The device will also be designed to help visually impaired people.

References

1. Yoffie, David B., Liang Wu, Jodie Sweitzer, Denzil Eden, and Karan Ahuja. "Voice war: Hey Google vs. Alexa vs. Siri." *Harvard Business School Case* 718, no. 519 (2018): 1.
2. Tulshan, Amrita S., and Sudhir Namdeorao Dhage. "Survey on virtual assistant: Google assistant, siri, cortana, alexa." In *International symposium on signal processing and intelligent recognition systems*, pp. 190-201. Springer, Singapore, 2018.

3. Terzopoulos, George, and Maya Satratzemi. "Voice assistants and smart speakers in everyday life and in education." *Informatics in Education* 19, no. 3 (2020): 473-490.

4. Shende, Deepak, Ria Umahiya, Monika Raghorte, Aishwarya Bhisikar, and Anup Bhange. "AI Based Voice Assistant Using Python." *Journal of Emerging Technologies and Innovative Research (JETIR)* 6, no. 2 (2019).

5. Kulhalli, Kshama V., Kotrappa Sirbi, and Abhijit J. Patankar. "Personal assistant with voice recognition intelligence." *International Journal of Engineering Research and Technology* 10, no. 1 (2017): 416-419.

6. Gowroju, Swathi, and Sandeep Kumar. "Robust Deep Learning Technique: U-Net Architecture for Pupil Segmentation." In *2020 11th IEEE Annual Information Technology, Electronics and Mobile Communication Conference (IEMCON)*, pp. 0609-0613. IEEE, 2020.

7. Swathi, A., and Sandeep Kumar. "A smart application to detect pupil for small dataset with low illumination." *Innovations in Systems and Software Engineering* 17, no. 1 (2021): 29-43.

8. Swathi, A., and Sandeep Kumar. "Review on pupil segmentation using CNN-region of interest." In *Intelligent Communication and Automation Systems*, pp. 157-168. CRC Press, 2021.

9. Gowroju, Swathi, and Sandeep Kumar. "Robust Pupil Segmentation using UNET and Morphological Image Processing." In *2021 International Mobile, Intelligent, and Ubiquitous Computing Conference (MIUCC)*, pp. 105-109. IEEE, 2021.

10. Dasari L. Prasanna, Suman Lata Tripathi. "Machine and Deep-Learning Techniques for Text and Speech Processing," in *Machine Learning Algorithms for Signal and Image Processing* , IEEE, 2023, pp. 115-128, doi: 10.1002/9781119861850.ch7

11. Kanak Kumar, Kaustav Chaudhury, Suman Lata Tripathi. "Future of Machine Learning (ML) and Deep Learning (DL) in Healthcare Monitoring System," in *Machine Learning Algorithms for Signal and Image Processing*, IEEE, 2023, pp. 293-313, doi:10.1002/9781119861850.ch17.

7

Image Forgery Detection: An Approach with Machine Learning

Madhusmita Mishra[1]*, Silvia Tittotto[2] and Santos Kumar Das[1]

[1]Dept. of ECE, NIT Rourkela, Rourkela, Odisha, India
[2]CECS, UFABC, Santo Andre, Sao Paulo, Brazil

Abstract
Before the camera was invented, verification processes were done manually. With the advancement in technology, now it is impossible to predict the difference between the actual and edited image. This is because of the growing varieties of advanced image editing tools. These editing tools have low cost and are open-source tools meant for the handlers and commonly utilized to create memes for uploading to social media websites. The present work illustrates forgery detection of an image via the error level analysis (ELA) method. Here the binary decision of convolutional neural networks (CNN) based model is taken in declaring the aptness of image intended for official applications. In the CNN model, trained Kaggle dataset is applied. The comprehensive simulations confirm the accuracy and precision of the suggested model.

Keywords: CNN, image forgery detection, machine learning (ML), error level analysis (ELA), convolutional neural network (CNN), deep learning (DL), joint photographic experts' group (JPEG)

7.1 Introduction

Images provide much information to the viewer. In the present-day societal media and the internet, digital images have undoubtedly evidenced their powerfulness and suitability. The need for images is never-ending in medical imaging, intelligence, journalism, digital forensics, photography, and

---

*Corresponding author: madhusmita.nit@gmail.com

Suman Lata Tripathi and Mufti Mahmud (eds.) Explainable Machine Learning Models and Architectures, (105–122) © 2023 Scrivener Publishing LLC

courts of law as evidence [1]. Therefore, in the present period the integrity of images is a subject of research [2, 3]. As the technologies are expanding to the human interest, image editing is not a new idea. Availability of contemporary technologies in the form of software with an easy user interface, such as Photoshop, GIMP, Premiere, Vega, CorelDRAW, etc., make its use even more widespread. Editing the image tampers with its originality, and such practice is called image forgery. Image forgery generally is any manipulation of the digital image to hide some meaningful and significant data in the image.

Several Image forgery detection techniques (IFDT) are as follows:

1. Active methodology: The active technique adds some reliable details (watermark) or signatures with the photo at the capturing time or after that. In the latter case, modification is done by digital watermarking or digital signature or both [2]. Subsequently it is shared with others.
2. Passive methodology: The passive method does not insert any details for validation motive. It functions totally by studying the binary data of digital images. Such images, in which no watermarking and signatures are there to cross verify, are called blind images. Researchers divided the passive approach in different ways based on editing techniques. The passive tools can be nearly classified into five classes [3]:
   i.   Pixel-level: procedure distinguishes measurable inconsistencies presented at the pixel level.
   ii. Format-level: procedures influence the measurable relationships presented by a lossy pressure scheme.
   iii. Camera level: procedures abuse ancient rarities offered by the camera focal point, sensor, or on-chip post-handling.
   iv. Physical techniques: explicitly determine and identify singularity in the three-dimensional cooperation amongst physical items, the camera and light.
   v.   Geometrical methods: create estimations of articles on the planet and their locations.

Passive image forensic tools are divided into three categories:

- Copy-move image forgery
- Image splicing
- Image retouching

All these techniques, along with techniques of machine learning (ML), detect different types of forgery with different accuracies [4, 5]. Prior knowledge of the pre-existing techniques to detect image forgery is needed to develop a new detection technique. Convolutional neural network (CNN/ConvNet) is a deep learning (DL) rooted algorithm that receives images from input and assigns weights to various components of the image and uniquely identifies different images. The processing involved in ConvNet is much lower than processing in other competing algorithms. Error level analysis (ELA) identifies the area of forgery with difference in compression levels. For an image in JPEG format, the compression level should be approximately at the same level. Digital forgery is detected when there is a significant difference in the error level.

The rest of the paper is as follows. Section 7.2 delivers the exhaustive state of the art historical background behind image forgery detection while providing the need for doing the image forgery detection. Section 7.3 discusses the ConvNet architecture and some important terminologies related to ConvNet. Section 7.4 focuses on the error level analysis of image. A proposed model of image forgery detection along with results and analysis is discussed in Section 7.5. Section 7.6 offers the closing remarks on this work.

7.2   Historical Background

Image forgery detection techniques (IFDT) for any type of forgeries have the goal of detecting forged regions with accuracy, improving the accuracy, regionalizing the forgery and making the time of detection as low as possible. IFDTs are categorized in two different types, as image processing and deep learning.

The authors of [8–10] used ELA and the authors of [11–14] used CNN for image forgery detection, which are an integral chunk of image processing and deep learning, respectively. Basavarajappa *et al.* [2] survey different techniques for approaching the detection of image forgeries. H. Farid [3] categorizes image forgeries in different passive approaches which were of great importance for the development of initial knowledge and learning of IFDT. Dureja *et al.* [4] survey the techniques on how to recover a forged image based on different retrieval techniques. Krizhevsky *et al.* [5] discuss the use of CNN to classify different images categories they obtained from the ImageNet database. Mishra *et al.* [6] discuss speed up robust features (SURF) and hierarchical agglomerative clustering (HAC) techniques for image forgery specifically for images which use region duplication. They detect forgery based on statistical features such as average entropy, entropy, skewness, and kurtosis of a forged image. Popescu and Farid in [7] use the image capturing technique used by cameras, employing a sensor in combination with a color filter array (CFA) to detect a forgery in images. Uliyan *et al.* [15] discuss the detection of a forged blurred area with a new system which combines blur metric evaluation and phase congruency. Walia and Kumar in [16] survey systematically the problems, questions, and existing techniques in the arena of digital image forgery. Zhang *et al.* [17] discuss the detection of image forgery using CNN. Zhang *et al.* [18] discuss the detection of regions of image forged with the support of neural networks and deep learning. Zhou *et al.* [19] discuss a new approach of block-based CNN for image forgery detection which consists of regions with convolutional neural networks (RCNN) for processing of each block.

Deogar *et al.* [20] have used the AlexNet model of object detection to detect image forgery. Bharti *et al.* [21] survey various techniques by which forged images are detected. The article comes with a useful conclusion with comparison of some parameters, merits, and demerits. Online resources in [22] have shown great impact in the ELA knowledge and development. Chen *et al.* [23] discuss CNN for image forensics using median filtering, a nonlinear digital filtering technique. Ansari *et al.* [24] review the passive image forgery detection based on pixels. In this article, various ideas are given on pixel-based forgery detection. Krawetz *et al.* [25] elaborate on ELA and its use in image forensics, and Birajdar *et al.* [26] surveys a wide range of passive techniques used to detect image forgeries. The latest advancement of convolutional neural networks in IFD, its use and analysis has been discussed by Gu *et al.* [27]. Liu *et al.* [28] show how to complete CNN training effectively with a small data size for pre-processing of models. Han *et al.* [29] provide a discussion for CNN on any generic data and discusses the difference in approaches for an image and other data. Bayar and Stamm in [30] presented the detection of image forgeries with a new convolutional layer as a part of deep learning.

The need for selecting this work is due to fake news. Fake news is news which is not true and is only generated to do social damage to a society, agency, person, or an entity. Fake news in the form of a forged image or edited video or with a wrong subtitle can exert a great influence on many unaware and innocent people and can result in social losses to societies.

The use of a reliable IFDT can help media houses to cover the news for large geographical areas and verify fake news as part of the process. The work is also interesting because of its relationship with image modification and its study using deep learning. So, it gradually becomes an interesting research field to get involved in. Usage of machine learning or deep learning technique [30–32] was an obvious choice for this work when considering its popularity, fastness, accuracy, and reliability. The repetitive passing of new data in a machine learning model makes it independently adaptable. By training a model with large data sets, the reliability of a model increases.

7.3   CNN Architecture

Convolutional neural networks (CNN/ConvNet) consists of three different words which describe the functioning of the Deep Learning–based model. The three words are Convolution, Neuron, and Network. Convolution is the operation between two functions and it produces a third function which describes the relation between the two original functions. Here, one of the original functions is input data and the other is the parameters which change with each training figures to get the desired output. A convolution is fundamentally sliding a filter over the input image data. In machine learning a neuron is the basic building block of a model that calculates a weighted average of its inputs with necessary biases and at last adds non-linearity to the result. In data communication, we pass data through many layers of routers, access points, or hubs, thus forming a network. Hence, here we pass input data and its modifications through many layers; thus the model is called a network. CNN accepts an image's data as input. Taking an image directly as input saves several variables and confusions in the model. The model does dot product between inputs and filter matrix basically of small size sliding all over the image. The output at the end of the network however is given with a percentage value for each possibility.

Basic neural network (BNN) takes a single vector input. It consists of many hidden layers and like CNN, these layers further consist of many neurons. Layer wise study shows that every neuron of the next layer is linked to the neurons of the previous layer. At the end, a fully connected (FC) layer is attached to all previous layer neurons and produces an output in the form of percentage values. A basic neural network structure is presented in Figure 7.1.

A BNN takes single vectors as inputs so a 2D image cannot fit in such a model. Colored image is 3D and third dimension of basic colors red, green, blue (RGB) make colored images real. In general, a Canadian Institute for Advanced Research (CIFAR-10) image is used in CNN. A CIFAR-10 image has a dimension of $32 \times 32 \times 3$ (i.e., 32 pixels each side and 3 shades). Also, if we consider making a 3D vector into a single vector, the size of the vector for a CIFAR image will be $32 \times 32 \times 3 = 3072$ parts along with a number of parameters for reconverting the vector back to a 3D matrix. For an image of size $256 \times 256 \times 3$ the number climbs up to 196,608 for the first layer.

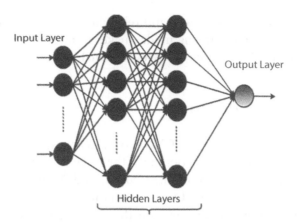

Figure 7.1 A basic structure of neural network.

This type of high numbers also gives rise to overfitting in a model, which is discussed later. Hence a BNN is not the right choice for involving thousands of images.

A ConvNet model contains neurons in a 3-dimensional fashion. The three dimensions of the ConvNet are named: width, height, depth (here, depth does not signify the full depth of the model). One Layer has one 3-dimensional filter (kernel) which slides on the whole dimension of the image and dot products to give a 3D volume. As the NN goes deeper from one layer to another the depth of the volume increases and the height and the width both decrease. Hence, the volume is a differentiated conclusion from the image after processing with the filters. The perception of this procedure is presented in Figure 7.2. In Figure 7.2, the model follows from left to right.

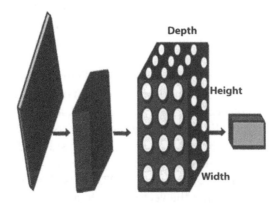

Figure 7.2 The 3-D structure of CNN model.

The ConvNet layers are basically distributed into three portions; the input, hidden and output layers. The hidden layer does all the work and the work of input and output layers can easily be concluded. The input layer receives the input data as image and the output layer gives out the result. The hidden layer is the most important for researchers and is classified as the Conv layer. It contains the activation function of the developer's choice. In this work, a rectified linear unit (ReLU) is used. The pooling layer is the fully linked layer.

A simple ConvNet model for CIFAR-10 images can have the following arrangement [INPUT -> CONV -> RELU -> POOL-> FC].

INPUT layer contains pixel values in a matrix form for the image dimensions ([$32 \times 32 \times 3$]). Convolution layer does the dot product amid the receptive field of the input image and weights in the form of filters (kernels). The process is done by a sliding filter which slides all over the image to perform dot product with the filters. A rise in the number of filters raises the depth of output volume.

ReLU is an activation function for each element in the volume. The function can be written as max (0, x). POOL layer performs a process called pooling, which is decreasing the size of the volume; basically it decreases the height and the width. The function used is called max pooling. Fully connected (FC) layer is completely linked to all the values in the former volume and helps to come to a desired conclusion. Hence, ReLU and pool layer are predefined functions. The main layers to work on are Conv layer and FC layer. The Conv layer contains a filter or kernel which transforms the input to required output and a FC layer is the final layer to produce a binary result for declaring an image forged or not. Hence an FC layer can be a normal neuron and using proper activation function the output can be declared.

Hence the key points are as follows. A ConvNet model contains different layers to transform the input volume into final classes' probabilities. Hidden layer contains different types of layers such as Conv layer, ReLU, pool layer, FC layer. Conv layer, pool layer and ReLU take a 3D input volume as input and give a 3D output volume. ReLU and the pool layer do not contain any parameters (filter/kernel).

Hyper-parameters, on which the learning rate depends do not belong to ReLU layer.

Pooling layer is occasionally embedded in the mid of progressive Conv layers during ConvNet implementation. It is used to decrease the spatial extent of the depiction with dynamism to reduce the amount of boundaries and calculation in the system. This layer works freely on each solidity to resize the information spatially by employing the MAX activity.

The pooling activity in case of 3-D volume is represented in Figure 7.3. From Figure 7.3, it is worth noticing that the profundity measurements after pooling activity remain unchanged (i.e., only height and width decrease, and depth remains unaltered).

The mathematical steps for pooling layer is given below:

- Initialization: Width = W, height = H and depth = D.
- Receive a volume of dimensions $W_1 \times H_1 \times D_1$
- Call two hyper-parameters: Spatial degree F, Stride S
- Regenerate a volume of dimensions $W_2 \times H_2 \times D_2$ where:
  $W_2 = (W_1 - F)/S + 1$; $H_2 = (H_1 - F)/S + 1$ and $D_2 = D_1$
- Announces zero boundaries as it processes a fixed capacity of the information
- For pooling layers, rarely to cushion the info utilizing zero-cushioning.

There are two types of maximum pooling, a pooling with S=3, F=2 (also termed as covering pooling) and pooling with F=2, S=2. Pooling with higher open fields is excessively devastating.

In entirely connected layers Neurons have complete associations with all initiations in the past layer. The advantage of keeping the spatial sizes fixed after Conv improves execution to a great extent. If there is a chance that the Conv layers will not protect the data sources to zero and only perform significant turns, the size of the volumes would scarcely decrease after each Conv. At this point the data at the edges would be "washed away"

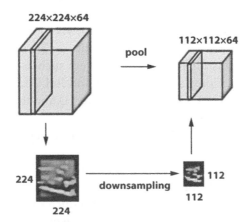

Figure 7.3 MAX pooling of 3D volume.

speedily. The considerable bottleneck during developing ConvNet models is the memory bottleneck. Even after enormous advancement in the GPUs there is still a constraint of 3/4/6 GB memory.

7.4   Analysis of Error Level of Image

Error level analysis (ELA) highlights the contrasts in the JPEG pressure rate. Areas with even concealing like a solid blue sky or a white divider will presumably have a poorer ELA result (darker concealing) than high-separate edges.

Analogous edges should have equivalent brilliance in the ELA result. Each highly distinguished edge must appear to be like the others, and all low-differentiate edges should appear to be comparative. With a unique photograph, low-differentiate edges ought to be nearly as brilliant as high-differentiate edges. Similar surfaces ought to have comparable shading under ELA. Zones with increasingly surface detail will probably have a better ELA ensue than a smooth out surface. Irrespective of the genuine shade of the surface, every level surface ought to have about a similar shading under ELA.

There is a wide range of picture document groups. A few arrangements are lossy, while others are lossless. Lossless record designs hold careful pixel shading data. On the off chance that you load an image, spare it, and burden it once more, every pixel will have precisely the same value. Indeed, even a change between two lossless configurations will hold precisely the same shading values. For instance, portable network graphics (PNG) and bitmap (BMP) are two diverse lossless configurations. On the off chance that you convert an image from a BMP to a PNG, it will hold precisely the same pixel values, even though the document position changed.

A lossy record design does not ensure that the shades will remain the equivalent. With JPEG, sparing requires indicating a quality level. The quality level alters the pressure sum (lower quality makes littler documents); however, it packs by expelling some shading data. With JPEG, sparing an image makes the shades change a bit. The resaved record may outwardly look equivalent to the source image; however, the specific pixel esteems to be contrast.

Along with ELA, each matrix that is not upgraded for the quality level will demonstrate lattice squares which have been changed during a resave. Unique pictures from computerized cameras must get a high level of progress during any resave (high ELA esteems). Each ensuing resave will bring down the blunder level potential, yielding a darker ELA result.

With enough resaves, the network square will in the end arrive at its base blunder level, where it will not change any longer. Recognizing the high recurrence territories such as edges and objects as a rule will elevate ELA esteems than the rest of the image.

ELA clients can figure out the methods to recognize picture scaling, quality, editing, and resave changes. For instance, if a non-JPEG picture comprises noticeable network boundaries (1-pixel wide in 8 × 8 squares), at that point it implies the image began as a JPEG and was changed over to the non-JPEG design. On the off chance that a few zones of the image need framework lines or the lattice lines move, at that point it means a join or attracted partition the non-JPEG picture. Another model, a PNG record is a lossless document design. If an image is a unique PNG, at that point ELA should create high qualities for edges and surfaces. Nonetheless, if ELA produces feeble outcomes (dim or dark shading) along edges and surfaces, at that point the PNG is expected to be made from a JPEG. This is on the grounds that the change procedure from JPEG to PNG is lossless and will hold JPEG curios. At the point when joined with different calculations, ELA turns into an exceptionally incredible assessment instrument. While ELA is a superb device for identifying adjustments, there are various warnings:

- A pixel change, or slight shading modification, may not produce a recognizable change in the ELA.
- JPEG works on a framework, and a modification to every piece of the lattice will probably affect the whole matrix square. One will be unable to distinguish precisely which pixel in the network was changed.
- ELA just recognizes what districts have distinctive pressure levels. It does not distinguish sources. On the off chance that a lower quality picture is joined into a more excellent picture, at that point the poorer quality picture might show up as a bleaker locale.
- Recoloring, scaling, or adding clamor to a picture will alter the whole picture, making a higher mistake level potential.
- If a picture is resaved on different occasions, at that point it might be altogether at the very least blunder level. For this situation, the ELA will restore a dark picture and no adjustments can be distinguished utilizing this calculation.

7.5   Proposed Model of Image Forgery Detection, Results and Discussion

The flow chart of the novel CNN model for image forgery detection is revealed in Figure 7.4. The model consists of the multilayer ConvNet with more than one convolution, ReLU and pooling layers. The proposed model is trained with a Kaggle dataset named CASIA1. The CASIA1 is further divided into two parts: dataset 1 and dataset 2. During the testing phase, the input layer has been fed with image with the size of $256 \times 256 \times 3$. The image goes under different layers of multilayer ConvNet. This model uses "ReLu" as an activation function and max pooling as pooling activity. In the output layer to acquire the binary decision, the image is forged and the simple activation function "sigmoid" is used. After obtaining the binary output, if the output is "1" the image is forged, otherwise a normal image. On training the network with two datasets obtained from Kaggle website

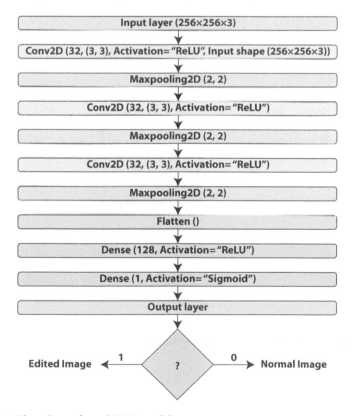

Figure 7.4 Flow chart of novel CNN model.

(CASIA1), the graphs of loss functions (LF) and accuracy are described below for both training and validation. The network training and validation has been performed with Google Colab notebook. Figure 7.5 shows training loss and accuracy for dataset 1. In Figure 7.5, the Y-axis represents the normalized accuracy and X-axis defines number of epochs.

From Figure 7.5 it can be deduced that the proposed model has achieved around 99% accuracy during the tanning process and around 91% accuracy during validation process. The complete simulation models have been tested for 100 epochs. The outcomes of the dataset 2 with respect to loss function and accuracy has been presented in Figure 7.6. The simulation setup for dataset 2 is the same as discussed in the earlier case. With dataset 2 also the proposed model shows the stable performance with the image forgery detection accuracy of around 87%. Thus, the simulation results validating the proposed model for image forgery detection has an accuracy of around 90%.

For the proposed ConvNet model, the confusion matrix of test dataset 1 and dataset 2 is represented by Figure 7.7 and Figure 7.8, respectively.

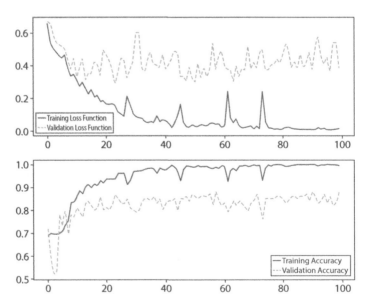

Figure 7.5 Training losses and accuracy for dataset 1.

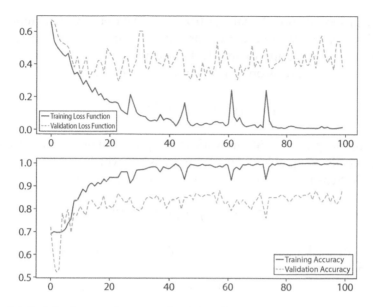

Figure 7.6 Training losses and accuracy for dataset 2.

197	3
43	257

Figure 7.7 Confusion matrix of dataset 1.

179	21
43	257

Figure 7.8 Confusion matrix of dataset 2.

Accuracy of the proposed model: As per the confusion matrix the normalized accuracy of ConvNet model is represented as follows:

$$Accuracy = (TP + TN)/(TP + TN + FP + FN)$$

The proposed model achieves 0.908 for dataset 1 which implies the model is approx. 91% accurate. For dataset 2 it is around 0.872 which implies the model is approximately 87% accurate.

Precision: The precision of a system is given as follows:

$$Precision = TP/(TP + FP)$$

The model presented in this work shows precision of 0.985 for dataset 1, which is truly acceptable and 0.895 for dataset 2, which is really acceptable.

Recall (Sensitivity): The recall of the system can be given by:

$$Recall = TP/(TP + FN)$$

The proposed model has a recall of 0.82 for dataset1 and 0.80 for dataset 2 which is useful for this model.

F1 score: F1 Score is the weighted normal of precision and recall and given by:

$$F1\ Score = 2 \times (recall \times precision)/(recall \times precision)$$

For the model presented here, the F1 score is 0.89 for dataset 1 and 0.84 for dataset 2.

7.6   Conclusion

In this research work, a novel CNN model along with error level analysis has been presented for image forgery detection. The suggested model has been validated with Kaggle's CASIA1 dataset. It has been found that the model performs with 91% accuracy for dataset 1 and around 87% accuracy for dataset 2. The detailed efficacy of the system is measured based on the confusion matrix for both the datasets. It is concluded that the system has a normalized precision of 0.98 and 0.89 for dataset 1 and dataset 2, respectively. Further, the proposed model is tested for recall and F1 score. For all the performance major criteria, performance of the model was found satisfactory. On the basis of the proposed novel model an android application can be developed in the near future. The application will determine whether the particular image is digitally altered/edited or not.

7.7   Future Research Directions

ICT along with cloud computing techniques ensures a robust scheme for machine learning (ML) and deep learning (DL) skills. Recently researchers investigated the 5G system as a candidate to offer groundwork for intelligent wireless networks to deal with congregated claims. ML-centered signal processing algorithms can pave the way to the progress of future intelligent wireless networks (B5G). DL typically comprises two phases, viz. training and testing. In practical application of real communications systems only the testing phase is useful. The training phase is customarily finished offline. A trained DL model can thus accomplish many objectives lacking the requirement for retraining. In this regard, we can use the proposed CNN algorithm with some modifications.

The implementation of CNN in Automatic modulation classification (AMC) has revealed hopeful accuracy. AMC is the method of categorizing the modulation pattern of a signal and is an essential method of non-cooperative communication. By using time-frequency channelized input to CNN, an enhancement of feature dimension will occur for CNN input. Henceforth the lost info like phase or frequency deviation can be simply caught in energy variation of time-frequency map. Hence the CNN method proposed here can be applied in AMC for enhancing the classification capability.

References

1. Madhusmita Mishra; LDPC Codes and Digital Forensics – A Perspective Approach. *IETE Journal of Research* 2019, pp. 1–8.
2. S. B. Basavarajappa and S. Sathyanarayana; Digital image forgery detection techniques: a survey. *ACCENTS Transactions on Information Security* 2016; pp. 22–31.
3. H. Farid; Image forgery detection. *IEEE Signal Processing Magazine* 2009; pp. 16–25.
4. A Dureja; P Pahwa; Image Retrieval Techniques: A survey. *International Journal of Engineering & Technology.* 2018, pp. 215–219.
5. A Krizhevsky; I Sutskever; G E Hinton; Imagenet classification with deep convolutional neural networks. *Advances in Neural Information Processing Systems.* 2012, pp. 1097–1105.
6. P Mishra; N Mishra; S Sharma; R Patel; Region duplication forgery detection technique based on SURF and HAC. *Scientific World Journal.* 2013.
7. A C Popescu; H Farid; Exposing digital forgeries in colour filter array interpolated images. 2005, pp. 3948–3959.

8. J Chen; X Kang;Y Liu; Z J Wang; Median filtering forensics based on convolutional neural networks. *IEEE Signal Processing Letters*. 2015, pp. 1849–1853.

9. M D Ansari; S P Ghrera; V Tyagi; Pixel-Based Image Forgery Detection: A Review. *IETE J Education*. 2014, pp. 40–46.

10. N. Krawetz; A picture's worth... Digital Image Analysis and Forensics. *Hacker Factor Solutions*. 2007.

11. Birajdar GK; Mankar VH.; Digital image forgery detection using passive techniques: A survey, *Digital Investigation* 2013, pp. 226–245.

12. Gu J; Wang Z; Kuen J; Ma L; Shahroudy A; Shuai B *et al.*; Recent advances in convolutional neural networks. *Pattern Recognition* 2018, pp. 354–377.

13. Liu S; Deng W; Very deep convolutional neural network based image classification using small training sample size. *3rd IAPR Asian Conference on Pattern Recognition (ACPR)* 2015.

14. Han H; Li Y; Zhu, X.; Convolutional neural network learning for generic data classification. *Information Sciences* 2019, pp. 448–465.

15. D M Uliyan; H A Jalab; A W A Wahab; P Shivakumara; S Sadeghi; A novel forged blurred region detection system for image forensic applications", *Expert Systems with Applications* 2016, pp. 1–10.

16. S Walia; K Kumar; Digital image forgery detection: a systematic scrutiny. *Australian Journal of Forensic Sciences* 2018, pp. 1–39.

17. J Zhang; W Zhu; B Li; W Hu; J Yang; Image copy detection based on convolutional neural networks, *Chinese Conference on Pattern Recognition* 2016, pp. 111–121.

18. Y Zhang; J Goh; L L Win; V L Thing; Image Region Forgery Detection: A Deep Learning Approach. *Proceedings of the Singapore Cyber-Security Conference (SG-CRC)*. 2016, pp. 1–11.

19. J Zhou; J Ni; Y Rao; Block-Based Convolutional Neural Network for Image Forgery Detection. *International Workshop on Digital Watermarking*. 2017, pp. 65–76.

20. Doegar Amit; Dutta Maitreyee; Gaurav Kumar; CNN Based Image Forgery Detection Using Pre-trained AlexNet Model. *International Journal of Computational Intelligence & IoT.* 2019.

21. C. N. Bharti; P. Tandel; A survey of image forgery detection techniques. *International Conference on Wireless Communications, Signal Processing and Networking (WiSPNET). IEEE.* 2016, pp. 877–881.

22. Factor H Foto; Forensics Online for ELA. 2012.

23. J Chen; X Kang; Y Liu; Z J Wang; Median filtering forensics based on convolutional neural networks. *IEEE Signal Processing Letters*. 2015, pp. 1849–1853.

24. M D Ansari; S P Ghrera; V Tyagi; Pixel-Based Image Forgery Detection: A Review. *IETE J Education*. 2014. pp. 40–46.

25. Yan Zhao *et al.*; Digital Image Manipulation Forensics. *Technical Report No. UCB/EECS- 2015-85*. 2015.

26. Birajdar GK; Mankar VH; Digital image forgery detection using passive techniques: A survey. *Digital Investigation*. 2013. pp. 226–245.

27. Gu J; Wang Z; Kuen J; Ma L; Shahroudy A; Shuai B; Recent advances in convolutional neural networks. *Pattern Recognition*. 2017.

28. Shengwei Zhou; Caikou Chen; Guojiang Han; Deep Convolutional Neural Network with Dilated Convolution Using Small Size Dataset. *Chinese Control Conference (CCC)*. 2019.

29. Han H; Li Y; Zhu X; Convolutional neural network learning for generic data classification. *Information Sciences*. 2019. pp. 448–465.

30. B. Bayar; M. C. Stamm; A deep learning approach to universal image manipulation detection using a new convolutional layer. *Proceedings of the 4th ACM Workshop on Information Hiding and Multimedia Security. AC.* 2016. pp. 5–10.

31. Deepika Ghai, Suman Lata Tripathi, Sobhit Saxena, Manash Chanda, Mamoun Alazab, *Machine Learning Algorithms for Signal and Image Processing*, Wiley IEEE Press, 2022.

32. Kanak Kumar; Kaustav Chaudhury; Suman Lata Tripathi, "Future of Machine Learning (ML) and Deep Learning (DL) in Healthcare Monitoring System," in *Machine Learning Algorithms for Signal and Image Processing* , IEEE, 2023, pp. 293–313, doi: 10.1002/9781119861850.ch17.

8

Applications of Artificial Neural Networks in Optical Performance Monitoring

Isra Imtiyaz[1], Anuranjana[1*], Sanmukh Kaur[2] and Anubhav Gautam[2]

[1]Department of Information Technology, ASET, Amity University Uttar Pradesh, Noida, India
[2]Department of Electronics & Communication Engineering, ASET, Amity University Uttar Pradesh, Noida, India

Abstract

The calculation and collection of numerous physical properties of transmitted signals and different optical network components is known as optical performance monitoring (OPM). Interest in OPM has increased as a result of advancements in optical networking, particularly with regard to signal quality metrics including optical signal-to-noise ratio (SNR), Q-factor, and dispersion. This paper reviews OPM algorithms and their advantages and disadvantages. It also reviews artificial intelligence (AI) methods in optical networks, and applications of AI in optical networking, optical impairments, and component faults.

Keywords: ANN, optical performance monitoring, LSTM, optical impaitments

8.1 Introduction

Optical communication is long-distance communication that uses light to transport information. It can be done visually or using electronic instruments. Optical wireless communication (OWC) is a type of optical communication wherein unguided infrared (IR), visible, or ultraviolet (UV) light is used to transmit a signal. It is mostly used for short-distance communication. Visible light communication (VLC) has been recognised as a possible indoor high-speed wireless solution for short-distance access as a

---

*Corresponding author: aranjana@amity.edu

Suman Lata Tripathi and Mufti Mahmud (eds.) *Explainable Machine Learning Models and Architectures*, (123–140) © 2023 Scrivener Publishing LLC

form of OWC integrating communication with illumination [1]. Free space optical communication (FSO) is another type of optical communication technology which uses free-space light propagation to wirelessly transport data via computer networking or telecommunications. Some merits of FSO are that free space optics is a versatile network that provides faster speeds than broadband and requires a small initial expenditure. High data rates comparable to optical fibre cable data rates can be attained, yet error rates are very low, and the incredibly narrow laser beam allows for an endless number of FSO lines to be established in a specific region. But along with this, there are some limitations too, for example, when flying birds, trees, and tall structures arrive in the line of sight (LOS) of the FSO system's broadcast, they can momentarily block a single beam. Also, temperature differences between air packets would occur as a result of heat rising from earth and man-made drivers such as heating ducts. Temperature differences can create amplitude fluctuations in the signal, resulting in "picture dance" at the FSO receiving end [2].

OPM is the assessment and acquisition of numerous physical properties of transmitted signals and optical network components. OPM features are critical to ensuring a stable network operation and play an important role in providing flexibility and improving overall network efficiency. OPM is key to ensure the reliability of optical networks and it comprises three levels as shown in Figure 8.1 [3]. The determination of the optical domain parameters necessary for transport and channel management at the WDM layer constitutes the first layer, known as the transport or WDM channel management layer monitoring. Examples of real-time measurements at the transport layer include those of channel existence, wavelength registration, power levels, and spectral optical sound to noise ratio (OSNR). The monitoring of the optical signal or channel quality layer, which locks onto a single wavelength and conducts tests that are sensitive to signal transitions, is the second level. The analogue eye and eye statistics, the Q-factor, the electronic SNR, and damage that arises inside the eye as a result of dispersion

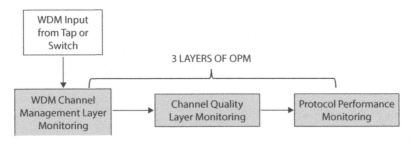

Figure 8.1 Different layers in OPM.

and nonlinear effects are examples of aspects that may be evaluated in the signal quality layer. Monitoring data protocol information and protocol performance constitute the third level of OPM named PPM. This involves the use of digital measurements to deduce characteristics of the analogue optical signal, such as the BER [4].

When other transmission distortions, including chromatic dispersion (CD) and polarisation mode dispersion (PMD), are adjusted in digital coherent optical receivers, OSNR is the metric that has the greatest impact on bit error rate (BER) [5]. Based on linear interpolation of either the noise level as from spectral gaps amongst signals, the conventional OSNR monitoring technique employed optical spectrum analysers (OSA). However, due to the low resolution of conventional diffraction-grating based OSAs, the spectral gap in ultra-dense wavelength division multiplexing (UDWDM) or super channel transmission systems is blurred or even non-existent (about 0.02 nm) [6].

Additionally, the ASE noise at the spectral gap may be significantly suppressed due to the cascaded filtering effect (CFE) caused by the optical filtering components contained in the optical nodes, such like optical add-drop multiplexers (OADM) but rather wavelength selective switches (WSS), rendering the interpolation-based method ineffective [7].

Optical networks will be extremely vulnerable to damaging and data-degraded fibre-based impairments as system capacity rises. Due to the wide spectrum of high-rate signals, some of the most significant impairments are CD, PMD, and OSNR. In order to sustain system performance, the network's capacity to determine the severity of the limitations is crucial. OPM can be accomplished out through monitoring data changes and identifying "real-time" changes brought on by different impairments, so that a change in one impact would alter a measured parameter [8]. This can use electrical post-processing procedures in the specific situation of coherent detection [9] or optical techniques to monitor the changes inside a radio frequency (RF) tone power or in the spectral channel power distribution [10].

Interest in OPM has increased as a result of advancements in optical networking, particularly with regard to signal quality metrics like OSNR, Q-factor, and dispersion. These sophisticated monitoring techniques may allow fault management and quality-of-service (QoS) monitoring to be expanded into the optical domain [11]. Table 8.1 lists different algorithms employed for optical performance estimation and monitoring along with their advantages and disadvantages.

In [3], the authors say that the need for optical network capacity has been rising substantially as a result of the development of 5G technology, high-definition video, and the internet of things. Low-margin optical

Table 8.1 Literature reviews.

Ref.	Algorithm	Advantages	Disadvantages
[12, 13]	ANN	• Enables a wide range of function representations • Capable of managing noisy data • An ANN with one or more corrupted cells can nevertheless produce output. Due to this feature networks are fault-tolerant.	• The trained model is difficult to interpret. • Few layers possible because of vanishing gradients • According to their structure, artificial NN demand processors having parallel processing power. The equipment's actualization is therefore dependent on this.
[14]	DNN	• Low cost of implementation. Deep NN–based inventory technology just requires the installation of the inventory application on an empty server. • Simple process for implementation, maintenance and operation	• For it to perform better than other strategies, a huge amount of data is necessary. • Due to the complicated data models, training is very expensive.
[15]	CNN	• Provides cutting-edge performance when working with two dimensional inputs • Time and cost benefit continue to be the top two of the three most popular advantages of neural networks. • Without human oversight, automatically identifies the key qualities.	• Significant computational difficulty • A large amount of training data is needed. • The orientation and position of an object are not encoded by CNN.

(Continued)

Table 8.1 Literature reviews. (*Continued*)

Ref.	Algorithm	Advantages	Disadvantages
[16]	SVR	• It is resistant to irregularities. • Updates to the decision model are simple. • It has a strong capacity for generalisation and good prediction accuracy. • It's simple to put into practice.	• For huge datasets, they are not appropriate. • When there is additional noise in the data set, such as when the target classes overlap, the decision model does not perform effectively.
[17]	SVM	• Effective in rooms with high dimensions • Memory-efficient since just a portion of the training points are used (support vectors)	• Heuristics are used to choose kernel functions. • Inability to use data outside of the class spectrum
[18]	KRR	• A benefit of kernel ridge regression is there are methods that compute the classification error rate and leave on-out mean-squared error using the results of a single training on the entire training set.	• The coefficients vector is not sparse, hence the idea of "support vectors" does not exist. Since support vector machines only need to sum so over set of support vectors and not the full training set, this makes the difference at the time of prediction.
[19]	LSTM	• Selection from a variety of LSTM parameters, such as learning rates with input and output biases. As a result, there is no need for fine adjustments.	• They require a significant amount of time and resource for learning in the real world, the linear layers available in each cell, they require high memory bandwidth, which the systems cannot often provide.

networks are getting attention in order to meet the capacity requirement. As a result, more precise planning tools are required, and the important components to achieving this are accurate models of transmission quality (QoT) and impairments. Additionally, since the margin is small, it is important to maintain the optical network's dependability, and OPM is necessary. OPM enables controllers to identify anomalies and modify the physical layer's setup. However, employing conventional analytical techniques to create such precise modelling and monitoring tools is challenging given the heterogeneity of the contemporary optical network, whereas in [12], with an infinite budget, comprehensive monitoring is available. Although optical networks' future is difficult to foresee, the value of OPM rises as transparency does. The way that networks are changing makes higher degrees of OPM desirable, if not necessary. To meet this OPM demand, numerous technologies have been developed. Applying these strategies in a way that strikes the correct balance between monitoring coverage, sensitivity, and cost will be the problem moving ahead.

In [2], the authors proposed 1D features (the IQHH and IQHD) and 2D IQH features to study OPM in FMF-based optical networks. Using a 10 Gbuad-DP-QPSK signal, they conducted simulations and experiments to assess OPM's performance. The findings demonstrated their ability to predict OSNR values between 8 and 20 dB, CD values between 160 and 1100 ps/nm, and various mode coupling coefficient values. However, the monitoring performance will be significantly impacted by the presence of impairment(s) with level(s), rendering IQH features almost indistinguishable for various circumstances.

In [11], the authors state that the deep neural network (NN)-based OPM technique currently in use lacks the capacity to select the input data. They always accept but also process everything, which could lead to major monitoring errors and undermine the monitoring system's credibility. Due to the diversity of the sent data in future heterogeneous BER-optic networks, which is likely to go beyond the capabilities of the monitoring system. In their new OPM architecture, they suggest an unsupervised generative adversarial network (GAN) as even the judgement module to choose the lawful material that falls within the purview of the monitoring system. Encoder-decoder-encoder (EDE) sub-network, which makes up the generator, jointly learns the image with hidden feature distribution of the legal data. Additionally, the OPM analyser network's training data are the same as the training data for the network in the newly added judgement module, so no additional data are acquired, saving money. To test the model's performance in the judgement module of the simulation, four modulation formats at two-bit rates are considered. The maximum area under the curve (AUC) value is 0.942 when a 60 Gbps 64QAM signal is used as unlawful data. A single image's judgement takes roughly 12ms. Additionally, the impact of task weights and latent feature shape on judgement performance is examined. The current OPM scheme's credibility and safety have been significantly improved by the newly included judging module.

8.2   Algorithms Employed for Performance Monitoring

8.2.1   Artificial Neural Networks

Information-processing systems called artificial neural networks (ANNs) provide appealing alternatives to traditional approaches like numerical modelling techniques, analytical techniques, or empirical modelling solutions because they generalise by abstraction and learn from observations [20, 21].

ANNs are straightforward to utilise and have the capacity to describe multi-dimensional nonlinear interactions. Additionally, the neural network approach is quick to respond and versatile (i.e., the same modelling technique may be utilised for passive/active devices/systems). These characteristics have made the ANN method popular as a strong tool in many fields, including pattern recognition, voice processing, control, and bio-medical engineering. More recently, it has also been used in RF modelling, microwave design, and optical performance monitoring. Often, the

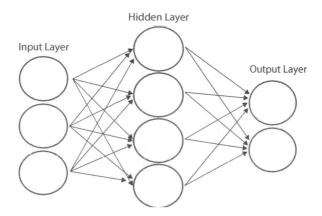

Figure 8.2 Layers of artificial neural networks.

electrical/optical behaviour of passive and active parts/circuits/systems is first modelled using neural networks. When employed in advanced modelling and design, these trained neural networks can provide quick solutions to the problem they were taught [8].

Multiple layers of processing units known as neurons make up an ANN. The coefficients below reflect the strength of the connections between each neuron and the neurons in the next layers. The correlations between sets of input-output data that represent properties of the device or system under examination are discovered by ANNs. The outputs of the ANN are compared to the desired outputs, and errors are determined, after the input vectors are given to the input neurons and the output vectors are generated. As soon as the network has seen all of the training sets, error derivatives are computed and added for each weight. The weights for the neurons are updated using the error derivatives, and training is continued until the errors achieve the desired low levels. The levels of ANN are shown in Figure 8.2.

8.2.2   Deep Neural Networks

Each link among the hidden layers of nonlinear processing units (neurons) used in ANN pattern recognition has a corresponding weight. In order for the ANN to learn how to represent complicated models, it must go through an iterative training process in which the input layer first receives raw data, which is then modified and processed by each succeeding hidden

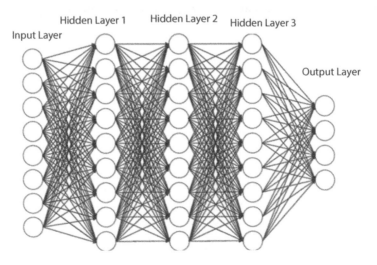

Figure 8.3 Layers of DNN.

layer. The number of hidden layers and neurons is a crucial design factor for ANNs since it affects the network's ability to learn [22].

Regardless of the fact that ANNs have been effectively employed for many years, technological advancements are forcing ANNs to perform at higher and higher levels due to the growing number of datasets. Deep neural networks (DNNs), models based on deep learning, may now be used to tackle these performance problems since they have the speed and accuracy to handle massive amounts of data in parallel using graphic processing units. A network is often referred to as a DNN when it includes two to ten hidden layers [Figure 8.3] and is capable of learning complicated functions more quickly than the conventional ANNs (also called shallow neural networks) [23]. Sigmoid activation functions have historically been utilised by DNNs; however, when hidden layers are added, the network starts to perform worse and converge more slowly. As a result, a unique DNN architecture known as deep rectifier neural networks was created, which replaced the sigmoid activation functions along with rectifier linear functions.

8.2.3   Convolutional Neural Networks

The weight matrices of a convolutional neural network (CNN), a particular type of neural network structure, are produced by convolution with filter masks. The better ability of CNNs to interpret organised arrays of data, such as pictures, talks, and audio signal inputs, sets them apart from other neural networks. In this part, we study the matrix form of CNNs in order to comprehend convergence of CNNs. We present an architecture of deep neural networks with larger widths that is inspired by CNNs [24]. CNNs have extensively adopted deep learning (DL) computations and the majority of certain NN categorization, especially in high dimensional information, such as images and recordings. It achieves Deep Neural Network's superiority, which hinders scaling well with multidimensional privately connected information [25].

As a result, CNN is crucial for information bases, where it was necessary to create a large number of hubs or boundaries. The diagram below shows the CNN architecture. Here is a definition of CNN's several levels in its architecture.

8.2.3.1   *Convolutional Layer*

The convolutional layer, which determines the yield of linked input in an open region, is the fundamental component of something like the convolutional neural network. A two-dimensional activation guide of the track

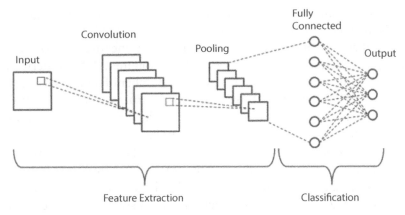

Figure 8.4 The CNN architecture.

is created by converging parts above the data information's height and breadth, registering the tiny piece between the input and channel values, and doing this. Figure 8.4 shows the basic CNN architecture.

8.2.3.2   Non-Linear Layer

The vast potential of non-linear systems must be greater than that of the individual. The info sign will be converted to the yield sign in this layer, and that signal will then be utilized to contribute to the layer below [26].

8.2.3.3   Pooling Layer

Its main function is to decrease the number of boundaries as well as counts with in model proportional to the spatial size of the depiction. It expedites estimates and avoids the overfitting problem. Maximum pooling is the different and most well-known variety of pooling layer.

8.2.3.4   Fully Connected Layer

Regular DNNs with fully connected layers aim to compile the motivation's forecasts to be used to identify relapse. It has a similar head as the standard MLP. A grid augmentation surveyed by an inclination counterbalance could be used to select representations for this type of layer, which receives entire connections with every actuation in the preceding layer.

8.2.4   Support Vector Regression (SVR)

SVMs, or support vector machines, are widely used to solve classification issues. However, there is little evidence supporting the use of SVMs in regression. Support Vector Regression is the name for these models (SVR). With SVR, we have the freedom to specify the level of error that we will tolerate in our model, and it will locate the best line (or hyperplane, in higher dimensions) that fits the data [16].

8.2.5   Support Vector Machine (SVM)

A popular discriminant method due to the statistical learning theory is the support vector machine (SVM) [27]. Its potent capacity to generalise to unknown data is one of its key advantages. The empirical risk minimization principle is used extensively in conventional methodologies to ensure that training-related errors are kept to a minimum [28]. SVM is based on the idea of structural risk reduction, which, in contrast to traditional methods, aims to reduce the upper bound of the promotion error in order to achieve an optimal network structure by achieving a balance between both the complexity of the model and the complexity of something like the training error [29].

8.2.6   Kernel Ridge Regression (KRR)

Ridge regression as well as classification are combined with the kernel trick in kernel ridge regression (KRR). In the space created by the relevant kernel and the data, it subsequently learns a linear function. This correlates directly to a non-linear method in the original space for non-linear kernels. The model developed by Kernel Ridge has the exact same structure as SVR. KRR employs squared error loss while SVR uses E-insensitive loss; both are paired with l2 regularisation. The loss functions, however, are different. In contrast to SVR, fitting Kernel Ridge is often quicker for medium-sized datasets and can be done in closed-form. As opposed to SVR, which adopts a sparse model for $E>0$ at prediction time, the acquired model is non-sparse and so as a result slower [30].

8.2.7   Long Short-Term Memory (LSTM)

In 1997, Hochreiter and Schmidhuber created the Long Short-Term Memory (LSTM), which consists of multiple neural layers with a few control gates in each neuron [31]. Recurrent neural networks of the LSTM type are able to learn order dependency. Four neural networks and a large number of memory cells arranged in a chain pattern form up the LSTM. A cell, an input gate, an output gate and a gate to eliminate previous data form a typical LSTM unit. The gates regulate the flow of information in and out of the cell, and the cell retains values for arbitrarily long periods of time. Time series of indefinite duration can be categorized and predicted with the LSTM algorithm [19]. These gate architectures increased long-term dependency prediction accuracy and addressed the vanishing gradient issue in recurrent neural networks. By using the sigmoid function on the concealed state from the previous time step as well as the current input data, the forget gate deleted the data regarding the current state [32].

8.3   Artificial Intelligence (AI) Methods, Performance Monitoring and Applications in Optical Networks

AI entities as well as systems have the capacity to perform biological processes, with a focus on human cognitive processes, to carry out activities similar to learning and decision-making. Virtual personal assistants, smart cars, purchase prediction, speech recognition, and smart home devices are just a few examples of AI applications that are almost universal. These and other AI-based technologies are already transforming our daily lives in ways that improve human productivity, safety, and health, even influencing how we communicate and have fun. For instance, throughout the past few decades, there has been a lot of research into how AI-based techniques might be used to enhance the performance in telecommunication networks, with implications for transmission, switching, and network management. Rather than sitting on the sidelines, optical communication networks and systems have begun to apply this discipline to AI-based optical networking, through photonic devices to control and management [33].

8.3.1   Performance Monitoring

Adapting to time-varying link performance metrics, such as optical signal to noise ratio (OSNR), nonlinearity factors, chromatic dispersion (CD), and polarisation mode dispersion, is a difficulty in network control and management (PMD). This subsection examines whether using AI approaches to monitor some of the factors mentioned are appropriate.

In order to perform network-diagnosis and take corrective action (such as fixing damage, operating compensators or equalisers, or rerouting traffic around less-than-optimal links), physical properties of transmitted optical signals must be estimated and acquired [25].

Another recent study that addresses the research listed the above's restricted scalability, which is dependent on the prior knowledge of a predetermined set of signals, and proposes using a deep neural network (DNN) trained using raw data that is asynchronously sampled by a coherent receiver to monitor OSNR. Results indicate that the OSNR is estimated correctly. However, for this DNN to produce correct results, it must be set up with nearly five layers and trained on 400,000 samples, which takes a lot of time. Both the SVM and the OSNR estimator use neural networks to train a continuous mapping function between input features taken from the power eye-diagram following the photo detector as well as the reference OSNR and modulation format, respectively. Although accurate results are obtained for the calculation of OSNR and the categorization of modulation formats, the study only takes white Gaussian noise into account and ignores linear and nonlinear optical fibre impairments at this time [33].

8.3.2   Applications of AI in Optical Networking

AI has a lot of options for automating activities and incorporating intelligent decision making in network planning, dynamic control, and management of network resources, covering challenges such as connection setup, self-configuration, and self-optimization. These opportunities are made possible by prediction and estimation using historical data and current network state [33].

8.4   Optical Impairments and Fault Management

Three basic forms of optical impairments include noise distortion and timing.

8.4.1   Noise

Random fluctuations in the signal that are frequently regarded as a Gaussian process and therefore can vary depending on the signal level.

8.4.2   Distortion

The average waveform of the signal is modified, for instance, when the marks and spaces are taken independently. Burst errors and BER floors can result from distortion, which can also be signal level and pattern dependent.

8.4.3   Timing

Timing jitter can happen instantly (bit-to-bit) or build up gradually over multiple bit cycles. There are countless underlying causes that fall under these categories, and many of the degrading effects appear in more than one area. The fundamental causes encompass all possible ways of component failure; hence they cannot be predicted in advance. It is useful to further categorise impairments into optical transmission impairments or component failure effects.

8.4.4   Component Faults

Incorrectly installed or configured equipment, individual or multiple component malfunctions, damage to or intrusion into the network are all examples of component problems. It is impossible to fully catalogue the effects of such problems since they affect networks and components with as many different configurations as possible. Consider the failure mechanisms of an optical amplifier as an example to understand the variety of possibilities. Reduced power will occur at specific locations along the transmission line or inside specific amplifier internal compartments as a result of failing pump lasers. These low power levels may be amplified further and become surplus noise, which will be seen in the optical spectrum. Although excessive noise on the signal can also be caused by unstable pump lasers, it might not be visible in the optical spectrum in this instance. The signal levels will be high if the pump laser's power control loop malfunctions and it runs high, which can promote a variety of nonlinear transmission phenomena like cross-phase (XPM) or self-phase modulation (SPM) [3].

Electronic switches, multiplexers, and regenerators—which typically incorporate SONET/SDH layer performance monitoring—are replaced by optical components in transparent networks. One trades off the greater capital equipment cost of integrating optical monitoring (to replace the electronic monitoring) against increased operating expenses due to more challenging troubleshooting by introducing the optical components with lower monitoring capacity. If the two costs scale similarly, this trade-off is acceptable. How network troubleshooting costs scale up is unclear. This trade-off was necessary in the past due to the high cost of optical performance monitoring. Critical optical technologies like tuneable filters and spectrometers have lately become more widely available and have reduced the cost of many optical monitoring solutions [34].

8.4.5   Transmission Impairments

In addition to poor network performance, there are numerous well-known and maybe countless negative effects of optical transmission that must be avoided or under control. Optically impairing factors such as amplifier noise, chromatic dispersion, and polarisation mode dispersion are carefully controlled in order to achieve extended connection lengths. As distance and channel count increase, inter-channel interactions cause noise to increase. Interactions between impairments make it difficult to predict, monitor, and control nonlinear impairments. XPM has a dispersion-dependent effect. As a result, the distance and channel configuration affect network performance [35].

While the usage of optical switching elements will influence how different impairments need to be monitored, distance is the main factor driving enhanced optical monitoring to mitigate transmission impairments. For instance, chromatic dispersion in static point-to-point systems might only be checked to ensure proper network installation or for in-service compensation. Chromatic dispersion may need to be checked for issues in a reconfigurable network since the accumulated dispersion and its effects will alter as the network evolves. Additionally, in an optical switching system, each channel will have a distinct history, therefore performance and cumulative impairments should be assessed per channel, identifying failures. Additionally, single-channel impairments are less likely to be linked to component alarms, especially when those components operate across the whole WDM spectrum. For these reasons, improved per-channel OPM may be needed for activities like wavelength routing as well as network reconfiguration to help with problem diagnostics [34].

8.4.6   Fault Management in Optical Network

The identification, diagnosis, resolving, and monitoring of defects in a network are referred to as fault management. Whenever a component or monitor alarm is set off or a customer report is submitted, the defect is identified. Many errors can be fixed by software tricks like remotely resetting a circuit pack, or they can be self-healing. The main defect indicators are bit error alarms at the network end terminals or in the client equipment. For instance, fibre cuts will cause alarm indication signals and launch a repair effort [3].

In optical network fault management systems, a failure that is signalled by an alarm at the end terminal often needs to be localised and diagnosed. Ideally, software would automate this process. A monitor must be able to identify the issue that led to the end terminal alarm in order to be effective. The monitors must, for this reason, have sensitivity that is equivalent to or greater than the end terminal receiver, where sensitivity is defined in relation to a certain impairment. The sensitivity specifications for a particular monitor will change based on where it is utilised in the network. The network becomes noisier as time goes on, and distortion moves throughout the dispersion map. The sensitivity requirements for a specific place are based on the noise and distortion combined at that point [34, 36].

8.5   Conclusion

Interest in OPM has increased as a result of advancements in optical networking. In this paper, we have reviewed the algorithms used for optical performance monitoring (i.e., ANN, DNN, CNN, SVR, SVM, KRR & LSTM) and found out about the advantages and disadvantages of each of them. This paper also demonstrates the different layers of OPM, application of AI in optical performance monitoring and the fault management in optical networks.

References

1. Zixian Wei, Zhaoming Wang, Jianan Zhang, Qian Li, Junping Zhang, H.Y. Fu, "Evolution of optical wireless communication for B5G/6G," *Progress in Quantum Electronics*, vol. 83, 2022.
2. Aditi Malik, Preeti Singh, "Free Space Optics: Current Applications and Future Challenges," *International Journal of Optics*, p. 7, 2015.
3. D. C. Kilper, R. Bach, D. J. Blumenthal, D. Einstein, T. Landolsi, L. Ostar, M. Preiss, A. E. Willner, "Optical Performance Monitoring," *Journal of Lightwave Technology*, vol. 22, pp. 294-304, 2004.
4. Francesco Musumeci, Cristina Rottondi, Avishek Nag, Irene Macaluso, Darko Zibar, Marco Ruffini, Massimo Tornatore, "An Overview on Application of Machine Learning Techniques in Optical Networks," *IEEE Communications Surveys & Tutorials*, pp. 1383-1408, 2019.
5. Savory, S. J., "Digital coherent optical receivers: Algorithms and subsystems," *IEEE J. Sel. Topics Quantum Electron*, vol. 16, p. 1164-1179, 2010.
6. Yibo Zhong, Sheng Cui, Hongwei Lu, Changjian Ke, Haoyu Wang, Peishan Jiang, Deming Liu, "A Robust Reference Optical Spectrum Based in-Band OSNR Monitoring Method Suitable for in-Band OSNR Monitoring Method Suitable for," *IEEE Photonics Journal*, vol. 12, 2020.

7. Moreolo, J. M. Fabrega and M. Svaluto, "On the filter narrowing issues in elastic optical networks," *J. Opt. Commun.*, vol. 8, 2016.

8. Xiaoxia Wu, Jeffrey A. Jargon, Ronald A. Skoog, Loukas Paraschis and Alan E. Willner, "Applications of Artificial Neural Networks in Optical Performance Monitoring," *Journal of Lightwave Technology*, vol. 27, pp. 3580-3589, 2009.

9. T. Luo, Z. Pan, S. M. R. Motaghian Nezam, L. S. Yan, A. Sahin, and A. E. Willner, "Chromatic-dispersion-insensitive PMD monitoring using optical off-center bandpass filtering," in *Optical Fiber Communications* (OFC), 2003.

10. H. Sun, K.Wu, and K. Roberts, "Real-time measurements of a 40 Gb/s coherent system," *Opt. Express*, vol. 16, p. 873-879, 2008.

11. Waddah S. Saif, Maged A. Esmail, Amr M. Ragheb, Tariq A. Alshawi, and Saleh A. Alshebeili, "Machine Learning Techniques for Optical Performance Monitoring and Modulation Format Identification: A Survey," *IEEE Communications Surveys & Tutorials*, vol. 22, pp. 2839-2882, 2020.

12. "1310 1550nm WDM Filter Integrated Optical Power Monitor," Lightwaves2020, 2019.

13. Haykin S., Neural Networks: A Comprehensive Foundation, Upper Saddle River, NJ: Prentice Hall, 1994.

14. Xin Fana, Xia Lyna, Fang Xiaoa, Tingting Caia, Chen Ding, "Research on Quick Inventory Framework Based on Deep Neural Network," *Procedia Computer Science*, pp. 40-51, 2021.

15. A. Krizhevsky, I. Sutskever, and G. E. Hinton, "Imagenet classification with deep convolutional neural networks," in *Proc. Adv. Neural Inf. Process. Syst. Conf.*, 2012.

16. Huang, H., Wei, X. And Zhou, Y., "An overview on twin support vector regression," Elsevier, pp. 80-92, 2021.

17. M. A. Hearst, S. T. Dumais, E. Osuna, J. Platt, and B. Scholkopf, "Support vector machines," *IEEE Intell. Syst. Appl*, vol. 13, pp. 18-28, 1998.

18. Guyon, Isabelle, "Kernel ridge regression," June 2005.

19. Schmidhuber, S. Hochreiter and J., "Long short-term memory," *Neural Comput.*, vol. 9, pp. 1735-1780, 1997.

20. Hassoun, M. H., *Fundamentals of Artificial Neural Networks*, MIT Press, 1995.

21. Gupta, Q. J. Zhang and K. C., *Neural Networks for RF and Microwave Design*, Norwood, MA: Artech House, 2000.

22. Lecun, Y., Bengio, Y., Hinton, G., "Deep Learning," *Nature* 521, pp. 436-444, 2015.

23. Srivastava, R.K., Greff, K., Schmidhuber, J., "Training Very Deep Networks," NIPS. Arxiv:1507.06228, 2015.

24. Yuesheng Xu, Haizhang Zhang, "Convergence of deep convolutional neural networks," *Neural Networks*, vol. 153, Sept. 2022, pp. 553-563, 2022.

25. Xiao L., Yan Q. and Deng S., "Scene classification with improved alexnet model," in *12th International Conference on Intelligent Systems and Knowledge Engineering, ISKE, IEEE*, 2017.

26. Z. Hong, "A preliminary study on artificial neural network," *6th IEEE Joint International Information Technology and Artificial Intelligence Conference,* vol. 2, pp. 336-338, 2011.
27. V. Vapnik, "Statistical learning theory. Adaptive and learning systems for signal processing," *Commun Control,* vol. 2, pp. 1-740, 1998.
28. Balasundaram S., and Gupta, D., "On optimisation based extreme learning machine in primal for regression and classification by functional iterative method," *Int J Mach Learn Cybern,* vol. 7, pp. 707-728, 2016.
29. Varatharajan R., Manogaran G. and Priyan M.K., "A big data classification approach using LDA with an enhanced SVM method for ECG signals in cloud computing," *Multimedia Tools Appl,* vol. 77, pp. 10195-10215, 2018.
30. Murphy, K. P, "Machine Learning: A Probabilistic Perspective," MIT Press, pp. 492-493, 2012.
31. Y. Hua, Z. Zhao, R. Li, X. Chen, Z. Liu and H. Zhang, "Deep learning with long short-term memory for time series prediction," *IEEE Commun. Mag.,* vol. 57(6), pp. 114-119, 2019.
32. Thanh-Phuong Nguyen, Chao-Tsung Yeh, Ming-Yuan Cho, Chun-Lung Chang, Meng-Jie Chen,"Convolutional neural network bidirectional long short-term memory to online classify the distribution insulator leakage currents," Elsevier.
33. Javier Mata, Ignacio de Miguel, Ramon J. Duran, Nowmi Merayo, Sandeep Kumar Singh, Admela Jukan, Mohit Chamania, "Artificial intelligence (AI) methods in optical networks: A comprehensive survey," *Optical Switching Networking,* Elsevier, vol. 28, pp. 43-57, 2018.
34. H. Chai, S. Yin, H. Liu, B. Guo, X. Li and S. Huang, "Algorithm research of routing and spectrum allocation based on OSNR impairment model in elastic optical network," *16th International Conference on Optical Communications and Networks (ICOCN),* 2017.
35. T. D. Vo *et al.,* "All-optical multi-impairment performance monitoring of 640 Gb/s optical signals using a chalcogenide photonic chip," *Conference on Optical Fiber Communication (OFC/NFOEC), collocated National Fiber Optic Engineers Conference, 2010.*
36. Sharma, K., Gupta, A., Sharma, B., & Tripathi, S.L. (Eds.). (2021). *Intelligent Communication and Automation Systems* (1st ed.). CRC Press, ISBN:9781003104599 https://doi.org/10.1201/9781003104599

9

Website Development with Django Web Framework

Sanmukh Kaur*, Anuranjana and Yashasvi Roy

Amity School of Engineering and Technology, Amity University Uttar Pradesh, Noida, India

Abstract

This chapter deals with the study of Django Web Framework, features of this framework and use of its inbuilt tools for web development. Further, it shows practical implementation of this framework through designing an architecture of a basic website and development of this website which has features like user registration, login-logout and user activity tracking through Django framework in backend. It highlights frontend development of user-friendly webpages using open-source CSS and Java Script–based design templates by Bootstrap, its customization and integration of these templates with Django Framework.

Keywords: Django, Python, HTML, CSS, MVT architecture, bootstrap

9.1 Introduction

Python is a generic programming language that can be used for making GUI applications and desktop applications as well as web applications [1]. It is also used for data analytics and visualization. Its simple syntax rules make its code more readable and maintainable than other languages. Due to various open-source Python frameworks, libraries, and development tools available it reduces software development cost significantly and any developer can use these frameworks for its product development and can integrate them.

**Corresponding author*: sanmukhkaur@gmail.com

Suman Lata Tripathi and Mufti Mahmud (eds.) Explainable Machine Learning Models and Architectures, (141–154) © 2023 Scrivener Publishing LLC

One of the open-source Python frameworks for web development is Django [2]. It is a high-level Python web framework that enables quick development of maintainable and secure websites. It is free and open-source web framework, has an active developer's community, great documentation, and various options for free technical support [3].

Django was at first developed between 2003 and 2005 by a website development group assigned to developing and maintaining a newspaper site. The process of creation of different websites by the group resulted in reusing the same codes and designing patterns which on further development took the form of a generic web development framework that was open sourced in July 2005 as the "Django" project.

9.2   Salient Features of Django

Some of the salient features of Django are discussed below.

9.2.1   Complete

Django works on the "Everything included" theory and gives nearly all that software engineers should develop "out of the box". Since all that is required is the one "product", then everything works flawlessly together, follows steady planned standards, and has broad and detailed documentation.

9.2.2   Versatile

Django can be used to develop any type of website whether it is content management systems, social networking, or news websites. It can be integrated with any framework and can transfer or show content in practically any configuration (counting HTML, JSON, XML, RSS channels and so on).

9.2.3   Secure

Django assists designers with staying away from numerous common security botches by giving a system that is designed to protect the website automatically. For instance, Django provides secure methods to manage user account and password details, eliminating common flaws like creating vulnerability through putting session information to the cookies or directly storing passwords in raw form instead of converting them to hash code (unidirectional) and then saving it in database. Django empowers insurance against numerous vulnerabilities by default, like SQL infusion, cross-site demand fabrication, clickjacking, and cross-site prearranging.

9.2.4   Scalable

Django follows a component/model-based "shared-nothing" architecture (i.e., every component of architecture works independently and doesn't interfere with others, therefore it can be customized as per need). Due to proper separation between its different components, it can be scaled up for increasing traffic by addition of hardware (servers) at any point like caching servers, application servers, or database servers. Some of the heavy traffic sites, like Instagram, have successfully managed to scale up using Django to fulfill their demands.

9.2.5   Maintainable

Django code is coded using well-defined design principles and well-defined patterns that help in development of easily maintainable and code which can be reused. It uses the DRY (Don't Repeat Yourself principle) so there is no unwanted duplication, and hence results in reduction in the amount of coding. Django also encourages the grouping of somewhat related functionalities into reusable applications and, at a lower level, same group related code into a module under the MVC (Model View Controller) pattern.

9.2.6   Portable

Django, which is written in Python, supports many platforms. It means that the developer is not bound to have its own specific server platform and can use many systems like Linux, Mac OS X, and Windows. Moreover, Django is also supported by various web-hosting cloud services, which often provide Django specific services.

9.3   UI Design

Django is a high-level Python Web framework. It has an easy to use UI. It has a pragmatic design to encourage fast web development. It has HTML, CSS and JavaScript support. It also includes multiple templates as it follows the model–template–views architectural pattern.

9.3.1   HTML

The Hyper Text Markup Language, or HTML, is the standard markup language for various component designing which is to be displayed in a web browser, which is further assisted by CSS and Java script for enhancing user experience.

9.3.2 CSS

Cascading Style Sheets is a style sheet language which describes how the content in HTML file where it is called will be displayed in a browser screen. CSS is a most important technology of the World Wide Web, alongside JavaScript and HTML.

9.3.3 Bootstrap

Bootstrap is one of the free and open-source CSS frameworks developed for responsive, mobile-first front-end web development [4]. It contains CSS- and JavaScript-based design templates for typography, forms, buttons, navigation, and other interface components.

9.4 Methodology

For web development the first step is to design its architecture as shown in Figure 9.1. It is planning of technical, functional and visual component of a website before its development. Our basic website contains home page, login page, re-login page, registration page, authenticated user console, logout and user tracking table.

Model View Template architecture is used for development of this website. In this approach a user requests a resource/operation in the form of a URL from Django framework [5] (acting as a controller) which looks for the same URL as requested by a user in urls.py and also looks for its corresponding view in view.py which contains a template for frontend operation, procedure and instance of a model (for database management) from models.py for backend operation as shown in Figures 9.2, 9.3, 9.4, 9.5, 9.6 and 9.7.

9.5 UI Design

Bootstrap is an open-source CSS Framework which provides various design templates for web development based on CSS and Java script which can be used for webpage designing by customizing the template code provided by the platform [6].

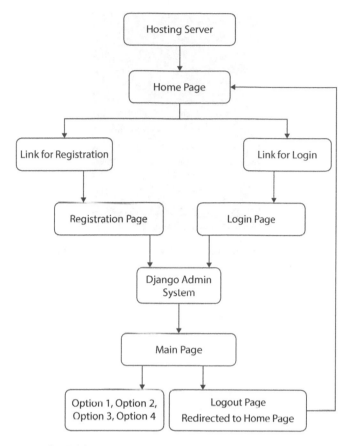

Figure 9.1 Django's MVT.

```
home )  urls.py ) ...
18      path('register/success/',views.regsuccess, name='regsucess')
```

Figure 9.2 Website architecture.

```
home )  views.py ) ...
115    def regsuccess(request):
116        num_visits = request.session.get('num_visits', 1)
117        request.session['num_visits'] = num_visits + 1
118        print(num_visits)
119        return render(request,"regsuccess.html")
120
```

Figure 9.3 View function defined in views.py for URL (register/success/) of urls.py in the project.

Figure 9.4 Resources for the template, i.e., HTML file, images, CSS file and Java stored in base directory of project.

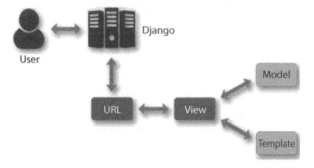

Figure 9.5 Model for table management in database for user tracking in models.py.

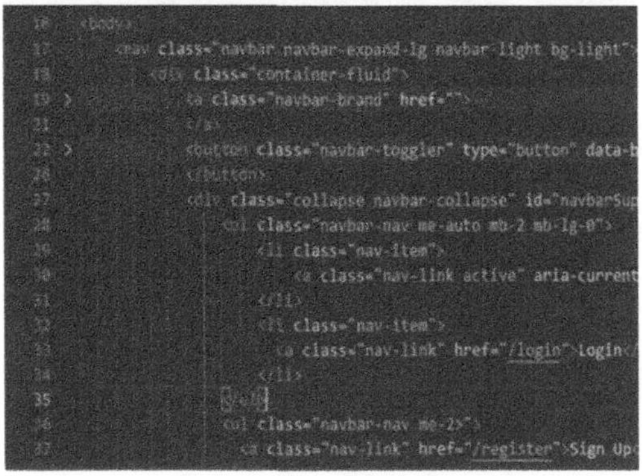

Figure 9.6 Log-data model's instance in log-entry view function in views.py executed during logout request.

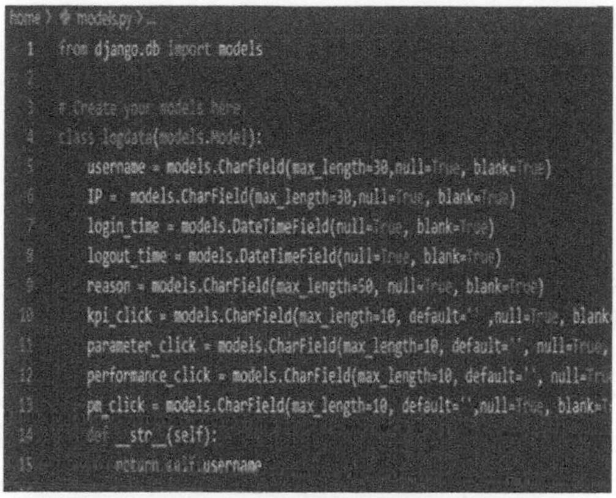

Figure 9.7 MVT (Model View Template) Architecture of Django.

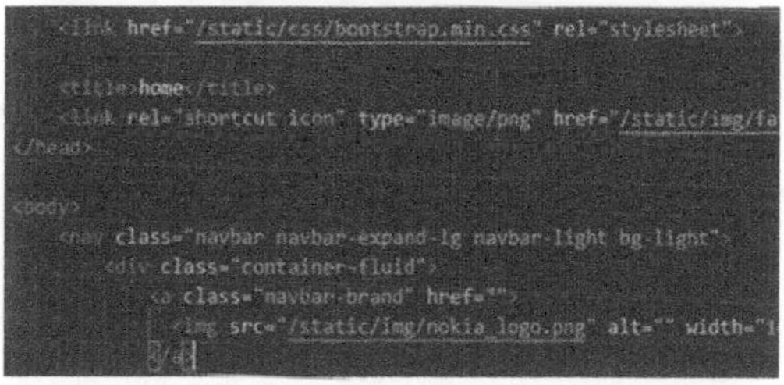

Figure 9.8 Customized Navbar template code for home page with URLs for the login page and Sign Up page.

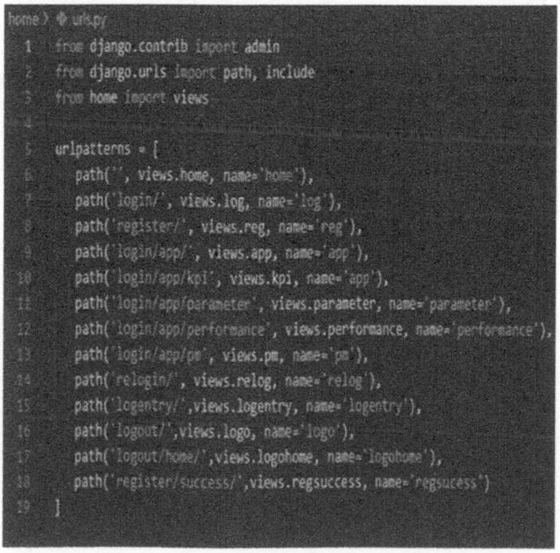

Figure 9.9 CSS file and image link integration with the home page template.

```
home ) ⊕ views.py ) ⊊ logentry
85    ins= logdata(username=username, IP=ip, login_time=login_time, logout_time=logout_time)
86    ins.save()
```

Figure 9.10 URLS in urls.py for href in template code.

For designing a home page Bootstrap's components Navbar and Carousel is used. The required CSS, Java Script files and images for the template is added to static named folder in base directory. Once the corresponding URL is triggered for home page the template using its support files gets displayed in browser screen [7]. To add consecutive page the URL for that page is added to the template code so when a user clicks on that URL, Django MVT architecture comes into play and provides the corresponding template to that URL present in urls.py (Figures 9.8–9.10).

9.6   Backend Development

Django is a world class tool for backend development. It is very stable and versatile. Django takes care of user authentication, content administration, side maps, RSS feeds, and many more tasks.

9.6.1   Login Page

The Django Admin System can only be accessed by the Super User by /admin inbuilt URL. The Django Admin can add new user, delete new user and can edit the accessibility of the user and can set only specific operations for any user.

```
20    def log(request):
21        if request.method=="POST":
22            username = request.POST['userid']
23            password = request.POST['password']
24            log.reason = request.POST['reason']
25            if log.reason:
26                log.reason= log.reason
27            else:
28                log.reason = "reason not specified"
29            print(log.reason)
30            user = authenticate(request,username=username,password=password)
31            if user is not None:
32                if user.is_active:
33                    login(request,user)
34                    return redirect("/login/app")
35                else:
36                    return redirect("/relogin")
37            else:
38                pass
39        return render(request,"login.html")
```

Figure 9.11 Code for login page.

For user login firstly a new user is created in admin console by super user. The view for login form page is coded by capturing post request and copying form contents using CSRF (Cross-Site Request Forgery) token in form code and authenticate it with user table and if user is present in table, it will be logged in and redirected to user console page (Figure 9.11).

9.6.2   Registration Page

Instead of creating new users from admin console, form template for registration is used. The view for registration page is copied from template after post request from submit button. No two users can have the same username and the two passwords entered by the user should match, which can be checked using if else statement to reload the form to get correct details from the new user (Figures 9.12, 9.13).

9.6.3   User Tracking

Django's authentication module can be used for user tracking by using its user object which can provide username and last login time. Logout Time can be captured using Python's datetime module at time of logout. The clicks on the user console are counted using sessions and basic counter in backend and all this data is saved to the tracking table in db.sqlite3 file at the time user logs out from his/her profile [8–12].

Figure 9.12 The registration page asks the user to enter the name, email, username, create password and confirm password and feed this data into the Django Admin as soon as we click on the 'Register' button.

Figure 9.13 The Login Page asks the user to enter the username, password and reason for login for logging in and as soon as the login verifies, the user is redirected to the Main Page of the website.

9.7 Ouputs

All the above culminates in an incredibly detailed web page. The webpage starts with the home screen (Figure 9.14). The home page will further direct you to the main page (Figure 9.15). The user will also have access to the admin console (Figure 9.16) where they can see the details of the other users that used the website (Figure 9.17). There is a logout option on the main screen (Figure 9.18) which the redirects you to the post logout screen (Figure 9.19).

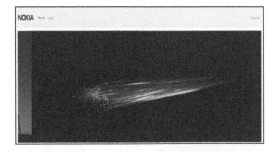

Figure 9.14 The Home page consists of three images moving in a slideshow manner and the navigation bar menu shows link for home, Sign up and Login.

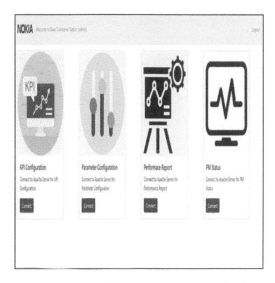

Figure 9.15 The Main Page consists of four sections, i.e., KPI Configuration, Parameter Configuration, Performance Report and PM Status. All four sections have links to the Apache Server where the user will be redirected. The navbar of the page also shows username of user logged in and contains a logout button to redirect to the logout page.

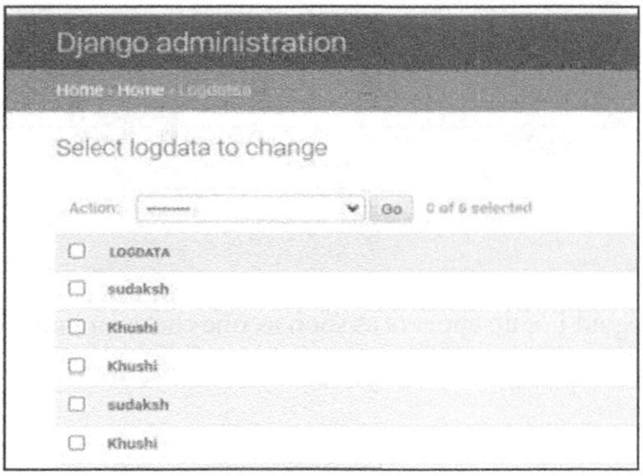

Figure 9.16 Admin console having username of users who recently used the website.

Figure 9.17 After clicking on usernames of users who recently used the website it shows their login and logout time, IP address, clicks on different links in main page and reason for login.

Figure 9.18 The Logout popup appears as soon as one clicks on Logout link on nav bar for logout confirmation.

9.8   Conclusion

Python Django Web Framework is an open-source robust web framework which can be used for many frameworks like HTML, JSON, PHP, etc.) for web development application. Django can be used for development of secure web applications and provides strong developer community support. Basic websites can be developed using Django with minimalistic coding knowledge. Deployment of Django applications relatively require less resources than other frameworks with reduced overall cost of service.

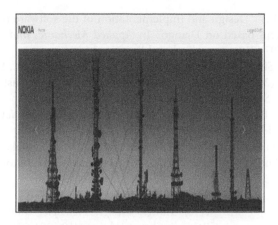

Figure 9.19 Post logout screen.

AI features can be introduced in web development using Django by integration of Python's rich AI libraries and frameworks. Development of customized templates using open-source Bootstrap CSS reduces frontend development requirements and makes web application compatible for other devices. Django will be helpful for businesses to promote their products online with their own website through minimal investment, and as the consumer base increases it can be easily scaled up for heavy traffic management.

References

1. Forcier, J., Bissex, P., & Chun, W. J. (2008). *Python web development with Django*. Addison-Wesley Professional.
2. Rubio, D. (2017). "Beginning Django." Apress
3. Burch, C. (2010). "Django, a web framework using python: Tutorial presentation." *Journal of Computing Sciences in Colleges*, 25(5), 154–155.
4. Spurlock, J. (2013). "Bootstrap: responsive web development." O'Reilly Media, Inc.
5. Ghimire, D. (2020). "Comparative study on Python web frameworks: Flask and Django".
6. Shyam, A., & Mukesh, N. (2020). "A Django Based Educational Resource Sharing Website: Shreic". *Journal of Scientific Research*, 64(1).
7. Li, S., & Si, Z. (2016, November). "Information publishing system based on the framework of Django". In *China Academic Conference on Printing & Packaging and Media Technology* (pp. 375–381). Springer, Singapore.

8. Li, Z. (2014). "Design and implementation of the software testing management system based on Django". In *Applied Mechanics and Materials* (Vol. 525, pp. 707–710). Trans Tech Publications Ltd.

9. Gore, H., Singh, R. K., Singh, A., Singh, A. P., Shabaz, M., Singh, B. K., & Jagota, V. (2021). "Django: Web Development Simple & Fast". *Annals of the Romanian Society for Cell Biology*, 25(6), 4576–4585.

10. Forcier, J., Bissex, P., & Chun, W. J. (2008). *Python web development with Django*. Addison-Wesley Professional.

11. Suman Lata Tripathi, Abhishek Kumar and Jyotirmoy Pathak, "Programming and GUI Fundamentals: TCL-TK for Electronic Design Automation (EDA)", Wiley-IEEE, 2021–22.

12. Thillaiarasu, N., Lata Tripathi, S., & Dhinakaran, V. (Eds.). (2022). *Artificial Intelligence for Internet of Things: Design Principle, Modernization, and Techniques* (1st ed.). CRC Press. https://doi.org/10.1201/9781003335801

10

Revenue Forecasting Using Machine Learning Models

Yashasvi Roy and Sanmukh Kaur*

Amity School of Engineering and Technology, Amity University Uttar Pradesh, Noida, India

Abstract

Machine learning (ML) has come a long way and has a significant impact on how we analyze data nowadays. In this chapter, we consider financial data of an organization with different variables and categories. All the categorical data has been encoded so that an ML algorithm can comprehend it. The data is run through different ML algorithms to find the one suitable or best fit for the data and providing maximum accuracy. Different performance metrics have been employed to determine the best fitting model. It has been observed that gradient boosting algorithm and a combination of multiple ML algorithms provide the best results for financial forecasting.

Keywords: Forecasting, encoding, machine learning, quantitative forecasting

10.1 Introduction

In this work we analyze forecasting of a company's revenue. It is a technique of making financial predictions. The organization's state is ultimately determined by its sales figures.

Financial forecasting also requires accurate predictions of future fixed and variable costs as well as various sources of income. On the basis of previous performance data, predictions are created. These assist in predicting future trends.

Corresponding author: sanmukhkaur@gmail.com

Suman Lata Tripathi and Mufti Mahmud (eds.) *Explainable Machine Learning Models and Architectures*, (155–170) © 2023 Scrivener Publishing LLC

Businesses and entrepreneurs use financial forecasting to determine how to spend their resources or what the estimated costs for a given time period will be. Financial forecasting is a tool used by investors to predict how specific events will affect a company's stock.

However, today, with the data and information being on such a large scale, that is very tedious and time consuming. Thus, the era of Artificial Intelligence has begun. Artificial Intelligence algorithms consisting of multiple analysis models analyze any given data set. Here the predictive variable and the target variable are set and large-scale data can immediately be processed.

Traditional Forecasting: MS Excel uses spreadsheets to arrange and examine data that has been stored. Excel is used by businesses for reporting, budgeting, analyzing, forecasting, and recognizing patterns.

Investors conduct financial analysis in one of two ways, generally speaking. The first, known as a fundamental analysis, focuses on information taken from a company's financial accounts and can give Excel the components for complex equations. The second is mostly concerned with graphing, probability, and what-if analysis [1].

Excel has multiple tools which help in organizing the data, one of them being power query. It allows users to combine multiple data sheets, while at the same time transforming the data as per their needs. Pivot Tables are also a great tool; they allow all data in an Excel sheet to be sorted under specific headers and then the combined values can be viewed according to the preference of the user.

10.2   Types of Forecasting

10.2.1   Qualitative Forecasting

An organization can use qualitative forecasting to develop forecasts about its financial situation based on internal perceptions. Forecasts can be used by managers and other high-level employees to evaluate and modify their company's budget [2].

Using expert judgement, qualitative forecasting is a technique for producing projections about a company's financial health. By identifying and analysing the relationship between current knowledge of previous operations and projected future operations, skilled professionals carry out qualitative forecasting. This enables the experts to predict a company's performance in the future based on their predictions and the data they get from other sources, such as staff surveys or market research [3].

Executives need qualitative forecasting to aid in decision-making for the business. Making decisions about how much inventory to keep on hand, whether to hire new employees, and how to modify a company's sales procedures can all be informed by qualitative forecasting. Qualitative forecasting is also essential for creating initiatives like marketing campaigns because it can identify the aspects of a company's service that should be highlighted in advertisements.

Some benefits of qualitative forecasting include the ability to predict future trends and phenomena in business and the usage of knowledge from experts in a company's industry. The ability to use sources other than numerical data is one of the benefits as well.

10.2.1.1   Industries That Use Qualitative Forecasting

1. Sales: Companies in sales can use qualitative forecasting to assist them in making decisions about how much of a product to manufacture and when to order extra inventory.
2. Agriculture: Based on the goods that consumers most frequently buy, farmers can utilize qualitative forecasting to evaluate their sales and choose which crops to sow for the upcoming season.
3. Pharmaceutical: Qualitative forecasting in the field of pharmaceuticals can assist in determining which medications are popular with customers and which demands people are addressing with pharmaceuticals in order to foretell the types of pharmaceuticals that might be developed in the future.
4. Healthcare: Employees in the healthcare industry might utilize qualitative forecasting to determine public health trends and which health care services may see a spike in demand in the near future.
5. Higher education: To forecast the number of students who might enroll for the upcoming term or academic year, colleges and universities might employ qualitative forecasting.
6. Construction and manufacturing: Qualitative forecasting can help these industries determine the resources or equipment they could need for their upcoming projects by displaying the quantity of various materials that they currently utilize.

10.2.1.2   Qualitative Forecasting Methods

Delphi Method

The Delphi method entails asking each member of a group of experts questions in order to get their perspectives. In order to avoid prejudice and guarantee that any consensus regarding business predictions comes from the experts' individual viewpoints, it is preferable to interview or obtain information from the experts one at a time as opposed to in a group. The experts' responses are then analysed by other staff members, who send them back with more inquiries until they arrive at a forecast that makes sense for the business.

Market Research

Market research examines the viability of a company's offers by exposing them to possible customers and monitoring their responses. Companies can either utilise their own workers to assist with the research or hire outside companies who specialise in such activities. A few techniques for performing market research include focus groups, consumer surveys, and blind testing of the product, in which a customer evaluates a product without ever having heard of it. Based on participant comments, businesses can decide which products or services to continue developing and which may need change throughout the production phase.

Informed Opinion and Judgment

This strategy is based on the judgments of experts from the sales, finance, purchasing, administrative, or production teams. By using executive opinion in forecasting, teams may generate forecasts efficiently and consider a variety of viewpoints from other departments. Some businesses might combine a quantitative approach with executive opinion forecasting.

10.2.2   Quantitative Forecasting

To analyse performance and anticipate future sales based on historical trends and data, sales teams use quantitative forecasting, a data-based statistical technique. By predicting results, businesses may make informed decisions regarding tactics and procedures to guarantee continuous success.

Quantitative forecasting differs from qualitative forecasting, which depends on subjective data like expert insight and viewpoints, because it is based on statistics and arithmetic and is objective. This forecasting will likely be done by sales operations teams so they can get a high-level view of performance and communicate with stakeholders about pertinent information and the future plan. Depending on a company's demands, the focus can be on a variety of quantitative strategies.

10.2.2.1   Quantitative Forecasting Methods

1. Naive Forecast
The naive approach is an easy strategy that counts on continued performance in the same manner as in the past. This method simply generates estimates based on historical performance data without taking trends, patterns, or other effects into account.

2. Seasonal Forecasting
Seasonal forecasting, also known as seasonal indexing, makes predictions about the same future seasons based on prior seasonal data. This approach can assist in developing a strategy for a challenging season that can still meet goals and ensure that the company performs as its management would like, as all businesses experience change [4].

It is necessary to collect all the information regarding business activity during the various seasons in order to perform a seasonal prediction. Average performance for each season will be revealed as a result of this forecast.

3. Straight-Line Method or Historical Growth Rate Method
This approach is quite straightforward and frequently utilised by organisations that are experiencing growth and anticipate continuing gains in revenue. Finding the historical revenue growth and extrapolating it to the future is how the straight-line technique is computed.

4. Moving Average Method
Comparable to the straight-line approach, the moving average method only considers the bits of historical data that are chosen to be most useful for a certain business, rather than the complete set.

5. Weighted Moving Average
The weighted moving average approach considers the likelihood that more current data is more reliable than older data.

This results in a more accurate forecast that takes the altering sales trends into account by giving the more recent years a numerical weight to boost their impact on the estimate. This process is referred to as exponential smoothing, and it can be used with other techniques as well, such the straight-line method [5].

6. Simple Linear Regression

Although this strategy is more difficult than the others, it can produce useful forecasting data. One independent variable is compared to one dependent variable in a model to ascertain their relationship. The outputs of the model can be plotted using Excel or other forecasting tools, but this takes some statistical expertise.

7. Multiple Linear Regression

A variation of simple linear regression, multiple linear regression compares several independent factors to one dependent variable as opposed to only one independent variable. This approach is useful since it takes into account a number of variables and can offer more accurate forecasts regarding consumer behaviour and upcoming marketing expenses.

10.2.3   Artificial Intelligence Forecasting

An AI-based forecasting approach optimizes forecasts using a combination of ML techniques. After that, the system chooses a model that is specially tailored for the specific business metric that is being forecast.

10.2.3.1   Artificial Neural Network (ANN)

ANNs are computing systems modelled after the biological neural networks found in human brains.

Artificial neurons, a group of interconnected nodes or units that roughly mimic the neurons in a human brain, are the foundation of an ANN. Similar to how synapses in the human brain function, every link can interact with neighbouring neurons. A perceptron can trigger neurons that are attached to it after processing signals given to it. The total of a neuron's inputs is determined by a non-linear function that determines the output of each neuron. Edges are the terms for connections. The weight of neurons regularly varies during learning [6].

A connection's signal strength might be raised or lowered depending on the weight. It's possible for neurons to have a threshold they must pass through in order to send a signal. Neurons frequently combine together to form layers. Different layers may change their inputs in different ways. Signals move through the layers from the first one (the input layer) to the last one, maybe several times (the output layer). The Figure 10.1 shows the comparison between a biological neuron and a neural network. It highlights the inputs and outputs of a biological neuron and compares them to an artificial neuron.

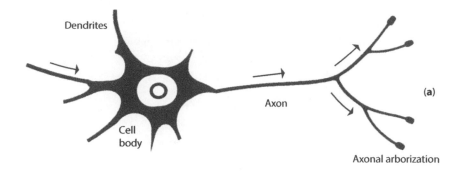

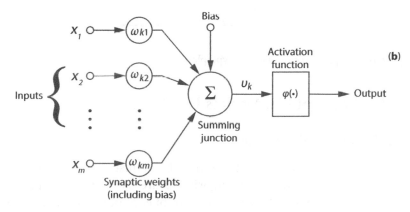

Figure 10.1 Comparison of biological neuron to artificial neural network.

10.2.3.2 Support Vector Machine (SVM)

SVMs are supervised learning models that evaluate data for regression and classification. They also include associated learning methods.

In order to increase the difference between two categories, SVM assigns training data to spatial locations. New samples are then projected into that same area and anticipated to fall into categories based on which end of the gap they fall [7].

Unsupervised learning is required when the data has no labels or is unlabeled as supervised learning is not a possibility. This method clusters the data to look for inherently occurring groupings, then transfers fresh data to these newly formed groups (Figure 10.2).

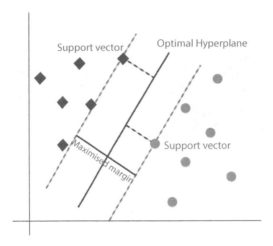

Figure 10.2 Support vector machine hyperplane.

10.3   Types of ML Models Used in Finance

10.3.1   Linear Regression

Linear regression is an ML algorithm and it is unsupervised. A regression task is carried out. Regression algorithms are used for target prediction tasks using variables that are independent of each other. It is used to create a function or demonstrate relationship between variables and predictions.

The dependent (y) variables are shown to have a linear relationship also known as linear regression. Given that linear regression shows a linear relationship, it is utilized to predict how the value of the dependent variable changes in relation to the value of the independent variable (Figure 10.3).

10.3.1.1   Simple Linear Regression

A linear regression procedure is referred to as simple linear regression if only one independent variable is utilized to predict values of a numerical dependent variable.

10.3.1.2   Multiple Linear Regression

A linear regression process is referred to as multiple linear regression if it uses more than one independent variable to predict the values of a numerical dependent variable.

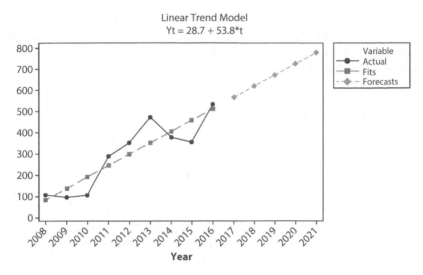

Figure 10.3 Linear regression forecasting.

10.3.2   Ridge Regression

The model-tuning technique called as ridge regression can be used to evaluate any data that displays multi-collinearity. This method performs L2 regularization. When the issue of multi-collinearity emerges, least-squares are unbiased, and fluctuations are considerable, predicted values diverge significantly from actual values (Figure 10.4).

In ridge regression, the means of the variables—both dependent and independent—are subtracted, and their standard deviations are divided. Since we need a means to indicate whether the variables in a particular formula are standardised or not, this is a challenge for notation. In terms of standardisation, all ridge regression calculations are based on standardised variables. Before being shown, the computed regression coefficients are scaled back to their initial value [8].

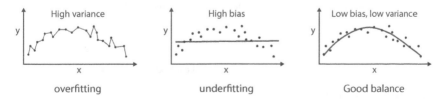

Figure 10.4 Ridge regression balancing of data.

The three assumptions made by ridge regression are independence, linearity, and constant variance. Since ridge regression does not provide confidence intervals, it is not required to believe that the error distributions are normally distributed.

10.3.3   Decision Tree

Decision trees are used by artificial intelligence to draw conclusions based on the data available from prior judgments. These conclusions are also given values and utilised to predict the expected future course of action.

Decision trees are quantitative, algorithmic models for ML that assess and discover answers to a range of problems and possible outcomes. Decision trees are therefore aware of the rules for making decisions in particular settings based on the information at hand. The learning process is ongoing and feedback-based. As a result, learning outcomes get better over time (Figure 10.5).

10.3.3.1   Prediction of Continuous Variables

Continuous variables can be predicted using one or more predictors. A continuous variable decision tree is the name of the decision tree model that is employed to represent such values. Different types of continuous decision trees address regression-type issues. In these circumstances a continuous, variable, and numerical output is predicted using labelled datasets.

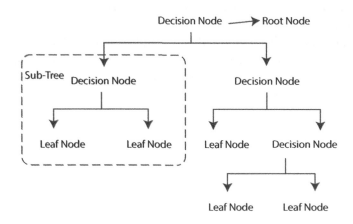

Figure 10.5 Decision tree structure.

10.3.3.2   Prediction of Categorical Variables

Additional categorical variables may also be used to predict categorical variables. However, this topic is about categorizing a new dataset into the existing classes of datasets rather than forecasting a value. Categorical variable decision trees address classification-type issues in which a class rather than a value is the output.

10.3.4   Random Forest Regressor

After numerous classifications, decision tree algorithm have now been trained to different datasets, a random forest learning method is made use of, which uses averaging to increase projected accuracy and reduce overfitting.

The outcome is dependent on multiple decision trees instead of just one because each one was precisely trained using that specific sample of data, so there is less volatility when we mix them all at once.

In a classification problem, the solution is determined by the simple majority classifier. In a regression problem, the overall output is the mean of each result. This is described as an aggregation.

Using several decision trees and a process called Bootstrap and Aggregation, sometimes known as bagging, Random Forest is an aggregation technique that can perform both classification and regression tasks.

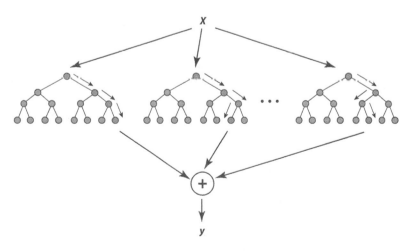

Figure 10.6 Random forest regressor structure.

The key idea behind this strategy is to integrate several decision trees in order to get the desired result rather than depending solely on one decision tree (Figure 10.6).

10.3.5   Gradient Boosting Regression

"Boosting" is an ML approach for combining several simple models into a single merged model. Boosting is also described as an additive model since it adds a single basic model while keeping the structure of the model's existing trees.

Boosting is also described as an additive model since it adds a single basic model while preserving the structure of the model's existing trees. The final, complete model improves as we merge even more simple models, making it a better predictor. Since the process employs gradient descent to minimize the loss, the term "gradient" in "gradient boosting" refers to this technique [9].

Gradient Boosting Regression finds difference between the present forecast and the known exact target value. This variation is referred to as residual. After that a poor model maps the features to that residual and is further trained.

This procedure moves the model closer to the desired outcome by adding the residual forecasted by a weak model to the input of the current model. This process can be repeated numerous times to enhance

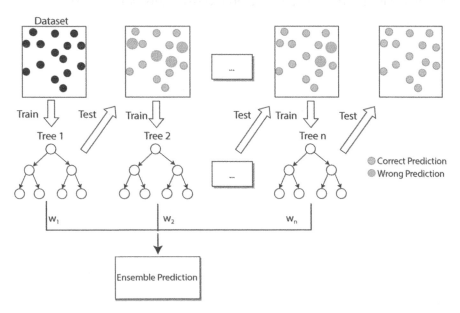

Figure 10.7 Gradient boosting model.

the overall model forecast. Gradient boost is utilized for regression when it is used to predict a continuous value. This differs from applying linear regression. The Figure 10.7 shows the working of a generic gradient boosting model. Where in it moves the model closer to the desired outcome by combining multiple trees.

Gradient Boosting Classification is used to predict classes, such as if a patient has a specific disease, whereas Gradient Boosting Regression is used to forecast continuous variables, such as house price.

10.3.5.1 *Advantages of Gradient Boosting*

1. Better accuracy: On average, Gradient Boosting Regression offers more accuracy.
2. Less pre-processing: Gradient Boosting Regression involves the least amount of data preparation, allowing us to implement this model more quickly and with less complexity.
3. Missing data: One of the problems when training a model is missing data. The missing data is handled by Gradient Boosting Regression on its own; handling it manually is not required.

10.4   Model Performance

How much the regression line fits the data set is determined by the goodness of fit. Optimization is the process of selecting the best model from a group of competing models.

10.4.1   R-Squared Method

A statistical technique that assesses the goodness of fit is R-squared.

On a scale of 0-100 percent, it evaluates the strength of the correlation between the dependent and independent variables.

A good model is one in which the R-square value is high since it indicates that there is little variation between the predicted and actual values.

It is called coefficient of determination or a coefficient of multiple determination for a multiple regression task.

10.4.2   Mean Squared Error (MSE)

The mean squared error tells us how much a regression line fits a set of data points. It is a function that gives the relationship with the anticipated value of the squared error loss. The term "mean square error" refers to the average (or the mean) of mistakes squared from the data relating to the function [10].

A smaller MSE suggests a close clustering of data points around the centre instant (mean), whereas a larger MSE shows the opposite. A smaller MSE is preferred since it demonstrates how the data points are evenly spaced around its central moment (mean). It shows how the values are primarily distributed, are not skewed, and most importantly, have less errors.

10.4.3   Root Mean Square Error (RMSE)

RMSE, referred to as root mean square deviation, is a technique used to evaluate the correctness of forecasts. It showcases the Euclidean separation between forecasts and observed true values.

To calculate the root-mean-square error, calculate the residual (difference between prediction and truth) for each data point together with its norm, mean, and square root (RMSE).

When evaluating a model's performance in ML, whether during training, cross-validation, or tracking after deployment, it is very helpful to have a single number. The root mean square error is one of the most widely used metrics for this. It is a suitable scoring system that is easy to understand and coherent with a number of the common statistical hypotheses. RMSE values between 0.2 and 0.5 shows that the model can relatively predict the data accurately [11–13].

10.5   Conclusion

All categorical data is to be encoded using label encoding, having order set as alphabetical order. This data was then imported into a data frame using the pandas library and empty rows were dropped using the dropna function of the data frame. The data was then trained using five models: Linear Regression, Ridge Regression, Decision Trees, Random Forest Regressor and Gradient Boosting Regressor.

The Decision Tree, Random Forest Regressor and the Gradient Boosting Regressor were found to be the most optimal training models having the highest R Square Value among all the models. The Root Mean Squared Error values for these models was between 0.2 and 0.5, meaning they were accurately predicting the target values. This meant that these models were the best fit for the given data and optimal for using for a forecast model.

References

1. Karolina Mateńczuk, Agata Kozina, Aleksandra Markowska, Kateryna Czerniachowska, Klaudia Kaczmarczyk, Paweł Golec, Marcin Hernes *et al.*, Financial Time Series Forecasting: Comparison of Traditional and Spiking Neural Networks, *Procedia Computer Science*, Volume 192, 2021, pp. 5023–5029, ISSN 1877-0509, https://doi.org/10.1016/j.procs.2021.09.280.
2. Kamalov, F., Gurrib, I. & Rajab, K. (2021) Financial Forecasting with Machine Learning: Price Vs Return. *Journal of Computer Science*, 17(3), 251–264. https://doi.org/10.3844/jcssp.2021.251.264
3. Cindy Candrian, Anne Scherer, Rise of the machines: Delegating decisions to autonomous AI, *Computers in Human Behavior*, Volume 134, 2022, 107308, ISSN 0747-5632, https://doi.org/10.1016/j.chb.2022.107308.
4. Sebastian Gnat, Impact of Categorical Variables Encoding on Property Mass Valuation, *Procedia Computer Science*, Volume 192, 2021, pp. 3542–3550, ISSN 1877-0509, https://doi.org/10.1016/j.procs.2021.09.127.
5. Karlo Kauko, Peter Palmroos, The Delphi method in forecasting financial markets—An experimental study, *International Journal of Forecasting*, Volume 30, Issue 2, 2014, pp. 313–327, ISSN 0169-2070, https://doi.org/10.1016/j.ijforecast.2013.09.007.
6. Jian Cao, Zhi Li, Jian Li, Financial time series forecasting model based on CEEMDAN and LSTM, *Physica A: Statistical Mechanics and its Applications*, Volume 519, 2019, pp. 127–139, ISSN 0378-4371, https://doi.org/10.1016/j.physa.2018.11.061.
7. Yevgeniy Bodyanskiy, Sergiy Popov, Neural network approach to forecasting of quasiperiodic financial time series, *European Journal of Operational Research*, Volume 175, Issue 3, 2006, pp. 1357–1366, ISSN 0377-2217, https://doi.org/10.1016/j.ejor.2005.02.012.
8. Chi-Jie Lu, Tian-Shyug Lee, Chih-Chou Chiu, Financial time series forecasting using independent component analysis and support vector regression, *Decision Support Systems*, Volume 47, Issue 2, 2009, pp. 115–125, ISSN 0167-9236, https://doi.org/10.1016/j.dss.2009.02.001.
9. D. L. Prasanna and S. L. Tripathi, Machine Learning Classifiers for Speech Detection, *2022 IEEE VLSI Device Circuit and System (VLSI DCS)*, 2022, pp. 143–147, doi:10.1109/VLSIDCS53788.2022.9811452.
10. Kyoung-jae Kim, Financial time series forecasting using support vector machines, *Neurocomputing*, Volume 55, Issues 1–2, 2003, pp. 307–319, ISSN 0925-2312, https://doi.org/10.1016/S0925-2312(03)00372-2.
11. Iebeling Kaastra, Milton Boyd, Designing a neural network for forecasting financial and economic time series, *Neurocomputing*, Volume 10, Issue 3, 1996, pp. 215–236, ISSN 0925-2312, https://doi.org/10.1016/0925-2312(95)00039-9.

12. Thillaiarasu, N., Lata Tripathi, S., & Dhinakaran, V. (Eds.). (2022). *Artificial Intelligence for Internet of Things: Design Principle, Modernization, and Techniques* (1st ed.). CRC Press. https://doi.org/10.1201/9781003335801

13. Kanak Kumar; Kaustav Chaudhury; Suman Lata Tripathi, "Future of Machine Learning (ML) and Deep Learning (DL) in Healthcare Monitoring System," in *Machine Learning Algorithms for Signal and Image Processing*, IEEE, 2023, pp. 293–313, doi: 10.1002/9781119861850.ch17.

11

Application of Machine Learning Optimization Techniques in Wind Resource Assessment

Udhayakumar K.[1*] and Krishnamoorthy R.[2†]

[1]Department of EEE, Anna University, Chennai, India
[2]Information Technology, TANGEDCO, Chennai, India

Abstract

Wind energy is a preferred energy in electricity production because reducing fossil fuels-based generations reduces pollution in the atmosphere. In this study, the wind characteristics and wind potential assessment in Onshore, Offshore and Nearshore location of India, viz., Kayathar, TamilNadu; Gulf of Khambhat; and Jafrabad, Gujarat, were statistically analysed with wind distributions methods. Weibull, Rayleigh, Gamma, Nakagami, GEV, Lognormal, Inverse Gaussian, Rician and Birnbaum Sandras and Bimodal Weibull-Weibull Distribution were used for resource assessment. The wind distribution parameters estimated with parameter methods is compared with Machine Learning optimization techniques Moth Flame Optimization method (MFO) for accuracy. The results show that the Moth Flame Optimization performed well on parameter estimation. The wind speed distributions mixed Weibull, Nakagami and Rician performed well in calculating potential assessments. The bimodal mixed Weibull distribution performed better than other distributions. The offshore Gulf of Khambhat area, Gujarat, has steady wind speeds ranging from 7 m/s to 10 m/s with less Turbulence Intensity and highest Wind power density, 431 watts/m2. Wind power generation peaks during South-West Monsoon periods from June to September with mean wind speed ranging from 9 m/s to 12 m/s.

Keywords: Wind assessment, weibull, mixed, bimodal, offshore, optimization, machine learning

Corresponding author: k_udhayakumar@annauniv.edu
†*Corresponding author*: krimoindia@gmail.com

Suman Lata Tripathi and Mufti Mahmud (eds.) Explainable Machine Learning Models and Architectures, (171–226) © 2023 Scrivener Publishing LLC

11.1   Introduction

As technological developments and populations grow, the electricity consumption need also increases, which leads to environmental pollution conditions regarding the type of fuels used for power production. The types of fuel like fossil fuel–based generation from coal, oil-based, threatens change in climatic condition with increased carbon emission and pollution particles suspended in air.

As per Paris Agreement commitments, to keep the rise in average global temperature closer to 1.5 °C, the government of India has set an ambitious target of achieving a total of 175 GW of renewable energy capacity including 60 GW of wind capacity by 2022 [1].

In depth analysis to be carried out wind characteristics and its potential is necessary for wind turbines installation in onshore, nearshore and offshore areas. The methodology adopted at least a period of one year, for data collection through local site survey, by installing anemometers, pressure and temperature humidity sensors, Lidar wind measurements in the land, coastal mast areas. The ground-level measurements are taken as a primary data for accuracy over satellite data. For wind potential history for past years, nearby wind stations and neighbouring stations like airport are taken for reference [2].

This study, focus on applying machine learning optimization techniques for analysing wind characteristics and wind distribution methods using the wind data collected in onshore location Kayathar (TamilNadu) and offshore location from Gulf of Khambhat (Gujarat) along with nearshore location from Jafrabad (Gujarat) for analysis. The analysis focuses on how wind characteristics behave in onshore, nearshore and offshore areas [3] by comparing the results obtained. Ten wind speed distributions methods are considered for analysis along with unimodal conventional distributions. Weibull [4, 5], Rayleigh, Gamma, Nakagami, Generalized Extreme Value, Log Normal, Inverse Gaussian, Rician and Birnbaum Sandras [6] and bimodal-WW were used for wind resource assessment. In the wind resource assessment earmarked locations, the impact of bimodality [7–9] is taken into consideration and mixed Weibull methods are adopted. The results and observations aid in effective deployment of wind farms in onshore and offshore areas.

11.2   Wind Data Analysis Methods

Wind energy is created on the earth surface due to uneven heating. Also, the wind resource varies with increase or decrease or is made turbulent by factors such as hilly area, bodies of water, buildings, and vegetative lands. Also, wind speeds in a location are subject to variation in nature by time of day, seasonal, and according to weather events. The wind data analysis of different landscapes such as onshore, nearshore and offshore are carried out in the subsequent sections. Wind characteristics at the selected location, wind power density in a location and wind distribution fitting are presented.

11.2.1   Wind Characteristics Parameters

The primary data collection sensors of most wind resource assessment are carried out by taking ground-level wind parameters using meteorological instruments mounted on tall towers and modern instruments like Sodar and Lidar devices [10]. The important parameters for any wind monitoring program are the wind speed, wind direction, and air temperature. The parameters normally measured in a wind location are shown in Table 11.1.

11.2.2   Wind Speed Distribution Methods

The wind speed [11] and its frequency of occurrence to form a wind distribution pattern is vital information and is used directly for estimating the wind turbine power output. The wind frequency distribution represents the number of times in the period of data collected that the observed speed falls within particular bins. The wind speed bins have a typically 0.5 or 1 m/s space and cover at least the range of speeds from 0 to 25 m/s or more which is defined for the turbine power curve. The usual reports for analysis are presented in bar chart/histogram and input as table. The probability density function is represented as mathematical one which visualizes the probable pattern of wind speed, which is random in nature in a continuous period. The wind distribution methods are analysed with cumulative distribution function (CDF) and probability density function (PDF).

Table 11.1 Basic parameters for ground-level measurements.

Parameters to be measured	Applications	Measured values
Wind speed, m/s	Wind generation suitability assessment and Turbine selection	Average, standard deviation, min/max
Wind direction, degrees	Optimizing wind turbines and understand the spatial distribution of wind	Average, standard deviation, max gust direction
Temperature °C	Air density	Average, min/max
Vertical wind speed, m/s	Turbulence	Average, min/max
Barometric pressure, kPa	Air density	Average, standard deviation, min/max
Relative humidity, %	Icing Analysis	Average, min/max
Solar radiation, W/m²	Atmospheric stability analysis	Average, min/max

11.2.3   Weibull Method [12]

The computation of PDF and CDF wind distribution parameters (k-shape and c-scale) using Weibull (WB) method is carried out using the following Equations:

$$f(v) = \left(\frac{k}{c}\right)\left(\frac{v}{c}\right)^{k-1} \exp\left(-\left(\frac{v}{c}\right)^k\right) \qquad (11.1)$$

$$F(v) = 1 - \exp\left(-\left(\frac{v}{c}\right)^k\right) \qquad (11.2)$$

For other wind distributions PDF and CDF carried out with respective equations.

11.2.4   Goodness of Fit

The goodness of fit is a statistical analysis method for qualifying the ten wind probability distributions taken for evaluation to match with actual data measured. The best Correlation Coefficient (R2) and Root Mean Square Error (RMSE) [7] scored the wind distribution method, which is the best suitable for the defined location. The fitness of ten distributions arrived at using R2 and RMSE and can be calculated as follows.

RMSE calculates the residuals of the measured data and frequency of examined PDF,

$$RMSE = \left[\frac{1}{n} \sum_{i=1}^{n} (y_i - x_i)^2 \right]^{0,5} \tag{11.3}$$

Where n stands for the number of bins, y_i is the observed data plotted in a histogram, and x_i is estimated probability distribution (PDF) of wind distribution. The evaluated RMSE value which is close to zero is the best fit.

The R2 evaluates the linear correlation between measured data and predicted values from PDF functions

$$R^2 = 1 - \frac{\sum_{i=1}^{n} (y_i - x_i)^2}{\sum_{i=1}^{n} (y_i - \bar{y})^2} \tag{11.4}$$

Where $\bar{y}$ is the mean of the total observed value. The evaluated value of R2 ranges between 0 to 1 and close to 1 is the best fit.

11.3   Wind Site and Measurement Details

The wind data collected from two Indian states with different landscapes, namely Gujarat and Tamilnadu, are considered. These two states contribute to the Indian power grid in a higher stake and are pioneers in wind energy generation. The wind data is segregated into three different landscapes such as Offshore from Gulf of Khambhat (Gujarat), Nearshore from Jafrabad (Gujarat) and Onshore from Kayathar (Tamilnadu) [13–23]. The statistics of each location are presented in Table 11.2.

Table 11.2 Measurement sensors data from wind stations.

Location	Landmass meas. sensor	Interval	Recovery rate	Lat., long.	Dataset period
Kayathar (Tamilnadu)	Onshore (Mast)	10 minutes	100%	8 °56'42.50" N, 77° 43'24.12" E	2014, 2015, 2016 (3 years)
Gulf of Khambhat (Gujarat)	Offshore (Lidar)	10 minutes	75.85 %	20° 45' 19.10" N, 71° 41' 10.93" E	12/2018 to 11/2019 (1 year)
Jafrabad (Gujarat)	Nearshore (Mast)	10 minutes	99.89%	20 53'29.81" N, 71 27'35.68" E	12/2018 to 11/2019 (1 year)

11.3.1 Seasonal Wind Periods

Concerning the classification of seasons for Gujarat and Tamilnadu states, the impact of seasonal winds from North-East Monsoon (NEM) and South-West Monsoon (SWM) are taking into consideration for analysis [24–26]. These seasons are categorised as seasonal months as follows:

> **Winter:** January and February, **Summer:** March, April, and May, **SWM:** June, July, August, and Sep, **NEM:** October, November, December.

11.3.2 Machine Learning and Optimization Techniques

Optimization is the process where the model to be trained iteratively that results in a maximum and minimum function evaluation. Also, the role of optimization techniques in machine learning plays a most important role in getting better results.

11.3.2.1 Moth Flame Optimization (MFO) Method

The application of artificial intelligence and soft computing along with optimization techniques [34] is adopted in various applications. In this work, the MFO method is implemented for estimating the parameters of the Bimodal Weibull-Weibull method. The MFO algorithm [27] is a naturally inspired algorithm where Moths are fancy insects and have similarity to the butterfly family. The navigation method through transverse orientation is the main inspiration of MFO algorithm. During the night, moths navigate by maintaining a fixed angle to the moon. This mechanism for traveling long distances occurs in a straight line. MFO is a promising metaheuristic algorithm and is applied in various optimization problems in a wide range of fields, such as medical applications, image processing, engineering design, power and energy systems, and economic dispatch.

The MFO working methodology is based on the individuals/set of moths (M) called population and flame (F). The best position of moths in the moth-flame combination contains one flame per moth. During each iteration, the flame will get updated on any better solution found. The matrix OM has the corresponding fitness (objective) value, which can be represented as follows:

$$M = \begin{bmatrix} m_{11} & m_{12} & \cdots & m_{1d} \\ m_{21} & m_{22} & \cdots & m_{2d} \\ \vdots & \vdots & \vdots & \vdots \\ m_{n1} & m_{n2} & \cdots & m_{nd} \end{bmatrix}$$

(11.5)

$$\text{and } OM = \begin{bmatrix} I\left(m_{11},m_{12},\cdots,m_{1d}\right) \\ I\left(m_{21},m_{22},\cdots,m_{2d}\right) \\ \vdots \\ I\left(m_{n1},m_{n2},\cdots,m_{nd}\right) \end{bmatrix} = \begin{bmatrix} OM_1 \\ OM_2 \\ \vdots \\ OM_n \end{bmatrix}$$

Where I is the objective function, n is the number of moths and d is the number of variables. Each moth flies around its corresponding flame. Therefore, the moths matrix and flames matrix is the same size. The matrix F, set of flames, while the matrix OF represents the corresponding fitness value and can be expressed as follows.

$$F = \begin{bmatrix} F_{11} & F_{12} & \cdots & F_{1d} \\ F_{21} & F_{22} & \cdots & F_{2d} \\ \vdots & \vdots & \vdots & \vdots \\ F_{n1} & F_{n2} & \cdots & F_{nd} \end{bmatrix} \text{ and } OF = \begin{bmatrix} I\left(F_{11},F_{12},\cdots,F_{1d}\right) \\ I\left(F_{21},F_{22},\cdots,F_{2d}\right) \\ \vdots \\ I\left(F_{n1},F_{n2},\cdots,F_{nd}\right) \end{bmatrix} = \begin{bmatrix} OF_1 \\ OF_2 \\ \vdots \\ OF_n \end{bmatrix}$$

(11.6)

The main difference between flames and moths is the way they are treated and updated in every iteration. The moths act as a search agents moving around the search space, while flames are the best position of corresponding moths obtained by the current iteration. The equation for getting best optimal value is given as

$$Mi = S(M_i, F_j) \tag{11.7}$$

Where Fj indicates the j-th flame, M_i indicates the i-th moth and S is the spiral function. The spiral function of the moth is represented as

$$S(M_i, F_j) = D_i \cdot e^{bt} \cdot \cos(2\pi t) + F_j \tag{11.8}$$

Where b is a constant for defining the shape of the logarithmic spiral, D_i indicates the distance of the i-th moth for the j-th flame and t is a random number. D_i is calculated as follows,

$$SD_i = |F_j - M_i| \tag{11.9}$$

When the position of a moth gets changed, the moth can converge or exploit in the given search space by changing the value 't'. A mechanism to solve the number of flames during each iteration is as follows,

$$\text{flame } no = \text{round}\left(N - l * \frac{N-1}{T}\right) \tag{11.10}$$

Where l is the number of current iterations, N is the maximum number of flames and T is the maximum number of iterations. The objective function considered for minimization of estimated Bimodal Weibull distribution parameters by MFO and observed actual wind speed distribution is derived as

$$\xi^2 = \sum (fest - fo)^2 \tag{11.11}$$

Where, *fo* is the observed data from the histogram and *fest* is the estimated value from BM-MFO

$$fest = w1\left(\frac{k1}{c1}\right)\left(\frac{v}{c1}\right)^{k1-1} \exp\left(-\left(\frac{v}{c1}\right)^{k1}\right)$$
$$+w2\left(\frac{k2}{c2}\right)\left(\frac{v}{c2}\right)^{k2-1} \exp\left(-\left(\frac{v}{c2}\right)^{k2}\right) \tag{11.12}$$

The MFO Pseudocode algorithm with program logic is derived below and the flow chart for the MFO algorithm is described in Figure 11.1.

```
Update flame no using Equation
OM = Fitness Function(M);
if iteration == 1
        F = sort(M);
        OF = sort (OM);
else
        F = sort (M_{t-1}, M_t);
        OF = sort (M_{t-1}, M_t);
end
for i = 1: n
        for j = 1: d
        Update r and t
        Calculate D using Eq with respect to the
        corresponding moth
        Update M (i, j) using Eqns. with respect to
        the corresponding moth
        end
end
```

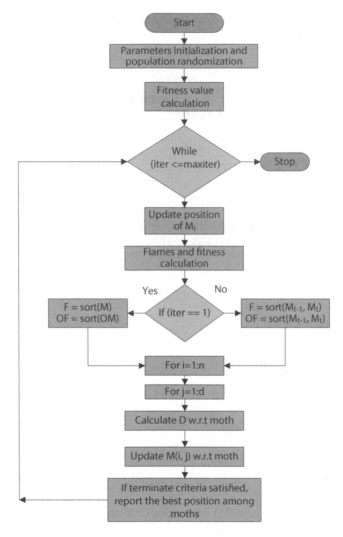

Figure 11.1 MFO algorithm flow chart.

11.4   Results and Discussions

The statistical investigation of the wind data measured through LIDAR, SODAR and Mast sensors in the three different landscapes are analysed in the subsequent sections. The ten popular wind distribution functions are adopted to estimate the correctness of the distribution that best fits the wind speeds of the targeted location. Later, the optimization method, i.e., MFO method is applied for parameter estimation and compared with ten wind distribution parameters. The MATLAB R2018b software with in-house developed code is used for estimating the parameters of ten Wind distribution functions along with the Maximum Likelihood method. Then, it is compared with the parameters estimated through Moth Flame Optimization method using bimodal (Weibull-Weibull) distribution. It is stated earlier, the goodness of fit to evaluate the best wind distribution method with a lower rate of RMSE value nearer to zero, the higher rate of R^2 nearer to one, and minimized error fit for evaluating Wind Power Density. Further, the results are grouped for Best wind power density with the selected distribution. Subsequently, the Annual mean wind speed along with mean turbulence intensity (15m/sec) are considered for categorizing the Turbulence class for Turbine selection to form a stand-alone Wind Turbine/Wind Farm. The wind resource assessment methodology, complete steps/procedures for the assessment of wind resources are given in Figure 11.2.

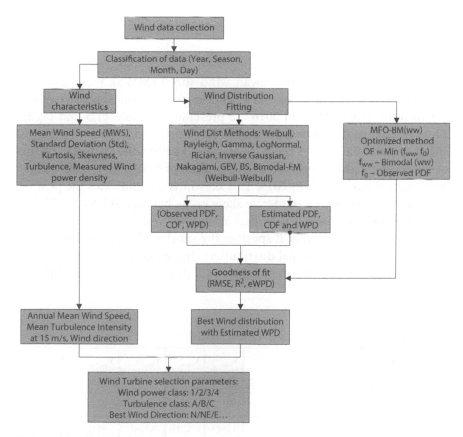

Figure 11.2 Wind resource assessment flow chart.

11.4.1   Wind Characteristics

The detailed wind statistical analysis for Jafrabad Station (Mast-Nearshore), Gulf of Khambhat station (Offshore) and Kayathar station (Onshore) are presented in the subsequent sections. The primary wind characteristics of any wind studies to ascertain the wind resource feasibility are Mean wind speed, Standard deviations of wind, wind directions, and Turbulence Intensity. To make the wind project technically viable, the collected statistical analysis is used to determine the site eligibility for wind turbines selection and energy yield from the turbines. The statistical analysis of wind speed, wind direction, along its relation is represented by the Wind rose plot. The mean wind speed over the periods for seasonal, monthly, and annual analysis represent the energy contained in the wind and also for the analysis of turbulence intensity to turbines class of operation. The Probability Density Functions (PDF) for fitting the wind power potential analysis, wind speed distribution and statistical characteristics are presented in the following sections.

11.4.1.1   Kayathar Station (Onshore)

The data collected for annual mean wind speed (MWS), standard deviation, maximum wind speed, skew, and kurtosis in the Kayathar region between the years 2014 and 2016 are presented in Table 11.3 and Figure 11.3 (a). The maximum wind speed of 20.92 m/s and highest mean wind speed of about 6.62 m/s is recorded in 2014. Further, the skewness factors of the wind speed are observed as a maximum of 0.8086 m/s in 2014 and a minimum of 0.5589 m/s in 2015. This skewness rate indicates the positive wind distribution with a moderate skew range between 0.5 to 1 [28]. The annual average kurtosis is recorded as -0.3190 and -0.7038 in the years 2014 and 2016, respectively. It specifies the shorter Wind Distribution and thinner tails than the normal distribution. The wind speed at various altitudes is measured and shown in Figure 11.3 (b). It is observed for different

Table 11.3 Annual wind speed (100m) statistics.

Year	V_{mean}	V_{rmc}	V_{std}	V_{max}	V_{min}	V_{skew}	V_{kurt}	V_{median}	MTI
2014	6.6272	8.8409	4.1491	20.9217	0.2800	0.8086	-0.3190	5.3425	0.1723
2015	5.9839	7.8121	3.5609	19.2750	0.4150	0.7733	-0.3235	4.9617	0.1820
2016	6.3884	8.1642	3.6560	18.8400	0.1983	0.5589	-0.7038	5.5117	0.1779

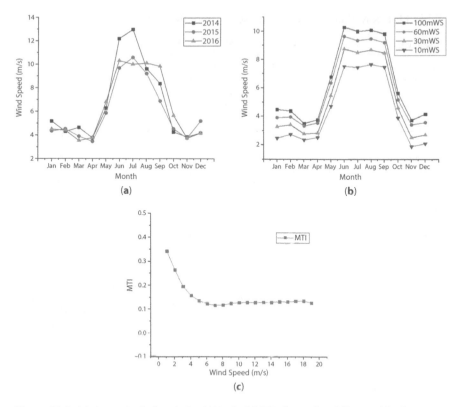

Figure 11.3 (a) Annual wind statistics (100m), (b) Wind speed at different altitude, (c) Turbulence intensity.

ranges such as 10mWS, 30mWS, 60Mws, and 100Mws. Also, the shear analysis power-law coefficient is evaluated and observed as 0.170.

Table 11.4 shows the seasonal wind speed peaks on the South-West Monsoon period (SWM) of about 10.03 m/sec and maximum seasonal wind speed observed as 18.52 m/sec. Comparing with Monsoon periods, North-East Monsoon (NEM) fetches low wind mean speed of 4.5 m/sec. The monthly mean wind speed is observed as maximum during June of 10.29 m/s, and maximum wind speed during July is 19.81 m/sec. The monthly standard deviation is stable from January to March with an average value of 1.8. Further, it is observed as 3.99, 3.5, and 3.01 for May, July, and October, respectively, during the peaks in monsoon periods due to seasonal winds. The Mean Turbulence Intensity (MTI) is estimated as a ratio between standard deviation of the experiential wind speed in each 10-minute period and mean observed wind speed for same period. Also, the turbulence is higher at low wind speed.

Table 11.4 Kayathar wind characteristics – month-wise.

Season	V_{mean}	V_{std}	V_{max}	V_{Skew}	V_{Kurt}	MTI
Winter	4.433253	1.691653	10.365	0.509646	-0.01742	0.256
Summer	4.686508	2.652375	14.30	0.570554	-0.39192	0.164
SWM	10.03937	2.746123	18.52	-0.1393	0.006654	0.135
NEM	4.504691	2.211281	13.83	0.672958	0.342298	0.196
Annual	6.388437	3.656017	18.84	0.558942	-0.70377	0.177
January	4.481756	1.495894	9.66	0.453957	-0.0686	0.181
February	4.384749	1.887412	11.07	0.565335	0.033756	0.331
March	3.511405	1.728998	13.3	0.687503	0.411679	0.178
April	3.761083	2.235506	11.18	0.74955	-0.46496	0.171
May	6.787036	3.99262	18.44	0.27461	-1.12249	0.145
June	10.29795	2.670321	19.63	-0.09339	0.187692	0.134
July	9.986461	3.530227	19.81	-0.29675	0.000403	0.144
August	10.0743	2.487559	17.05	-0.05946	-0.15188	0.132
September	9.798785	2.296385	17.6	-0.1076	-0.0096	0.13
October	5.62802	3.019308	16.54	0.607327	-0.37755	0.181
November	3.730028	1.933597	12.85	0.836013	0.985876	0.227
December	4.156026	1.680937	12.1	0.575535	0.418568	0.181

The efined location, namely Kayathar wind station, falls in Turbulence category 'B' (as per IEC standard) with MTI at 15 m/sec of 0.132. i.e.. 13.2% (Table 11.5).

Furthermore, the annual maximum wind speed falls on wind direction, i.e., South-West (WSW) is observed as 38.66% at 10.262 m/sec followed with WSW 11.27% and WNW 7.57% as shown in Table 11.6 and Figure 11.6 (a). The second maximum wind generation with NEM in NE wind direction is observed as 6.51%, mean wind speed of 4.766 m/sec, and followed with NNE of 6.50%. The wind rose plots shown in Figure 11.5 indicate the influence of South-West and North-East Monsoons. The North-East

Table 11.5 Kayathar wind directions – annual occurrence.

Direction sector	Direction name	Mean	Max	Std. dev.	Wind occ.
348.75° - 11.25°	N	3.146	13.46	1.256	1.730419
11.25° - 33.75°	NNE	4.25	15.05	1.681	**6.500455**
33.75° - 56.25°	NE	4.766	20.63	1.829	6.51184
56.25° - 78.75°	ENE	4.824	14.03	2.03	4.678962
78.75° - 101.25°	E	4.627	13.38	2.249	2.846084
101.25° - 123.75°	ESE	3.735	16.54	1.684	4.166667
123.75° - 146.25°	SE	4.207	11.82	1.988	3.51776
146.25° - 168.75°	SSE	4.821	11.18	2.291	3.586066
168.75° - 191.25°	S	3.487	11.77	1.851	2.379326
191.25° - 213.75°	SSW	2.752	12.12	1.392	1.605191
213.75° - 236.25°	SW	2.973	10.11	1.537	1.867031
236.25° - 258.75°	WSW	5.442	19.87	3.502	11.27049
258.75° - 281.25°	W	10.262	22.86	3.3	38.6612
281.25° - 303.75°	WNW	6.067	18.82	3.005	7.570583
303.75° - 326.25°	NW	3.115	13.48	1.35	1.8898
326.25° - 348.75°	NNW	3.075	11.94	1.3	1.218124

monsoon influenced the wind direction during October-December and West direction shifts to N-NNE. During South-West Monsoon periods (i.e., June-September) it is found to be W and WSW wind directions.

Figures 11.4 (a) to 11.4(e) shows the wind rose plot of annual, winter, summer, SWM, NEM monsoon periods of wind direction. The main wind direction from western direction ranges between 258.75° - 281.25° during South-West Monsoon. The summer wind rose plot experiences wind from south-west monsoon and the wind direction from SE-SSE and western direction. The winter season falls on North-East Monsoon winds and influence starts at the end of the south-west monsoon period.

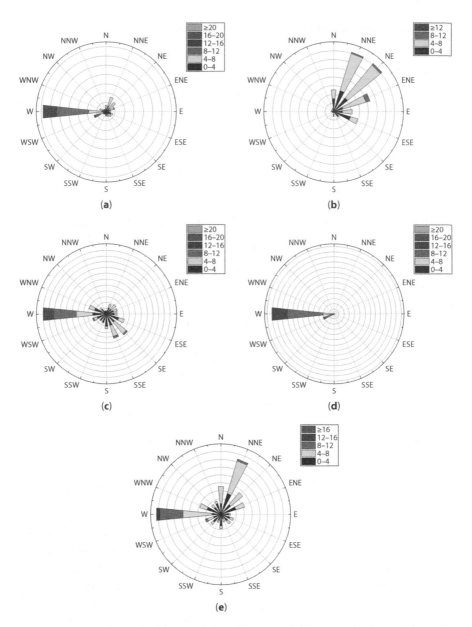

Figure 11.4 Windrose plot (a) Annual plot, (b) Winter, (c) Summer, (d) SWM, (e) NEM,
(*Continued*)

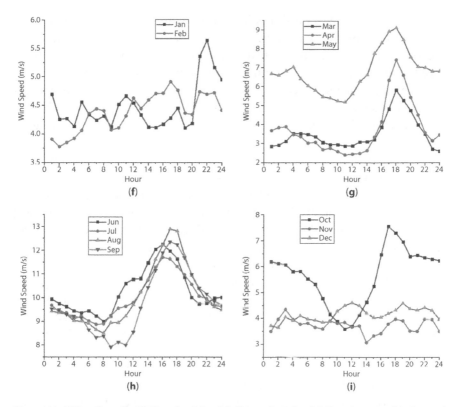

Figure 11.4 (Continued) (f) Kayathar Monthly Diurnal – Win, (g) Kayathar Monthly Diurnal – Summer, (h) Kayathar Monthly Diurnal – SEM, (i) Kayathar Monthly Diurnal – NEM.

The daily wind speed behaviour in Kayathar Onshore location with month-wise under seasonal changes is shown in Figure 11.4 (f) as Winter Season months such as January and February, Summer Season months in Figure 11.4 (g), and SWM and NEM monsoon plots in Figure 11.4 (h) and Figure 11.4 (i). Among all, May month (year 2016) wind speed peaks with the early sign of south-west monsoon start with mean speed from 7 m/s to 9 m/s. The October month wind varies from 6 m/s to 8 m/s due to northeast monsoon winds. November to February have low wind speed with a mean wind speed of 4 m/s.

11.4.1.2   Gulf of Khambhat (Gujarat Offshore) Station

The Gulf of Khambhat, Gujarat, Mean Wind Speed (MWS) data collected from Lidar measurements at altitudes from 40m to 200m for the period of December 2018 to November 2019 at various heights are presented in

Figure 11.5 (a). Table 11.6 shows low mean wind speed in November 4.81 m/s and the monthly maximum mean wind speed in July 10.13 m/s. The 100-meter measurements are taken for analysis; the annual mean wind speed observed as 7.59 m/s and maximum wind speed as 22.99 m/s during June. Based on the measured wind speeds at various altitudes, the shear analysis power-law coefficient is perceived as 0.0782. The Gulf of Khambhat is less due to its offshore landscape by nature when comparing with Kayathar onshore shear coefficient. The wind rose plot representing wind direction, for seasonal periods is plotted and presented in Figure 11.6. The major wind directions occur during NE-Monsoon on the North NE direction and during SW-monsoon in SW South direction. The annual and seasonal wind rose plots are shown in Figure 11.6. The maximum range of annual wind speed occurred in SSW and SW direction. Regarding seasonal changes, the winter season took maximum wind that occurs on North to NE direction.

Table 11.7 shows the maximum seasonal wind speed parameters of about 20.26 m/s and maximum mean wind speed of 9.04 m/s during Jun-September (SWM) season. The standard deviation is stable with an average value of 3.2 throughout the year in all the seasons. The minimum mean wind speed during North-East monsoon periods (October – December) is recorded as 5.74 m/s. Also, the annual wind speed of 7.511 m/s maximum wind speed of 20.263 m/s is observed. The NEM period of Gulf of Khambhat recorded the low wind speed of 5.74 m/s and the remaining periods show the average range of about 7 m/s during winter and summer.

The maximum wind speed during Jun 22.99 m/s and month-wise wind speed peaks at July 10.13 m/s due to south-east Monsoon. The Low wind speed dominates due to North-East Monsoon during October 5.4 m/s and Nov 4.8 m/s. The skewness factor of wind speed was observed with

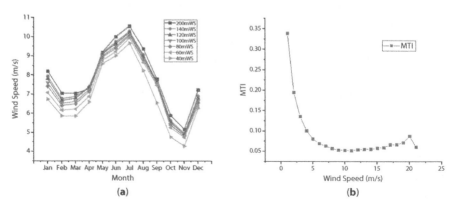

Figure 11.5 Gulf of Khambhat (a) Wind different altitude, (b) Turbulence intensity.

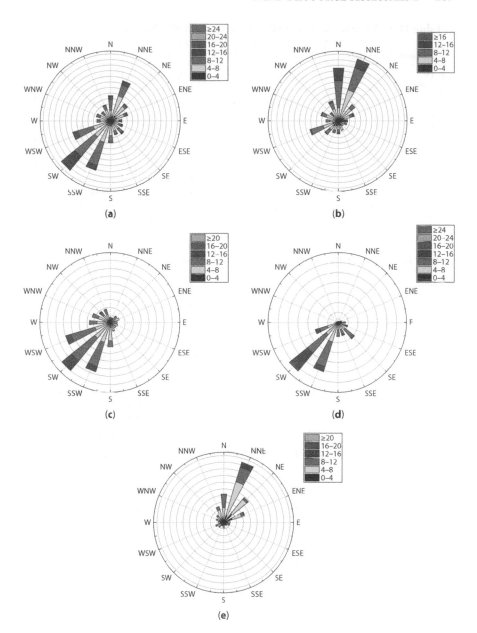

Figure 11.6 Gulf of Khambhat Offshore Wind rose (a) Annual, (b) Winter, (c) summer, (d) SWM, (e) NEM.

Table 11.6 Annual and Seasonal parameter Gulf of Khambhat.

Param	Winter	Summer	SWM	NEM	Annual
V_{mean}	7.127801	7.560787	9.045668	5.747251	7.511933054
V_{std}	3.312202	3.078941	3.44793	3.012046	3.446632
V_{max}	15.2883	16.8733	20.2633	17.0267	20.2633
MTI	0.06546	0.07021	0.07800	0.1084	0.080518
V_{Skew}	0.155809	0.087471	0.052146	0.728901	0.258659
V_{Kurt}	-0.83782	-0.70006	-0.52122	0.225859	0.57949

Table 11.7 Gulf of Khambhat monthly wind parameters.

Month	V_{mean}	V_{rmc}	V_{std}	V_{max}	V_{min}	V_{skew}	V_{kurt}
January	7.610495	9.068981	3.649033	15.34	0.43	0.024095	-1.06965
February	6.525176	7.644364	2.913069	15.89	0.3	0.114074	-0.65879
March	6.622904	7.625312	2.718898	15.93	0.4	0.300566	-0.37479
April	7.250485	8.363482	3.044569	16.42	0.35	0.080937	-0.6518
May	9.010916	9.974533	3.183418	17.27	0.49	-0.40806	-0.43811
June	9.510477	10.63388	3.465538	22.99	0.37	-0.00716	-0.43601
July	10.13571	11.18198	3.547624	18.74	0.54	-0.57574	-0.26271
August	8.867841	10.07355	3.387475	20.39	1.1	0.507237	-0.04934
September	7.567488	8.479169	2.798815	15.25	0.5	-0.06932	-0.66327
October	5.406942	6.845564	2.902275	17.98	0.42	1.070219	1.357721
November	4.819781	5.97269	2.51649	19.39	0.43	0.600687	0.703141
December	6.650116	8.021865	3.225335	17.37	0.2	0.436379	-0.55433

maximum of 1.07 during October. The annual skewness is 0.258659. The skewness indicates the wind distribution is positive with moderate skew as the range falls between 0.5 to 1. The annual kurtosis 0.57949 indicates that Wind Distribution is shorter, tails are thinner than the normal distribution.

Table 11.8 Wind direction annual statistics.

Direction	Direction	Mean	Median	Min	Max	Std. dev.	Wind occ.
Sector	Name	(m/s)	(m/s)	(m/s)	(m/s)	(m/s)	
348.75° – 11.25°	N	7.8378	7.75	0.37	15.05	3.1236	10.174288
11.25° – 33.75°	NNE	7.0987	6.73	0.4	17.98	3.1305	11.073271
33.75° – 56.25°	NE	5.7323	5.09	0.42	18.12	3.023	5.8221065
56.25° – 78.75°	ENE	5.4737	4.53	0.47	20.21	3.4377	3.7286523
78.75° – 101.25°	E	6.4851	4.79	0.41	22.99	4.5151	2.924826
101.25° – 123.75°	ESE	6.6518	5.49	0.44	20.27	3.8941	2.9348425
123.75° – 146.25°	SE	7.2785	7.3	0.41	16.95	3.4295	4.0742225
146.25° – 168.75°	SSE	6.3539	5.66	0.43	15.74	3.2954	3.5358341
168.75° – 191.25°	S	6.7609	6.7	0.47	14.05	2.8566	4.6677017
191.25° – 213.75°	SSW	8.4432	8.73	0.3	18.17	2.8963	13.059047
213.75° – 236.25°	SW	9.8051	10.06	0.48	20.39	3.4841	15.80608
236.25° – 258.75°	WSW	8.1353	8.44	0.49	18.74	3.2279	8.7544448
258.75° – 281.25°	W	6.2233	5.93	0.35	14.06	2.8906	3.2428507
281.25° – 303.75°	WNW	5.6979	5.55	0.68	11.82	2.5664	2.8647268
303.75° – 326.25°	NW	5.9608	5.7	0.41	16.42	3.1893	3.0825863
326.25° – 348.75°	NNW	6.5063	6.63	0.61	13.84	2.9067	4.25452

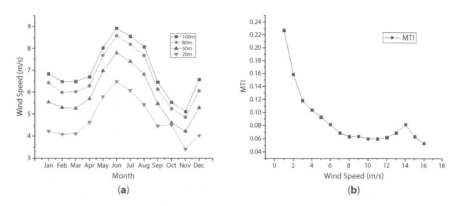

Figure 11.7 Jafrabad (a) Wind pattern different altitude, (b) Turbulence intensity.

The annual wind direction obtained with a mean wind speed of 9.8501 m/s and maximum value at SW direction was about 15.8%. Further, SSW and WSW obtained about 15.8% and WSW 8.7%, respectively, due to South-West Monsoon as shown in Table 11.8. The next maximum wind direction occurred in NNE was about 11.07% with a mean wind speed of 7.0987 m/s followed with N direction (10.17%) with a mean wind speed of 7.83%. The wind direction starts at N-NNE-NE direction during winter season initially and moves towards South-South-West direction during summer with the traces of south-east monsoon season picking up. Later, the peaks have taken during South-West Monsoon (SWM) with SW-S direction and finally through NEM season in N-NE direction. The major wind directions are obtained on S-SW and N-NE direction during seasonal periods. The turbulence intensity for offshore Lidar data is plotted in Figure 11.7 (b). Its mean value took place at 15 m/s of about 5.9%. As per the IEC standard, it falls on the Turbulence Ç category. On comparing with onshore Kayathar station, MTI value is low due to the offshore area.

11.4.1.3   Jafrabad (Gujarat-Nearshore)

The wind data collected for the period of December 2018 to November 2019 from mast Anemometers with various altitudes (20m-100m) is considered. The Mean Wind Speed (MWS) data collected from Mast measurements at various heights (10m to 100m) for the same period is presented in Figure 11.7. The monthly maximum mean wind speed of 8.92 m/s at 100m in June and low mean wind speed of in 5.11 m/s November is perceived. Further, the comparison of Mean wind speed gain while increasing the altitudes during June at 20 meters and 100 meters is 6.48 m/s, and

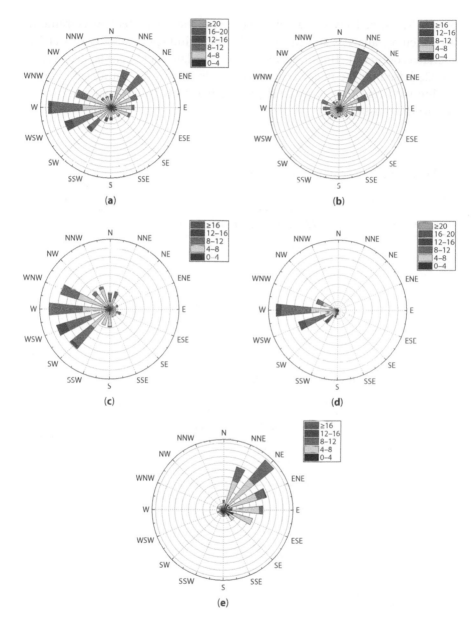

Figure 11.8 Wind rose: Jafrabad (a) Annual, (b) Winter, (c) Summer, (d) SWM, (e) NEM.

8.92 m/s, respectively, is evaluated. Wherein, the 100 meters measurements are taken for analysis and the annual mean wind speed of 6.99 m/s at 100 meters is observed. The shear analysis power-law coefficient is observed as 0.0228 based on the measured wind speeds at various altitudes. On comparing with Kayathar onshore shear coefficient, Jafrabad nearshore is less due to the coastal area.

Table 11.9 Seasonal parameter - Jafrabad.

Wparm	Winter	Summer	SWM	NEM	Annual
Vmean	6.671606926	7.082649592	8.015581992	5.749275181	6.991171
Vstd	2.589916191	2.639309659	2.977539329	2.435723167	2.837821
Vmax	13.3803	14.7525	17.4752	13.7208	17.4752
Skew	-0.00814	0.099369	0.278546	0.309722	0.299699
Kurtosis	0.85177	-0.4277	0.36875	0.47468	0.26657

Table 11.10 Monthly wind profile – Jafrabad.

Month	V_{mean}	V_{rmc}	V_{std}	V_{max}	V_{min}	V_{skew}	V_{kurt}
January	6.841446	7.761309	2.687005	14.499	0.429	-0.04353	-0.85235
February	6.487472	7.389023	2.581813	13.704	0.372	0.039756	-0.74116
March	6.498724	7.243676	2.313472	13.135	0.529	0.104691	-0.4758
April	6.708012	7.606093	2.625718	15	0.316	-0.02884	-0.42678
May	8.029128	8.938122	2.881918	15.561	0.514	-0.14875	-0.47036
June	8.925299	10.11441	3.415905	19.095	0.367	0.285194	-0.62292
July	8.564448	9.415539	2.908076	17.34	0.536	-0.4365	-0.38157
August	8.076447	8.889504	2.615936	17.799	1.803	0.552958	0.306734
September	6.456349	7.378807	2.540506	14.052	0.477	0.466343	-0.14508
October	5.535514	6.389749	2.280889	13.78	0.281	0.412565	-0.00276
November	5.118365	6.017146	2.283802	19.365	0.242	0.310674	-0.06034
December	6.573595	7.501067	2.632688	13.173	0.547	0.073535	-0.87302
Annual	6.991171	8.028212	2.837821	17.4752	0.5428	0.299699	-0.26657

The annual wind direction from the wind rose plots are shown in Figure 11.8. The maximum wind direction occurs in a SW to West direction. Regarding winter season and North-East Monsoon (NEM), wind direction towards NNE to East direction. During SWM season and Summer Monsoon periods, the majority of wind occurs in the SW to WNW direction.

Table 11.9 and Table 11.10 show the annual, seasonal, and monthly wind parameters.

11.4.2   Wind Distribution Fitting

For estimating the wind energy potential to extract wind power meritoriously, accurate wind distribution modeling is essential. The performance of targeted location wind potential assessment hinges on the selection of the PDF to picture the computed wind speed behavior plotted in the frequency distribution.

The collected wind speed data is to fit into ten numbers of wind distribution. These are Weibull, Rayleigh, Birnbaum Sandras (BS), Gamma (GM), Inverse-Gaussian (IG), Rician (RI), Log-Normal (LN), Nakagami (NK), Generalized Ext. Value (GEV) and Bimodal Weibull-Weibull (BM) distribution methods. The bimodal-WW method is adopted because the visual traces of probability distribution function have similarity on Bimodal with two peaks. The bimodal nature is predicted by numerical calculations of mean and standard deviation [29, 30]. The goodness of fit and best-fitted wind distribution is ascertained with RMSE and R^2 methods by comparing actual measured data with individual wind distribution methods through probability density functions. In this work, three methods, namely the Maximum Likelihood (ML), Expectation-Maximization algorithm (EM) for the Bimodal-Weibull-Weibull method, and the Moth Flame Optimization (MFO) for Bimodal-Weibull-Weibull Methods are used to estimate the parameters of wind speed distributions. The EM method consists of two steps, namely Expectation-step (E-step) and the Maximization-step (M-step). The E-step computes the conditional expectation and the M-step maximizes the expectation. The parameters of the bimodal and multimodal distribution are estimated by an iterative procedure until convergence is reached. Also, the Bimodal (Weibull-Weibull) parameters shown in Table 11.2 and Figure 11.4 are estimated through MFO with objective function by minimizing the error between Estimated and Observed Probability Density Function (PDF).

The distribution of wind speed data, also known as wind frequency distribution, is presented by histogram plots which is a usual method of presenting wind data for a specific year. The histogram displays the percentage of time of occurrence of each wind speed ranges.

11.4.2.1   Kayathar Station (Onshore)

Figure 11.9 shows the annual wind speed observed at 100m hub height with estimated parameters by the ten distributions through probability distribution function (PDF) and cumulative probability distribution (CDF) plots. The observed wind speed plotted into frequency distribution is fitted with other distributions to observe the difference in the fitting of each distribution with real histogram data.

Figure 11.10 shows the seasonal wind speed pattern by estimated parameters with distribution functions and plotted with PDF functions. The PDF visual examination likely Rayleigh distribution behavior distinct from other distributions during winter, summer, and SEM monsoon periods. During winter, Rayleigh performs well owing to the incidence of low wind speed.

11.4.2.2   Bimodal Behaviour

Table 11.11 shows the Bimodal WW method applied to observe the data in two parts with different weightage. It is estimated by bimodal methods through EM (Expectation-Maximization) algorithm and the values are plotted on each part along with weightage, mean speed, standard deviation, shape, and scale parameters. The bmc1 and bmc2 are the bimodality numerical check apart from Visual analysis, where bmc1 $=|\mu2 - \mu1|$ / $(2*(\sigma1 * \sigma2)^{(1/2)})$ when bmc1 > 1. Likewise, bmc2== $|\mu2 - \mu1|$ / $(2*$ min

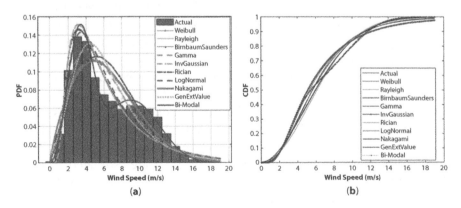

Figure 11.9 Annual wind behaviour with ten wind distributions. (a) Annual PDF, (b) Annual CDF.

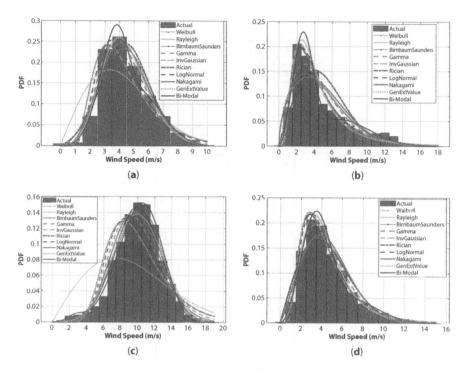

Figure 11.10 Seasonal plots: (a) Winter PDF, (b) Summer PDF, (c) SWM PDF, (d) NEM PDF.

($\sigma 1$, $\sigma 2$)) when bmc2 > 2. (Where, $\mu 1$ and $\mu 2$ are means, and $\sigma 1$ and $\sigma 2$ are standard deviations of 2 parts of bimodal model.

The wind distribution analysis in Kayathar region falls on multiple peaks and differs from normal bell-shaped histogram curves. The bimodal behavior is exclusively analyzed with the Bimodal Weibull-Weibull method. Figures 11.11 (a) and (b) shows the bimodal behavior of Annual and Winter season. Annual Season has more bimodality than winter through visual analysis as given in Table 11.13, i.e., bmc1 and bmc2 estimation. Wherein, winter comprises a lesser range of bmc1 and bmc2 of 0.64 and -0.1511, respectively, and the annual value of 1.4357 and 3.0533 for bmc1 and bmc2, respectively.

Table 11.12 shows the yearly and seasonal parameters from the observed wind speed by ten wind distribution models with the parameter estimation from the Maximum Likelihood method.

Table 11.13 shows the goodness of fit methods of RMSE and R^2 between estimated wind distribution parameters and observed parameters by the ten distribution PDF. The annual wind distribution for Kayathar region

Table 11.11 Kayathar bimodal estimated parameters.

Seasons	V_{mean}	mu1	mu2	sigma1	sigma2	w1	w2	k1bm	c1bm	k2bm	c2bm	bmc1	bmc2
Annual	6.38	3.36	8.960	1.272	2.989	0.459	0.540	2.870	3.7697	3.2945	9.9902	1.4357	3.05
Winter	4.43	3.51	5.061	0.847	1.688	0.405	0.594	4.690	3.8454	3.294	5.6434	0.64529	-0.15
Summer	4.69	2.74	7.289	1.054	3.088	0.570	0.429	2.827	3.081	2.5407	8.2123	1.2594	2.43
SWM	10.03	8.54	10.48	3.278	2.321	0.228	0.771	2.829	9.5904	5.1397	11.399	0.35148	-2.70
NEM	4.51	3.45	6.711	1.297	2.513	0.675	0.324	2.899	3.8766	2.906	7.5264	0.90146	0.66

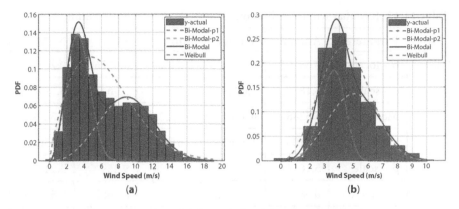

Figure 11.11 (a) Kayathar - Bimodal Annual plot, (b) Winter Bimodal plot.

Table 11.12 Kayathar wind distribution estimated parameters.

Dist	Parameter	Annual	Winter	Summer	SWM	NEM
	V_{mean}	6.3884	4.4349	4.6966	10.039	4.5131
WB	k – shape	7.2171	4.9643	5.2833	11.027	5.1141
	c - scale	1.8411	2.9385	1.6172	4.1904	2.0472
	Mean	6.4116	4.4291	4.7323	10.021	4.5307
	Std	3.6114	1.6399	2.9988	2.6955	2.3191
RY	σ – scale	5.2047	3.3338	3.9907	7.3507	3.597
	Mean	6.5231	4.1783	5.0016	9.2128	4.5082
	Std	3.4098	2.1841	2.6144	4.8157	2.3565
NK	μ – shape	0.88932	2.0036	0.75934	3.2433	1.1261
	ω – scale	54.177	22.229	31.851	108.07	25.877
	Mean	6.4323	4.4323	4.8288	10.004	4.5664
	Std	3.5781	1.6074	2.9213	2.8262	2.2416
IG	μ – mean	6.3884	4.4349	4.6966	10.039	4.5131
	λ – shape	12.275	19.584	9.023	80.131	13.792
	Mean	6.3884	4.4349	4.6966	10.039	4.5131
	Std	4.6088	2.1104	3.3884	3.5535	2.5817

(*Continued*)

Table 11.12 Kayathar wind distribution estimated parameters. (*Continued*)

Dist	Parameter	Annual	Winter	Summer	SWM	NEM
RI	b – location	0.68257	4.0616	0.22823	9.6326	0.26813
	a – scale	5.1836	1.6929	3.988	2.764	3.5926
	Mean	6.5248	4.4362	5.0023	10.039	4.5089
	Std	3.4106	1.5965	2.6148	2.6998	2.3569
BS	β – scale	5.1662	3.9977	3.8091	9.459	3.9145
	γ – shape	0.68275	0.46358	0.68277	0.3487	0.55146
	Mean	6.3703	4.4273	4.697	10.034	4.5097
	Std	4.4374	2.0874	3.272	3.5401	2.536
GM	θ – scale	2.8218	6.9442	2.5373	11.002	3.9132
	k – shape	2.264	0.63864	1.851	0.91251	1.1533
	Mean	6.3884	4.4349	4.6966	10.039	4.5131
	Std	3.803	1.6829	2.9485	3.0267	2.2815
GEV	μ – location	0.059586	-0.13198	0.31303	-0.28097	0.069464
	σ - scale	2.8121	1.4316	1.8015	2.7864	1.7032
	ξ – shape	4.5827	3.7751	3.0078	9.0713	3.4038
	Mean	6.3813	4.4343	4.8447	10.058	4.512
	Std	3.9263	1.5902	4.5938	2.7839	2.4153
LN	μ - mean	1.667	1.4158	1.337	2.2604	1.3738
	σ - scale	0.64842	0.41758	0.65443	0.33264	0.53036
	Mean	6.5351	4.495	4.7169	10.132	4.5469
	Std	0.64842	0.41758	0.65443	0.33264	0.53036

follows, Bimodal-WW wind distribution with a lower RMSE value of 0.004 and R^2 value of 0.9878. Regarding seasonal wind distribution fitness analysis, winter season best fit by Gamma method, summer with Inverse Gamma, SWM with Rician method and Winter season with GEV method.

Table 11.13 Kayathar wind distribution PDF fitness.

Distribution metrics						
Season	Fitness	Annual	Winter	Summer	SWM	NEM
V_{mean}		6.3884	4.4349	4.6966	10.039	4.5131
BM	RMSE	0.00491	0.00996	0.01265	0.00762	0.00834
	R^2	0.98798	0.98871	0.96082	0.98097	0.98679
WB	RMSE	0.01802	0.02431	0.0225	0.00664	0.01693
	R^2	0.82152	0.93121	0.86689	0.98657	0.94457
RY	RMSE	0.02117	0.04763	0.03207	0.04209	0.01708
	R^2	0.76435	0.75954	0.72581	0.45767	0.94478
NK	RMSE	0.0186	0.01638	0.0259	0.01201	0.01611
	R^2	0.80975	0.96831	0.82146	0.95464	0.94747
IG	RMSE	0.01524	0.02957	0.00787	0.02621	0.01212
	R^2	0.90596	0.89734	0.98489	0.77615	0.97282
RI	RMSE	0.02118	0.02533	0.03207	0.00642	0.01709
	R^2	0.76421	0.92328	0.72568	0.98702	0.94473
BS	RMSE	0.01426	0.02936	0.0083	0.02604	0.01091
	R^2	0.9111	0.89932	0.98176	0.77924	0.97726
GM	RMSE	0.01602	0.00939	0.01779	0.01684	0.00621
	R^2	0.86416	0.98997	0.91474	0.90939	0.992
GEV	RMSE	0.01919	0.01188	0.01075	0.00926	0.00464
	R^2	0.81312	0.98314	0.97539	0.97568	0.99691
LN	RMSE	0.01502	0.01563	0.00971	0.02317	0.00825
	R^2	0.89798	0.97248	0.97578	0.8263	0.98789
Good Fit	RMSE	BM	Gamma	IG	Rician	GEV
Good Fit	R^2	BM	Gamma	IG	Rician	GEV

There is a similarity between Rician and Weibull; both follow each during high wind seasons.

11.4.2.3   Gulf of Khambhat (Offshore) Wind Distribution

Figure 11.12 shows the annual wind speed observed at 100m with estimated parameters by the ten distributions through probability distribution function (PDF) and cumulative probability distribution (CDF) plots in the Gulf of Khambhat region.

Figure 11.13 shows the seasonal wind speed pattern by the estimated parameters using distribution functions and plotted with PDF functions. Table 11.14 shows the Bimodal WW method parameters. The bmc1 and bmc2 are the bimodality numerical check apart from Visual analysis.

The wind distribution analysis in the Gulf of Khambhat region falls on multiple peaks. Figure 11.15 shows the bimodal behavior of the Annual and Winter season. Annual Season has less bimodality than winter through visual analysis. As per bmc1 and bmc2 estimation, it is more as 1.2955 and 2.3584, respectively. The annual value has lower score of bmc1 and bmc2 of about 1.0904 and 1.5078, respectively.

Table 11.15 shows the yearly and seasonal parameters from the observed wind speed by ten wind distribution models with the parameter estimation from the Maximum Likelihood method. Table 11.16 shows the goodness of fit methods RMSE and R^2 between estimated wind distribution parameters with observed parameters by the ten distribution models. The annual wind distribution pattern follows the Bimodal-WW wind distribution model with lower rate of RMSE and R^2 values.

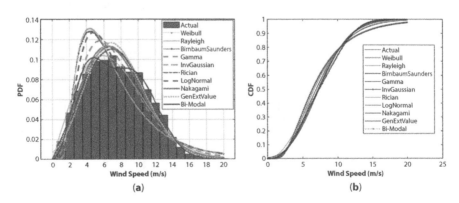

Figure 11.12 Gulf of Khambhat (a) Annual PDF, (b) Annual CDF.

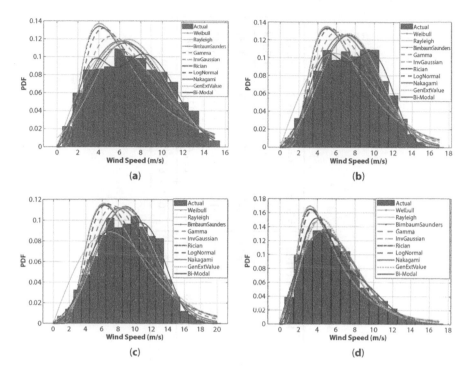

Figure 11.13 Gulf of Khambhat seasonal (a) Winter PDF, (b) Summer PDF, (c) SWM PDF, (d) NEM PDF.

Comparing the annual best fit, Bimodal-WW distribution performed well comparing with other distributions as indicated with R^2 and RMSE of about 0.98669 and 0.00463 respectively. During seasonal periods, Bimodal-WW performed well on summer and SWM periods. Weibull and BM shares best fit during winter season, and Rayleigh Distribution performed well during North-East Monsoon (NEM) period.

11.4.2.4   Jafrabad Station (Nearshore) Distribution Fitting

Figure 11.14 shows the annual wind speed observed at 100m hub height with estimated parameters by the ten distributions through probability distribution function and cumulative probability distribution plots in the Jafrabad nearshore region. Figure 11.15 shows the seasonal wind speed pattern of the estimated parameters by the distribution functions and plotted with PDF.

Table 11.17 shows the Bi-Modal WW method parameters. The bmc1 and bmc2 are the bimodality numerical check apart from Visual analysis.

Table 11.14 Gulf of Khambhat bimodal estimated parameters.

Season	mu1	mu2	sigma1	sigma2	w1	w2	k1bm	c1bm	k2bm	c2bm	bmc1	bmc2
Ann	4.1789	9.0125	1.6628	2.9542	0.31044	0.68956	2.7204	4.698	3.3579	10.038	1.0904	1.5078
Win	3.3501	8.3238	1.3076	2.8181	0.24046	0.75954	2.7779	3.7634	3.242	9.2876	1.2955	2.3584
Sum	4.6323	9.2917	1.6575	2.3209	0.37149	0.62851	3.053	5.1835	4.5106	10.18	1.1878	1.3443
SWM	5.6817	10.618	2.0393	2.7803	0.31858	0.68142	3.0428	6.3586	4.2857	11.669	1.0366	0.85811
NEM	3.7831	7.5851	1.5675	2.8748	0.48338	0.51662	2.6034	4.259	2.8681	8.5102	0.89552	0.667

Table 11.15 Estimated wind distribution parameters.

Dist	Param	Annual	Winter	Summer	SWM	NEM
V_{mean}		7.5119	7.1278	7.5608	9.0457	5.7473
WB	k – shape	8.4826	8.0497	8.5093	10.149	6.5034
	c - scale	2.3297	2.3028	2.6758	2.8735	2.0215
	Mean	7.5161	7.1315	7.5649	9.0461	5.7624
	Std	3.426	3.2846	3.046	3.4171	2.9833
RY	σ – scale	5.8441	5.5573	5.7724	6.845	4.5879
	Mean	7.3245	6.965	7.2346	8.5789	5.7501
	Std	3.8287	3.6408	3.7817	4.4844	3.0057
NK	μ – shape	1.2406	1.1977	1.5274	1.718	1.0452
	ω – scale	68.307	61.767	66.641	93.707	42.098
	Mean	7.4902	7.0986	7.5318	9.0094	5.7786
	Std	3.4934	3.3728	3.1485	3.5408	2.9506
IG	μ – mean	7.5119	7.1278	7.5608	9.0457	5.7473
	λ – shape	20.015	17.964	26.078	35.487	13.916
	Mean	7.5119	7.1278	7.5608	9.0457	5.7473
	Std	4.6021	4.4899	4.0711	4.567	3.6934
RI	b – location	5.9627	5.6008	6.605	8.1336	0.65497
	a – scale	4.0468	3.8986	3.3922	3.7116	4.5656
	Mean	7.5088	7.1301	7.5577	9.0442	5.7515
	Std	3.4532	3.3058	3.0857	3.4511	3.0064
BS	β – scale	6.3869	6.012	6.6442	8.0615	4.8243
	γ – shape	0.58779	0.6031	0.52106	0.49036	0.61432
	Mean	7.4903	7.1053	7.5461	9.0308	5.7346
	Std	4.4922	4.373	4.0067	4.5081	3.5954

(*Continued*)

Table 11.15 Estimated wind distribution parameters. (*Continued*)

Dist	Param	Annual	Winter	Summer	SWM	NEM
GM	θ – scale	3.9564	3.7688	4.9587	5.6311	3.4166
	k – shape	1.8987	1.8913	1.5248	1.6064	1.6821
	Mean	7.5119	7.1278	7.5608	9.0457	5.7473
	Std	3.7766	3.6716	3.3953	3.8119	3.1093
GEV	μ – location	-0.18995	-0.25267	-0.25961	-0.25133	-0.01657
	σ - scale	3.2147	3.1905	3.0072	3.3843	2.4277
	ξ – shape	6.1512	5.9136	6.439	7.7735	4.3707
	Mean	7.49	7.1023	7.5456	9.0375	5.7329
	Std	3.4055	3.24	3.0412	3.4395	3.0484
LN	μ - mean	1.8848	1.8255	1.9188	2.1109	1.5953
	σ - scale	0.55852	0.57477	0.49651	0.46603	0.58727
	Mean	7.6967	7.3206	7.7062	9.2024	5.8576

There is no bimodality comparing with other locations due to low bmc1 and bmc2 scores of 0.860 and 0.328, respectively. Figure 11.14 shows the bimodal behavior of winter season with bmc1 and bmc2 score of 1.321 and 1.088, respectively. There are no many visual changes on bimodality during the summer season because bmc1 and bmc2 have some indication with 1.115 and 1.382, respectively. Table 11.18 shows the yearly and seasonal estimated parameters from the observed wind speed by ten wind distribution models with the parameter estimation from the Maximum Likelihood method.

From Table 11.19, during winter periods particularly on SWM and NEM periods, Bimodal-WW performed well. The value of R^2 (0.989) shared the best fit during summer whereas Weibull shared the best fit with RMSE 0.006. By summarizing all the locations, annual wind distribution, wind estimation from probability density function for Kayathar and Gulf of Khambhat region, Bimodal-WW stands top and Jafrabad Weibull distribution ranked as best fit. The annual probability density function parameters

Table 11.16 Goodness of fit values.

Season	Fitness	Annual	Winter	Summer	SWM	NEM
BM	RMSE	0.00463	0.008187	0.005787	0.005149	0.008814
	R^2	0.98669	0.95241	0.98257	0.98347	0.97104
WB	RMSE	0.00679	0.006795	0.010809	0.007685	0.005915
	R^2	0.97474	0.92843	0.94507	0.96487	0.98613
RY	RMSE	0.008356	0.011158	0.017738	0.019121	0.005598
	R^2	0.95637	0.90881	0.84349	0.78715	0.98765
NK	RMSE	0.007369	0.01179	0.012305	0.009872	0.006318
	R^2	0.9695	0.92085	0.92696	0.94087	0.98425
IG	RMSE	0.020808	0.02649	0.024299	0.021487	0.018341
	R^2	0.77749	0.67819	0.73487	0.73263	0.9
RI	RMSE	0.006079	0.010237	0.01084	0.008027	0.00561
	R^2	0.97828	0.93777	0.94275	0.96131	0.9876
BS	RMSE	0.019828	0.025204	0.023575	0.020979	0.016777
	R^2	0.79221	0.69566	0.74568	0.74202	0.91302
Gamma	RMSE	0.01169	0.016514	0.016295	0.013774	0.006528
	R^2	0.924	0.85394	0.87404	0.88597	0.98645
GEV	RMSE	0.008793	0.012897	0.011335	0.007933	0.008826
	R^2	0.95641	0.89742	0.93884	0.96199	0.97386
LN	RMSE	0.01787	0.023337	0.021774	0.018976	0.014858
	R^2	0.82918	0.73583	0.78258	0.78832	0.93241
Good Fit	RMSE	BM	WB	BM	BM	Rayleigh
	R^2	BM	BM	BM	BM	Rayleigh

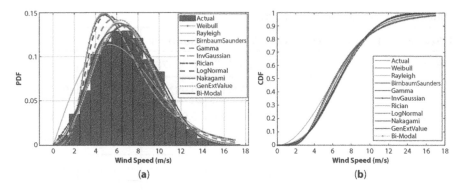

Figure 11.14 (a) Jafrabad annual PDF, (b) Jafrabad annual CDF.

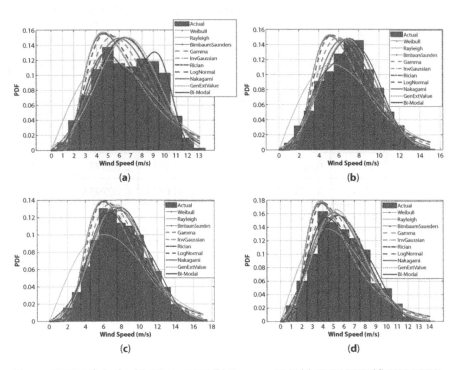

Figure 11.15 Jafrabad – (a) Winter PDF, (b) Summer PDF, (c) SWM PDF, (d) NEM PDF.

Table 11.17 Jafrabad bimodal estimated parameters.

Season	mu1	mu2	sigma1	sigma2	w1	w2	k1bm	c1bm	k2bm	c2bm	bmc1	bmc2
Annual	4.47	7.96	1.581	2.608	0.28	0.72	3.098	5.008	3.364	8.875	0.860	0.328
Winter	4.68	8.81	1.607	1.519	0.51	0.48	3.197	5.233	6.747	9.440	1.321	1.088
Summer	3.71	7.57	1.238	2.419	0.12	0.87	3.300	4.145	3.455	8.427	1.115	1.382
SWM	5.77	9.58	1.825	2.603	0.41	0.58	3.456	6.421	4.117	10.553	0.873	0.155
NEM	3.85	7.10	1.399	2.090	0.41	0.58	3.009	4.319	3.777	7.866	0.950	0.451

Table 11.18 Jafrabad wind distribution estimated parameters.

Dist.	Param	Annual	Winter	Summer	SW-Mon	NE-Mon
	Vmean	6.9912	6.6716	7.0826	8.0156	5.7493
WB	k – shape	7.8698	7.4958	7.9406	8.9928	6.4834
	c - scale	2.6582	2.8423	2.9392	2.9254	2.5444
	Mean	6.9948	6.6785	7.0846	8.0217	5.7551
	Std	2.8332	2.5476	2.6226	2.982	2.4241
RY	σ – scale	5.3352	5.0603	5.3445	6.0462	4.415
	Mean	6.6867	6.3421	6.6983	7.5777	5.5334
	Std	3.4953	3.3152	3.5014	3.9611	2.8924
NK	μ – shape	1.5804	1.666	1.8162	1.8879	1.4658
	ω – scale	56.929	51.213	57.127	73.112	38.984
	Mean	6.9797	6.6459	7.0612	8.0085	5.7418
	Std	2.8658	2.6544	2.6956	2.9959	2.4527
IG	μ – mean	6.9912	6.6716	7.0826	8.0156	5.7493
	λ – shape	26.862	25.987	31.597	40.51	20.267
	Mean	6.9912	6.6716	7.0826	8.0156	5.7493
	Std	3.5666	3.3804	3.3533	3.5655	3.0621
RI	b – location	6.1142	5.9552	6.4154	7.2687	4.8981
	a – scale	3.1262	2.8061	2.8257	3.1842	2.738
	Mean	6.9877	6.6694	7.0812	8.0143	5.7445
	Std	2.8462	2.5947	2.6427	2.9806	2.4463
BS	β – scale	6.2191	5.9423	6.3943	7.3187	5.0667
	γ – shape	0.49521	0.49202	0.46134	0.43467	0.51574
	Mean	6.9817	6.6616	7.0748	8.0101	5.7406
	Std	3.5203	3.3369	3.3192	3.537	3.0164

(Continued)

Table 11.18 Jafrabad wind distribution estimated parameters. (*Continued*)

Dist.	Param	Annual	Winter	Summer	SW-Mon	NE-Mon
GM	θ – scale	5.2608	5.4541	6.0472	6.4748	4.8474
	k – *shape*	1.3289	1.2232	1.1712	1.238	1.186
	Mean	6.9912	6.6716	7.0826	8.0156	5.7493
	Std	3.0481	2.8567	2.8802	3.1501	2.6113
GEV	μ – location	-0.1804	-0.31306	-0.25184	-0.19419	-0.18116
	o - scale	2.6471	2.5947	2.5825	2.7935	2.2544
	ξ – shape	5.862	5.7926	6.1134	6.8496	4.7817
	Mean	6.9828	6.6582	7.0771	8.0042	5.7351
	Std	2.8245	2.5501	2.6238	2.95	2.4041
LN	μ - *mean*	1.8466	1.8034	1.8727	2.0022	1.6424
	σ - scale	0.47502	0.47096	0.44412	0.42108	0.4951
	Mean	7.0953	6.7822	7.1801	8.0917	5.8413

Table 11.19 Jafrabad goodness of fit estimated parameters.

Season	Fitness	Annual	Winter	Summer	SWM	NEM
		6.991	6.672	7.083	8.016	5.749
BM	RMSE	0.005	0.007	0.007	0.005	0.009
	R^2	0.991	0.981	0.983	0.990	0.976
WB	RMSE	0.003	0.018	0.006	0.007	0.010
	R^2	0.995	0.887	0.988	0.977	0.972
RY	RMSE	0.018	0.026	0.026	0.023	0.018
	R^2	0.889	0.747	0.773	0.801	0.909
NK	RMSE	0.005	0.019	0.010	0.006	0.010
	R^2	0.991	0.871	0.965	0.986	0.975

(*Continued*)

Table 11.19 Jafrabad goodness of fit estimated parameters. (*Continued*)

Season	Fitness	Annual	Winter	Summer	SWM	NEM
IG	RMSE	0.021	0.030	0.027	0.016	0.024
	R^2	0.842	0.707	0.764	0.899	0.851
RI	RMSE	0.005	0.019	0.006	0.008	0.011
	R^2	0.991	0.877	0.989	0.968	0.963
BS	RMSE	0.020	0.029	0.026	0.015	0.023
	R^2	0.851	0.716	0.772	0.904	0.859
GM	RMSE	0.011	0.023	0.016	0.008	0.013
	R^2	0.957	0.827	0.908	0.973	0.956
GEV	RMSE	0.006	0.018	0.007	0.006	0.011
	R^2	0.989	0.886	0.985	0.983	0.967
LN	RMSE	0.018	0.028	0.024	0.014	0.020
	R^2	0.882	0.749	0.809	0.924	0.890
Good Fit	RMSE	Weibull	BM	Weibull	BM	BM
	R^2	Weibull	BM	Rician	BM	BM

estimated from the ten distributions are compared with the optimization method using the Moth Flame Optimization algorithm for accuracy in the subsequent section.

11.4.3   Optimization Methods for Parameter Estimation

11.4.3.1   Optimization Parameters Comparison

The parameters estimated from wind distribution methods in previous sections through the Parameter Estimation method for unimodal and EM Algorithm for Bimodal (BM-EM) are compared with Annual Bimodal Weibull Estimation parameters through Moth Flame Optimization (MFO-BM) method. The estimation of the Moth Flame method parameter is presented in Table 11.20. The optimization parameter is projected through MFO with the objective function for Bimodal Weibull distribution.

Table 11.20 BM-MFO wind distribution estimated parameters.

Method	Station	Mean	k1	c1	k2	c2	w1	w2
BM-EM	Kayathar	6.388437	2.87	3.7697	3.2945	9.9902	0.45927	0.5407
BM-MFO	Kayathar		2.626324	3.823721	3.013573	9.885349	0.460752	0.539248
BM-EM	GoK	7.511933	2.7204	4.698	3.3579	10.038	0.31044	0.68956
BM-MFO	GoK		2.437014	5.039469	3.370965	9.960301	0.30165	0.69835
BM-EM	Jafrabad	6.991171	3.098	5.008	3.364	8.875	0.28	0.72
BM-MFO	Jafrabad		2.95449	5.08246	2.98780	8.41179	0.16405	0.83595

Table 11.21 Optimization PDF fitness.

Method	Station	RMSE	R2	eWPD%	WPD
Pactual	Kayathar				334.1708
BM-EM	Kayathar	0.004907	0.98798	0.083552	333.8916
BM-MFO	Kayathar	0.004093	0.990776	5.42E-08	334.1707
Pactual	GoK				431.5318
BM-EM	GoK	0.004628	0.986713	0.224788	430.5617
BM-MFO	GoK	0.003807	0.991794	5.81E-10	431.5318
Pactual	Jafrabad				318.1847
BM-EM	Jafrabad	0.004816	0.99056	0.448712	316.7569
BM-MFO	Jafrabad	0.002892	0.99673	-1.409Ee-05	318.1846
WB-Unimodal	Jafrabad	0.003416	0.99544	0.67818	316.026

The wind parameters from the MFO method, PDF fitness analysis with RMSE and R^2 method, and the snapshot of WPD results are presented in Table 11.21. The MFO parameters are estimated in two stages by satisfying the PDF objective function firstly with minimum RMSE/R^2 value. Then, over fit and underfit of wind power density calculated from estimated parameters from Optimization is tuned with MFO optimization again for higher accuracy. The observed results satisfy both the lower RMSE/R^2 value and the annual wind power density. It is accurately estimated through the MFO method. The results of MFO for Kayathar, Jafrabad, and Gulf of Khambhat (GoK) outperform the bimodal parameters estimated through EM algorithm, and MFO stands top-ranked in all the stations.

11.4.4   Wind Power Density Analysis (WPD)

The WPD value is the major factor for the wind energy potential assessment of a wind location and also evaluating economic feasibility to form a potential wind farm. The model of WPD defines the distributions of wind energy at several wind speed values and proportional to the cube of wind speed. Its value is represented in W/m2 depends on the wind location, air density and the wind speed and derived as follows:

$$WPD = \frac{P}{A} = \frac{1}{2}\rho v^3 \tag{11.11}$$

Where P is a wind power measured in Watts, A stands for a swept area in m2, ρ states the air density ($\rho = 1.225kg/m3$) and v represents the wind speed in m/s. Considering all these, the distribution of wind speed is taken into account and then WPD can be expressed as

$$\frac{P}{A} = \frac{1}{2}\rho \int_0^\infty v^3 f(v) dv \tag{11.13}$$

For evaluating WPD of a particular distribution, the wind power density distribution function f(v) can be expressed as

$$\frac{P}{A} = \frac{1}{2}\rho v^3 f(v) \tag{11.14}$$

The best fit of WPD is calculated as follows,

$$eWPD = \left(\frac{(WPDo - WPDest)}{WPDo} \right) 100\% \tag{11.15}$$

Where *WPDo* is the observed Wind power Density from Measured values, *WPDests* the estimated values from Distribution Fitting and *eWPD* is the error between observed and estimated.

11.4.4.1 Comparison of Wind Power Density

The annual WPD comparison with MFO estimated parameters and seasonable wind power density for the three locations are given in Table 11.22 and Table 11.23, respectively.

The three locations of different landscapes such as offshore, nearshore, and onshore are considered. Wind power density is evaluated after carrying goodness of fit with RMSE and R^2 using probability distribution methods. The goodness of fit eWPD indicates the wind power density how best the particular distribution to suit the location.

Table 11.24 shows the Wind Power Density calculated from different distributions along with measured value during seasonal periods for three

Table 11.22 Annual WPD comparison with MFO and other methods.

WPD annual comparison				WPD annual fitness comparison			
Dist.	Kayathar annual	GoK annual	Jafrabad annual	Distribution	Kayathar annual	GoK annual	Jafrabad annual
Actual	334.17	431.53	318.18				
BM-MFO	334.1707	431.5318	318.185	BM-MFO	5.42E-08	5.81E-10	-1.409Ee-05
BM-EM	333.89	430.54	316.76	BM-EM	0.08	0.23	0.45
WB	325.23	430.55	316.03	WB	2.68	0.23	0.68
RY	319.76	445.6	330.17	RY	4.31	-3.26	-3.77
BS	319.05	447.39	324.34	BS	4.53	-3.67	-1.93
GM	323.06	448.22	323.65	GM	3.32	-3.87	-1.72
IG	312.96	443.16	322.83	IG	6.35	-2.69	-1.46
RI	320	431.11	315.26	RI	4.24	0.1	0.92
NK	325.25	434.01	317.14	NK	2.67	-0.58	0.33
GEV	310.55	423.73	314.85	GEV	7.07	1.81	1.05
LN	317.4	455.52	328.18	LN	5.02	-5.56	-3.14

locations. Figure 11.16 (e) shows the monthly Wind power density statistics using monthly WPD analysis for Kayathar station. Bimodal method scores better during February, April, July, August, and September (5 months), whereas GEV distribution scores best during March, October, November, and December (4 months) followed with Weibull during May and June as the best fit. For monthly wind power density of Gulf of Khambhat, BM scores better except February, June, and November, whereas Rician distribution scores best during February and November followed with Weibull during June as shown in Figure 11.16 (e). For Jafrabad region monthly WPD analysis, BM scores better except April, May, and August, whereas Rician distribution scores best during April. Generalized Extreme Value (GEV) distribution scored better during May and Weibull during August as the best fit.

Figure 11.16 (d) represents the different seasons wind power density share and comparing with each region. Gulf of Khambhat offshore shares 37% maximum Wind power density during South-West Monsoon (SWM) and minimum during North-East Monsoon period with 15%. The winter and summer have a steady share of 22% and 26% respectively. The Gulf

Table 11.23 Wind power density.

Dist.	Kayathar winter	Summer	SWM	NEM	GoK winter	Summer	SWM	NEM	Jafrabad winter	Summer	SWM	NEM
Actual	76.447	170.8	751.97	111.58	370.79	399.83	653.26	225.29	266.13	310.66	450.83	183.59
Bimodal EM (WW)	75.665	168.67	750.22	110.19	359.69	398.02	652.35	222.89	263.94	308.88	449.94	181.97
WB	75.535	156.24	748.65	106.16	341.26	395.26	649.57	219.07	255.79	307.45	447.1	180.98
RY	78.826	146.27	715.72	106.94	328.76	398.12	657.39	219.67	235.35	304.32	439.72	187.25
BS	78.202	161.23	762.86	112.67	283.22	379.98	637.78	225.76	222.95	296.18	428.9	182.7
GM	76.145	150.8	769.73	104.86	317.66	396.48	658.32	221.09	242.02	306.61	440.03	184.01
IG	77.996	161.12	761.83	113.11	278.06	376.72	633.71	223.84	221.01	294.55	427.05	181.56
RI	74.491	146.33	753.27	106.99	344.94	396.46	651.02	219.82	256.04	307.38	444.62	180.83
NK	74.997	155.61	757.78	104.41	335.75	395.91	652.69	218.08	250.37	306.87	443.05	181.33
GEV	74.766	153.03	766.27	106.14	349.27	392.36	650.64	214.73	259.2	307.47	443.06	178.76
LN	78.758	156.7	774.63	112.23	289.81	387.29	650.4	226.53	227.56	300.51	432.14	184.8

Table 11.24 WPD error metrics.

Season	Kayathar				Gulf of Khambhat				Jafrabad			
	Win	Sum	SWM	NEM	Win	Sum	SWM	NEM	Win	Sum	SWM	NEM
BM-EM	1.02	1.25	0.23	1.25	0.3	0.04	0.04	-0.29	0.82	0.57	0.2	0.89
WB	1.19	8.53	0.44	4.86	7.96	0.56	0.56	2.76	3.88	1.03	0.83	1.43
RY	-3.1	14.36	4.82	4.16	11.34	-0.63	-0.63	2.49	11.57	2.04	2.46	-1.99
BS	-2.3	5.6	-1.45	-0.97	23.62	2.37	2.37	-0.21	16.22	4.66	4.87	0.49
GM	0.39	11.71	-2.36	6.03	14.33	-0.77	-0.77	1.87	9.06	1.3	2.4	-0.23
IG	-2.0	5.67	-1.31	-1.37	25.01	2.99	2.99	0.64	16.95	5.18	5.27	1.1
RI	2.56	14.33	-0.17	4.12	6.97	0.34	0.34	2.43	3.79	1.05	1.38	1.5
NK	1.9	8.89	-0.77	6.43	9.45	0.09	0.09	3.2	5.92	1.22	1.73	1.23
GEV	2.2	10.4	-1.9	4.87	5.8	0.4	0.4	4.69	2.6	1.03	1.72	2.63
LN	-3.0	8.25	-3.01	-0.58	21.84	0.44	0.44	-0.55	14.49	3.27	4.15	-0.66
GF	BM	BM	BM	BM	BM	BM	BM	IG	BM	BM	BM	BS

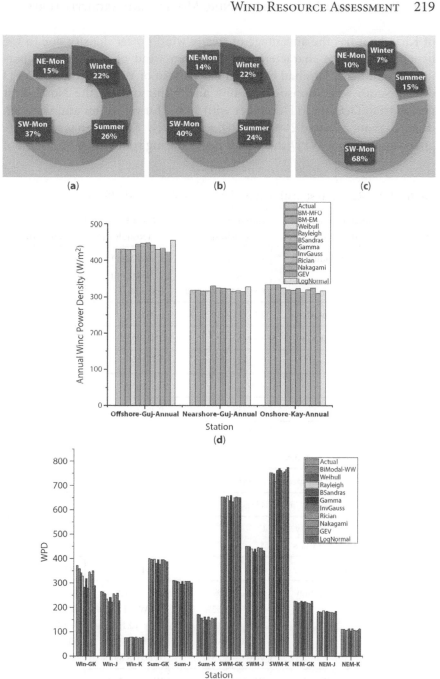

Figure 11.16 WPD region annual share: (a) Jafrabad, (b) Gulf Khambhat, (c) Kayathar, (d) Annual WPD plot comparison, (e) Seasonal WPD comparison.

of Khambhat has the advantage of steady wind power density due to the benefit of offshore characteristics free from wind obstruction comparing the landmass. Jafrabad has a similar pattern of WPD with peak WPD during south-west Monsoon of 40% and minimum on the North-East period from October to December with 14%. During winter and summer, it shares about 24% and 26% of WPD, respectively. Kayathar has wide marginal variations on WPD share with peaks during south-west Monsoon of

Table 11.25 Research statistics in onshore, nearshore, and offshore.

S. no.	Annual parameter (@100m)	Gulf of Khambhat (Offshore)	Jafrabad (Nearshore)	Kayathar (Onshore)
1	Wind Distribution Fit (Rank)	1. BM-MFO 2. Rician BM-EM & Weibull	1. BM-MFO 2. Nakagami BM-EM	1. BM-MFO 2. BM-EM Nakagami
2	Mean Wind speed	7.511933054	6.991171	6.388437
3	Standard Deviation	3.446632	2.837821	3.656017
4	Max. wind speed	20.2633	17.4752	18.84
5	Skew	0.258659	0.299699	0.558942
6	Kurt	0.57949	0.26657	-0.70377
7	MTI at 15 m/sec	5.9%	6.4%	13.2%
8	Shear Power Law Index	0.0782	0.0228	0.170
9	Mean cubic Wind speed	8.8881	8.028212	8.1642
10	WPD (observed) W/m^2	431.53	318.18	334.17
11	Turbulence Category Wind Power Class	C 3	C 2	B 2
12	WPD (Estimated)	431.11	317.14	333.89
13	Best Wind Direction	SW – 15.8% SSW – 13.05% NNE – 11.07% N - 10.17% WSW – 8.75%	W – 15.04% WSW – 11.63% NE – 10.158% NNE – 9.421% WNW-8.891%	W -38% % WSW – 11% WNW – 7.57% NE – 6.51% NNE – 6.50%
14	Wind power Density share	Winter – 22% Summer – 24% SWM – 40% NEM - 14%	Winter – 22% Summer – 26% SWM – 36% NEM - 15%	Winter - 7% Summer – 15% SWM - 68% NEM - 10%

about 68% and low WPD during North-East monsoon of 10% share. The winter share of about 7% and summer share of 15% of the rest Wind power density share. Kayathar region falls on Class 2, Gulf of Khambhat on Class 3, and Jafrabad on Class 2 wind power class [31].

11.5   Research Summary

The wind energy potential assessments evaluated using ten wind distribution methods along with Bimodal influence factors and MFO Machine Learning Optimization methods in the wind prone locations of onshore, offshore and nearshore with different landscape are summarized and shown in Table 11.25.

The application of Moth Flame Optimization in wind resource assessment for estimating the parameters is explored with multiple wind distributions and their behavior on different landscapes under bimodality influences. In India, Tamil Nadu and Gujarat stand top on wind energy generation. The major hurdle is the Low voltage ride through (LVRT) issue [32], because the power generating plants should not get disconnected from the grid and must continue to operate through short periods of low grid voltage. Wind Power Generating farms connected above 66 kV need to stay connected in the grid as per Indian Electricity Grid Code (IEGC). The power generating plants act as a fault recovery by generating reactive power compensation to support the grid during system faults. Some of the old wind turbines with stall regulation type, the provision of putting add on LVRT is technically not possible. It is noted that about 11,510 such turbines were installed till April 2014 in India which have to be replaced with new wind turbines to make smooth grid operation. The Active Network Management describes the control systems that manage generation and load for specific purposes to implement in India to control the wind turbines during high grid frequency. But SCADA integration and network communication have to be strengthened. During a higher rate of renewable energy injecting in the grid, the control of renewable energy [34–36] should be adopted to maintain the grid by modernizing network and information technology systems.

The field data measurements, history of data available in the archive, and satellite data are the basic data analytics sources for wind resource assessment. However, raising standards of data quality through big data [33] analytics will help to make the wind and solar resource assessment with high accuracy.

11.6   Conclusions

The application of Moth Flame Optimization technique in Machine Learning is applied in Wind resource assessment. The wind distribution pattern and wind speed characteristics in the offshore, onshore, and near-shore in India are compared at different timescales like annual, seasonal and monthly in detail to predict the behavior of wind. Based on the detailed wind behavioral analysis, the following conclusions are drawn.

1. The conventional wind distribution Unimodel are overridden by the Bimodal (Weibull-Weibull) method with the Moth Flame optimization method. Among wind distribution evaluated methods, Bimodal-WW performed well, followed by Nakagami, Rician, and Weibull distributions.
2. Comparing to onshore Kayathar wind station in Tamilnadu state, the offshore coastal area of the Gulf of Khambhat, Gujarat, the turbulence intensity is low of 0.0782 due to low surface roughness. During the South-west monsoon, the prevailing wind direction for the Gulf of Khambhat is observed on SW (15.8%) and SSW (13.05%). Low wind and prevailing wind direction with a wind speed of about 11.07% (NNE) and North direction of 10.17% wind speed from the north-east monsoon. The Wind Power Density measured at 100m of Gulf of Khambhat is highest with 431.53 watts/m^2 with annual mean wind speed of 7.51 m/s on comparing with Kayathar and Jafrabad.
3. The Wind Power Density obtained in the onshore area, the Kayathar region, a maximum of 68% share experienced during south-west monsoon which is highest compared with the Gulf of Khambhat and Jafrabad. The Gulf of Khambhat falls under the wind power Class 3 category and for Kayathar and Jafrabad belongs to wind power class 2 categories.
4. For Seasonal wind pattern analysis, the south-west and north-east monsoons influence in seasonal changes are taken. Comparing north-east monsoon periods, the south-west monsoon brings more wind power generation.

References

1. Ministry of New and Renewable Energy (MNRE). India-Paris Agreement commitments, Government of India; MNRE Annual Report 2018-19: India (2019).
2. Ministry of New and Renewable Energy (MNRE) India. Programme Scheme wise Physical Progress in 2019-20 and Cumulative up to March 2020 (2020).
3. Prabir, D. *et al.* Offshore wind energy In India. MNRE Report April 2019; MNRE website: India, (2019).
4. Global Wind Energy Council. *Global Wind Energy Report April 2019*: Brussels, Belgium (2019).
5. Tim, O. *et al.* Small Wind Site Assessment Guideline. *National Renewable Energy Laboratory (NREL) USA Technical Report: USA*, (2015).
6. Don, K.; Kyungnam Ko. Jon Huh. *et al.* Comparative Study of Different Methods for Estimating Weibull Parameters: A Case Study on Jeju Island, South Korea. *Energies* 2018, 11, 356. (2018).
7. Pobočíková I.; Sedliačková Z.; and Michalková M. *et al.* Application of four probability distributions for wind speed modeling. *Procedia Engineering* 192: 2017, 713–718. (2017).
8. Yilmaz, V.; Heçeli, K.A *et al.* Statistical approach to estimate the wind speed distribution: The case of Gelibolu region. *Doğuş Üniversitesi Dergisi* 9(1) 2008, 122–132 (2008).
9. Paula, M.; Andrés, M.; Eliana, Z.A. *et al.* Statistical analysis of wind speed distribution models in the Aburrá Valley, *Colombia. CT&F - Ciencia, Tecnología y Futuro*, Vol. 5 Num. 5 Dec. 2014, 121-136. (2014).
10. Mohamad, MA.; Youssef, K.; Hüseyin, C. *et al.* Assessment of wind energy potential as a power generation source: A case study of eight selected locations in Northern Cyprus. *Energies* 2018, 11, 2697 (2018).
11. Eugene, CM.; Matthew L.; Richard MV.; Laurie, GB. *et al.* Probability distribution for offshore wind speeds. *Energy Conversion and Management*, 2011, 15–26 (2011).
12. Emilio, GL.; María CB.; Mathieu, K.; Sergio MM. *et al.* Probability Density Function Characterization for Aggregated Large-Scale Wind Power Based on Weibull Mixtures. *Energies* 2016, 9, 91 (2016).
13. Tian, PC. *et al.* Estimation of wind energy potential using different probability density functions. *Applied Energy* 2011, 1848–1856 (2011).
14. Ravindra, K.; Srinivasa, RR.; Narasimham, SVL. *et al.* Mixture probability distribution functions to model wind speed distributions. *International Journal of Energy and Environmental Engineering* 2012, 3:27. (2012)
15. Ijjou, T.; Fatima, EG.; Hassane B. *et al.* Wind speed distribution modelling for wind power estimation: Case of Agadir in Morocco. *Wind Engineering* 2018, 1–11. (2018)

16. Jianxing Yu; Yiqin Fu; Yang Yu; Shibo Wu; Yuanda Wu. *et al.* Assessment of Offshore Wind Characteristics and Wind Energy Potential in Bohai Bay, China. *Energies* 2019, 12, 2879. (2019)

17. Mekalathur, BHK.; Saravanan, B.; Padmanaban, S.; Jens, BHN. *et al.* Wind Energy Potential Assessment by Weibull Parameter Estimation Using Multiverse Optimization Method: A Case Study of Tirumala Region in India. *Energies* 2019, 12, 2158. (2019)

18. Carla, FA.; Lindemberg FS.; Marcus, V.; Silveira, M. *et al.* Four heuristic optimization algorithms applied to wind energy: determination of Weibull curve parameters for three Brazilian sites. *International Journal of Energy and Environmental Engineering*, 2019, 1–12 (2019).

19. Kasra, M.; Omid, A.; Jon, GM. Use of Birnbaum-Saunders distribution for estimating wind speed and wind power probability distributions: A review. *Energy Conversion and Management 143* 2017, 109–122.

20. Jaramillo. OA.; Borja, MA. *et al.* Bimodal versus Weibull wind speed distributions an analysis of wind energy potential in La Venta, Mexico. *Wind Engineering* 2004, 225–234 (2004).

21. Seshaiah V.; Indhumathy D. *et al.* Analysis of Wind Speed at Sulur - A Bimodal Weibull and Weibull Distribution. *International Journal of Latest Engineering and Management Research (IJLEMR)* 2017, 29-37. (2017).

22. Feng, JL.; Hong, K.; Shyi, K.; Ying H.; Tian, C. *et al.* Study on Wind Characteristics Using Bimodal Mixture Weibull Distribution for Three Wind Sites in Taiwan. *Journal of Applied Science and Engineering* 2014, *283-292.* (2014).

22. Prem, KC.; Siraj, A.; Vilas, W. *et al.* Wind characteristics observation using Doppler-SODAR for wind energy applications. *Resource-Efficient Technologies 3* 2017, 495–505. (2017).

24. Wind Power Profile of Tamilnadu State. Indianwindpower.com web portal. http://indianwindpower.com/pdf/Wind-Power-Profile-of-Tamilnadu-State.pdf (2020).

25. Palaneeswari, T. *et al.* Wind Power Development in Tamilnadu. *International Journal of Research in Social Sciences* 2018. 1-9. (2018).

26. Wind Power Profile of Gujarat State. Indianwindpower.com web portal. Available Online: http://www.indianwindpower.com/pdf/Gujarat-State-Wind-Power-Profile.pdf. (2020).

27. Seyedali, M. *et al.* Moth-flame optimization algorithm: A novel nature-inspired heuristic paradigm. *Elsevier Knowledge-Based Systems* 2015, 228–249. (2015).

28. Diva jain. *et al.* Skew and Kurtosis: 2 important statistics terms you need to know in Data science. codeburst.io web portal. Aug 23, 2018 (2018).

29. Hajo, H.; Sebastian, V. *et al.* A likelihood ratio test for bimodality in two-component mixtures with application regional income distribution in EU. *Springer AStA* 2008, *57–69* (2008).

30. Javad, B.; Shiraz. *et al.* On the Modes of a Mixture of Two Normal Distributions. *Technometrics* 1970, 131-139. (1970).
31. Oh, K.Y.; Kim, J.Y.; Lee, J.K.; Ryu, M.S. *et al.* An assessment of wind energy potential at the demonstration offshore wind farm in Korea. *Energy* 2012, 555–563. (2012).
32. Thirumoorthy, AD. *et al.* LVRT Tamilnadu's Experience. Windpro portal (2018). http://www.windpro.org/Presentations-Forecasting-and-99+Grid-Availability/JAN-23-2018/ session/A. D. Thirumoorthy - LVRT Taminadu's Experience.pdf.
33. Amr, MA, Yasser; Mohamed, I. *et al.* Big data framework for analytics in smart grids. *Electric Power Systems Research* 2017, 369–380 (2017).
34. Kumari, C.L., Kamboj, V.K., Bath, S.K. *et al.* A boosted chimp optimizer for numerical and engineering design optimization challenges. *Engineering with Computers* (2022). https://doi.org/10.1007/s00366-021-01591-5
35. Suman Lata Tripathi , Souvik Ganguli , Abhishek Kumar, Tengiz Magradze, *Intelligent Green Technologies for Sustainable Smart Cities*, Wiley, 2022, doi: 10.1002/9781119816096 https://onlinelibrary.wiley.com/doi/book/10.1002/9781119816096
36. Arora, K., Tripathi, S.L., & Padmanaban, S. (2022). *Smart Electrical Grid System: Design Principle, Modernization, and Techniques* (1st ed.). CRC Press. https://doi.org/10.1201/9781003242277, ISBN: 9781003242277

12

IoT to Scale-Up Smart Infrastructure in Indian Cities: A New Paradigm

Indu Bala[1]*, Simarpreet Kaur[2], Lavpreet Kaur[3] and Pavan Thimmavajjala[4]

[1]SEEE, Lovely Professional University, Phagwara, Punjab, India
[2]Baba Banda Singh Bahadar Engineering College, Fatehgarh Sahib, Punjab, India
[3]Journalism and Mass Communication Department, Punjabi University,
Patiala, India
[4]Economic Policy Analyst, Nikore Associates, Hyderabad, India

Abstract

This paper presents a perspective regarding IoT, detailing its fundamentals linking it to technological evolution and further dwells on the nitty-gritty of IoT and the principles that need to be followed along with the technicalities involved. It emphasises how IoT is being implemented in a few Indian cities, as part of the drive to make Indian cities "smart" with the creation of a smart infrastructure which adds in a big way to the overall push to create a Digital India. Finally, the paper lays out the concerns that emerge from the use of such technology, in general, highlighting both the technological and financial challenges involved.

In this context, further research can be conducted at a more city-centric level to determine how individual cities are performing on the IoT front. In addition, it would be more interesting to see what business models Indian firms that are in the IoT business adopt, given the policy that has been outlined by MeITY on IoT. The importance of explainable AI-based multidisciplinary work to improve the scalability of various types of IoT services and their economic viability is discussed while reviewing the economic impact of the adoption of IoT at the city and state level using various econometric techniques.

Keywords: Internet of Things, smart city, network architecture challenges, protocols

**Corresponding author*: i.rana80@gmail.com

Suman Lata Tripathi and Mufti Mahmud (eds.) Explainable Machine Learning Models and Architectures, (227–250) © 2023 Scrivener Publishing LLC

12.1   Introduction

In today's day and age, it is necessary to embrace new technologies such as IoT, Blockchain, etc., and apply them for everyone's well-being. The world-renowned Nobel Laureate in Economics from Massachusetts Institute of Technology, Professor Robert Solow, noted in his path-breaking Solow–Swan Model, that it was technological advancements that drove economic growth. In contrast to the earlier chain of thought, this model was a mix of capital (implying heavy machinery, plants, and buildings), and labor (workers employed), that generated growth. In this background, the rapid changes that are occurring in the fields of electronics, communication, and other related aspects of engineering should be looked at from that perspective—aiding in overall progression. One can draw an analogy between such advancements from the fact that it was the invention of the wheel in ancient times, and then on to the spinning jenny, steam engines, and further on, modern locomotives and steel blast furnaces, that were developed in the Industrial Revolution in England in the 19th century, which then led to even faster technological growth in the West. The overall result was an increase in the net growth of the economy. Likewise, the development of the internet and its multidimensional applications has given birth to innovation, including the Internet of Things or IoT, which is fast becoming the new wheel of change; its impact on today's lifestyles and those of tomorrow is going to be quite phenomenal. To put things in perspective, while the internet has connected human beings living in different places through different media, it also has created a system, through which even devices can be connected in real time.

In this context, we treat IoT as having the potential to act as a catalyst for the growth of various cities, which are contributing in a major way to the growth in Gross domestic product (GDP) already. With large investments coming into our cities to make them "smarter" and more future-ready, it is imperative to apply such path-breaking technology to improve our cities and upgrade the existing physical and social infrastructure to meet the needs of changing times. In this chapter, we make a case for applying IoT in multiple sectors in different cities, as it aids in monitoring the status of existing infrastructure, and enables policymakers to track the changes over time. Such investments in new-age technology will promote growth, both directly and indirectly by first creating efficient systems and then creating a boom for domestic alternatives for IoT and reducing dependency on foreign technology [1].

In this chapter, we provide holistic coverage of IoT in Smart Cities projects. We start by discussing the fundamental components for an IoT-based

Smart City followed by the technical support that enables these domains to exist. We will also look at some of the most prevalent practices and applications in various Smart City domains—the challenges and the future scope.

12.2   Technological Progress: A Brief History

The spark of advancement was lit when man invented the wheel in the Chalcolithic Age. The wheel kept moving, and with that, the world progressed. The Industrial Revolution is a process of transformation from an agrarian and handicraft economy to an industry-dominated one. Many other changes, including socioeconomic and cultural changes, were involved in the Industrial Revolution. The first Industrial Revolution is marked by mechanization and dates back to the 1780s. This was the time when steam power was put into application and railroads started. The second Industrial Revolution was marked by mass production and electrical power as a stepping stone for technological advancements [2].

With the development of many natural and synthetic resources and with a combination of machines, this era gave rise to the automatic industry. Computers made their way after the 1960s, and advancements in technology automated the process of production. The era is marked by markets flooded with electronics. And then came the time when the need was felt for our devices to be smart! Three Industrial Revolutions later, we are now experiencing the fourth Industrial Revolution, or better called the Digital Revolution. The Internet is the wheel here, that is driving all the change. As shown in Figure 12.1, this industrial revolution has impacted every

Figure 12.1 Industrial revolution with technology.

industry, transforming the entire system of production, management, and even governance, driving the IoT adoption to full swing.

12.3   What is the Internet of Things (IoT)?

IoT has been the buzzword for quite a few years now. The idea of devices being able to communicate with each other just as efficiently as humans do with one another has paved the way for major developments in communication and related engineering fields. What exactly is IoT? The Internet of Things is a collection of devices, embedded with sensing and processing capabilities, that connect and communicate with each other over the internet. This enables seamless communication between people, processes, and things with minimal human intervention and using low-cost computing, data analytics, cloud, and advanced mobile technologies [3]. IoT can be thought of as a light bulb that can be controlled with a smartphone application or even a driverless car. Both of them are IoT and work on the same principle.

From a small LED to an airplane, it is possible to connect anything into the IoT. The sensors add an element of digital intelligence, by virtue of which, devices communicate without human intervention, leading to a smarter and more responsive environment around us. We are already investing in smart cities projects and sensors are deployed everywhere to help us understand and control the environment.

How big is IoT? Well, the network is getting bigger and bigger every day. IoT applications are everywhere—security cameras and devices, automotive, and healthcare (especially for monitoring of chronic diseases) are the fastest-growing sectors for IoT. Smart City projects are the key feature of IoT, generating large amounts of data with big infrastructure (including traffic lights, toll plazas, etc.) already in place. Sensors spread across the entire region produce large amounts of data that make use of cloud and big data analytics to add further intelligence to the system [4].

12.4   Economic Effects of Internet of Things

In [5] the authors note that the economic value of IoT is a continuous process and it is not merely a technology but connects various interdependent systems which are continuously evolving. An analogy can be drawn about the weather and agriculture and the overall setup wherein weather becomes the basis for the sustenance of agriculture and the farmer's profit and livelihood. The difference, however, lies in the scale and intensity of IoT's applications; the base being networking and use of AI along with data collected in real time. The emergence of IoT creates a multidimensional impact that translates into primarily three effects: Technological, economic, and social, in that order. The emergence of the market for IoT and IoT-based products in India as noted in [6] shows that the potential is very high. IoT in a sense can be called the catalyst that drives the discovery of oil (i.e., data). The markets still seem to be in an early phase of development but with start-ups focusing on IoT-based solutions to small problems such as checking levels of water as well as pollution in lakes and setting up a lake grid to aid in monitoring their toxicity. Therefore the technological aspect generates supply effects to meet rising demand in the society for such technology. To use economics jargon, we can say it follows Say's Law (which states that supply for a good finds its demand under certain assumptions). The market for IoT appears to be monopolistic (at the moment) with a varying degree of differentiated products (solutions) proposed or put forth by various IT companies and other tech firms.

While the net effect of IoT is positive on the economic front, many other effects need to be pointed out in this chapter. In terms of technology, there would be delays in implementation and constant maintenance of IoT infrastructure and this would raise a company's cost element. Furthermore, on the economic front, while things might seem hunky-dory with the adoption of IoT, there is a very good chance of the value of IoT-related products fluctuating in a big way due to the customization of such a technology. As argued by [5] it might even result in a digital divide with the fairly well off being able to utilize IoT for homes while others would miss out due to the costs involved in accessing such technology. But that said, the social consequences can be very hard to predict. Further on the economic front is the viability of switching to IoT; not every company would find a need to use the technology. In addition to this, the issue of financial prospects of companies engaged in developing such technology comes into the picture. The authors in [5] opine that IoT is hampered by a lack of compelling and sustainably profitable business models. Thus at this stage, we can only presume what the effects are going to be. It would take time to estimate the direct and indirect impacts, as modeling IoT business models or modeling the economic impact (which is subjective and goes sector-wise) becomes a tricky process due to many shortcomings which are beyond the scope of this chapter, given their technical nature.

12.5   Infrastructure and Smart Infrastructure: The Difference

Infrastructure, in general, refers to a physical framework such as airports, seaports, rail lines, roads, power, machinery and equipment, land, education and healthcare facilities, financial safety nets, and the organizational wherewithal at both the government and private industry level needed for a state to function efficiently. At the macro level, there is a clear distinction regarding the types of infrastructure:

1. Economic Infrastructure
2. Social Infrastructure

In the event of the Coronavirus disease (COVID-19) pandemic, many economists have for instance been advocating spending more on infrastructure to increase growth. The question that follows is, growth of what? Economic infrastructure at the outset is encapsulated by the broad umbrella of construction of buildings, colonies, retail chains, commercial markets for goods and services used on a day-to-day basis, railway networks, road networks—highways, outer ring roads, peripheral roads—waterways, and sea and airports along with the availability of internet and adequate power supply (which in turn requires a mix of power plants and renewable power sources). In a sense, economic infrastructure provides the necessary tools to boost growth. More often than not, cities are where economic infrastructure gets concentrated which then generates a process of urbanization and brings about changes in the occupational structure of the economy. Today, cities act as a nerve center for economic as well as financial infrastructure with manufacturing hubs related to each sector located around major cities as seen in the case of Mumbai, Hyderabad, Pune, Chennai, Delhi NCR, Chandigarh, and Bangalore. Building economic infrastructure is impossible without building the necessary technological infrastructure, and this is where IoT is playing a key role in terms of improving staffing, and it is expected to play an even bigger role in the future [7].

Likewise, when it comes to social infrastructure, it primarily refers to the broad elements that drive social change. Under this umbrella, social overheads such as schools, colleges, and research institutes along with the provision of healthcare, parks, green spaces, etc., can be considered. Therefore the broad network of educational institutions, the healthcare sector along with healthcare facilities (dealing with wide-ranging health ailments and providing the best care possible) come under the gamut of social infrastructure. Access to affordable and timely healthcare and quality education become important determinants of the quality of social infrastructure. Technology is equally important here as it not only streamlines the methods involved (be it teaching or improving health care and treatment) but also adds to the efficiency factor. It shows learning can be imparted more effectively while surgeries are done with much more precision causing minimum harm to the patients while enabling schools, colleges, and hospitals to monitor progress in various areas. IoT's applications in the health sector are already underway in various forms, be it for physicians to keep track of patients' health parameters or for hospitals to keep track of the status of medical equipment and status of patients in different rooms along with other essential requirements [8].

12.5.1   What is Smart Infrastructure?

Now that we have an understanding of the distinction between social and economic infrastructure, it is essential to know what smart infrastructure can consist of. Smart infrastructure leverages technological advancements and applies them to critical areas to boost the existing infrastructure. A smart system uses a data feedback mechanism to give evidence for making intelligent decisions. Based on data collected from sensors, the system may monitor, measure, evaluate, communicate, and act. To improve performance, smart infrastructure responds intelligently to changes in its surroundings as per user demands and other infrastructure [7]. Smart Infrastructure is the consequence of merging physical and digital infrastructure to provide adequate data for faster and less expensive decision-making. Smart infrastructure can revolutionize the efficient use of available infrastructure as well as a construction project, presenting a £4.8 trillion challenge and opportunity [8]. We can therefore say, smart infrastructure provides a medium for the entire infrastructural set up to be dynamic rather than static and respond to changes that occur in the system and thus connects the physical (both social and economic) to the digital world. A key outcome of this amalgamation is thus generation of real-time data for various purposes. We would now be able to identify which part of the city has more traffic than others and manage the congestion problem accordingly. In addition, this would tell us about the frequency of the metro rail or the number of passengers using it in real time.

Using IoT, the organizations involved would be able to generate big data for further analysis and better performance of operations. Airports, for instance, would now be able to better predict at what time the number of flights taking off and landing would be the highest (peak time of operations) and plan out the flight schedules better with airlines that serve the airports concerned. A mix of sensors, IoT applications, and networks along with GIS and GPS technology help generate big data and positively drive outcomes. Therefore, while it creates a complex network involving many agencies and parties, it enables smooth functioning and better synergy within and between organizations. When this is looked at from the perspective of Indian cities, we can say that we are embracing the change and using technology in a big way [9].

12.5.2   What are the Principles of Smart Infrastructure?

Smart infrastructure and systems would have to be versatile to changing requirements and environments, along with evolving technologies. This necessitates the development of a smart infrastructure framework, which will make its use more convenient [10].

It is necessary to adapt the broad framework as shown below to enable policymakers, engineers, and industry experts alike to know what is required. Data captured through IoT sensors and other device devices when analyzed provide the technical experts and data analysts a perspective of the scheme of things and progress. This would provide an interface for the system to interact with the infrastructure and minimize human errors and on the other hand improve human judgment of the parameters and improve the decision-making process. However, for that to happen, there needs to be constant feedback related to the decision-makers. As a result, current feedback mechanisms assist in ushering in sophistication, which is characterized as gathering data on how an asset is used and using that data to improve how well that system performs. Any smart system's data feedback loop is crucial (refer to Figure 12.2).

Feedback backed by data on the ground would promote adaptability of the system to changes within and outside in a big way and this can be enunciated with an example. Assume we have a metro rail system in a city; supposing due to unforeseen extrinsic shocks such as rise in petrol prices overnight, the service sees a much higher ridership than usual. IoT systems can help relay this to the main server which could then allow the system to explore the option of increasing frequency of the trains over a certain period to meet the increased demand for the specific mode of transport. IoT along with recorded historic trends thus could apply to local transit options and help ply more services as and when required. Likewise, it can, as has already been demonstrated by a few companies such as Staqo, help track bicycles that are provided for citizens' use by embedding sensors and

Figure 12.2 Futuristic smart infrastructure.

location devices so that the provider can keep track of the fleet of cycles that have been released.

12.5.3   Components of IoT-Based Smart City Project

As shown in Figure 12.3, the Internet of Things (IoT) is at the heart of Smart City initiatives, since it is the enabling technology that has fostered pervasive digitization by allowing devices linked to the internet to transfer data to the cloud and make decisions. Smart infrastructure is actively deployed in a Smart City, allowing processes to run without the need for human intervention. A Smart City has several components, including smart infrastructure, smart transportation, smart health, smart city services, smart housing, and so on [1]. Most of these applications have four aspects associated with the data collection: data transmission/reception, data storage, and data analysis for the final feedback. The development of sensors has been driven by the need to collect data in real time. Moreover, data collection is application-based, boosting the development of sensor technologies in specific fields. For data transmission from data collection units to the cloud for storage and analysis, several technologies such as city-wide Wi-Fi networks, 4G and 5G technologies are used. What is the location of the data? Data is saved in the cloud using various storage strategies to provide management it. Data analysis is the process of extracting patterns and inferences from obtained data to assist decision-making. It can be done using simple decision-making or statistical methods. For accurate

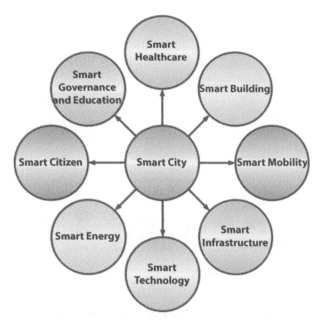

Figure 12.3 Components of smart city.

and efficient decision-making, we can also employ real-time machine and Deep Learning algorithms.

12.6   Architecture for Smart Cities

With the help of a generic five-layered structure, the IoT unifies various processes such as data sensing, collection, transmission/reception, storage, and processing. Each layer functions on the information from the preceding layer. The Sensing layer, also known as the Perception layer, is the first. This layer's primary function is to detect the external world, which it accomplishes through the use of sensors that may collect data on physical quantities of interest in any application [11]. It also contains actuators that may act on tangible objects, such as RFID scanners for scanning RFID tags. The data acquired by the sensing layer (through sensing) is then sent on to the Middleware layer using wireless network technologies such as Wi-Fi, cellular internet, Zigbee, and Bluetooth, among others, in the networking layer [12]. As the name implies, the Middleware layer primarily serves as a generic interface between the sensing layer hardware and the Application layer [13–15]. The acquired data is used in the application layer to provide customers with services via various APIs and database management services. It is the relationship between what the sensor collects and what we perceive as users (the decision). The Business layer is connected to the application layer and is responsible for defining plans and policies that aid in the administration of the entire system.

12.6.1   Networking Technologies

The functioning of the Internet of Things in a Smart City has mostly relied on the integration of information acquired by individual sensing devices strategically deployed across the smart city. The "smart" in the future city structure is defined by the collaborative use of data from these individual sensing units to make complicated decisions and provide seamless services to inhabitants [16]. Even in circumstances where devices are mobile, wireless technologies must be employed as physical links to enable the collective use of data from these devices to communicate data [17].

The internet allows mobile technology such as computers, smartphones, and other electronic devices all over the world to interface with one another, allowing for instant information transfer [18]. However, with IoT, the internet may not be the only communication channel; instead, an application may consist of a local network of sensing units that can exchange data and send data to a central node through a multi-hop communication protocol (or a hub or a gateway).

12.6.2   Network Topologies

In Smart City initiatives, three basic IoT network topologies are widely employed. These include point to point, star, and mesh topologies, as well as other non-IoT topologies like trees. Devices are connected in a point-to-point way in a point-to-point topology. If two nodes desire to share data, the data must hop and pass via each node in the network between them. This topology isn't the best choice because it has a low fault resilience rating, and packet delivery suffers when any of the intermediate nodes fail. However, under a Star architecture, data is exchanged to a central node rather than each node transmitting data to the cloud independently. The Mesh network topology enables all devices to communicate with one another. It has a wider range since data sent to a specific node might travel numerous hops over the network. This improves the packet delivery as alternate paths can be used in case of a faulty network.

12.6.3   Network Architectures

The structure of the network deployed for a particular application is known as network architecture. As mentioned in previous sections, IoT devices do not always need to be linked to the internet; instead, distributed connection architectures can be used, with only one device collecting and sending data to the cloud. In such instances, the arrangement of the devices is crucial. The three major types of network architectures deployed for IoT-based smart cities are as follows.

12.6.3.1   Home Area Networks (HANs)

These are short-range networks that often entail data transfer to a single central node that collects and sends data to the cloud. These networks use low-power communication protocols including Zigbee, Bluetooth, and Wi-Fi.

12.6.3.2   Field/Neighborhood Area Networks (FANs/NANs)

Field Area Networks (FANs) have a longer communication range than HANs and are used to connect a consumer to a utility provider (for example, in a smart grid).

12.6.3.3   Wide Area Networks (WANs)

Wide Area Networks (WANs) are network topologies that allow people to communicate across great distances. These networks are not as dense as HANs or FANs, and they rely on cellular services, physical connections like fiber optics, and a set of low-power protocols developed specifically for WANs. WANs are used in a variety of Smart City applications, including Smart Grids because they connect various substations.

12.6.3.4   Network Protocols

The application determines the network type, and the communication protocol employed in a smart city application must provide the desired Quality of services (QoS). Different networking protocols in the IoT can be used in a variety of applications, depending on their characteristics.

All parts of our lives are being digitized thanks to the Internet of Things. This digitization process is linked to the addition of enhanced sensing nodes in every domain of smart infrastructure in smart cities. Not only that, but because the application scope is so extensive, IoT system designers confront huge obstacles in designing and deploying smart city projects, which we shall examine in more detail in the following sections.

12.7   IoT Technology in India's Smart Cities: The Current Scenario

As noted earlier in the chapter, it was found that the IoT environment is very much active in Indian cities and towns, and cities like Kohima in Nagaland have already started developing expertise in applying IoT to various civic issues. Likewise, other cities have experimented with IoT to solve their respective issues in their manner. This section shall provide detailed information on the same.

At the outset, it is essential to state that from the government side, there has been a determined push to create 100 smart cities (from 2015) with an investment of up to Rs. 70 billion and the objective of creating them [19–23].

One of the important characteristics is the use of smart solutions to improve infrastructure and services in area-based development [20]. In addition, the Government of India's Ministry of Electronics and Information Technology (MEiTY) has released an IoT Policy Document (2016) that details the government's perspective on this new era of technology. It states that the key to the Internet of Things' success will be the creation of open platforms for simplicity of use and low cost, the development of scalable models, and the utilization of citizens as sensors. It was predicted that by 2020, India would have a USD 15 billion IoT market, accounting for at least a 6% share of the worldwide IoT sector (IoT Policy Document, Government of India, 2016). Key areas that the policy noted for IoT's applications were Smart water, smart environment, remote health monitoring, smart agriculture, smart waste management, smart safety, and smart supply chain and logistics are just a few examples of smart technologies. As is evident, it misses out on smart transport using IoT for which examples have been mentioned earlier in this paper. However, the policy goes on to illustrate all the right intentions from the government with plans to focus on R&D and capacity building with a five-pillar approach. Such an approach to changing the technological landscape is a welcome change.

Against this backdrop, with an IoT policy in place, we look at the progress made in a few cities in India and the technology that has been utilized. Cities like Dahod and Rajkot in Gujarat, Pimpri Chinchwad near Pune, and Kohima in Nagaland have taken up IoT to improve their civic infra-structure by going in for IoT-based smart street lighting which uses a sen-sor to light up the streets each time a car or a person passes by while saving power. A homegrown Indian company named iRAM Technologies was awarded the contract to undertake the series of projects mentioned above. iRAM, a homegrown product development and technology company with the most advanced solutions has secured four large, and for some major cit-ies, much-needed projects based on the IoT, which describes the network of physical objects embedded with sensors, software, and other technolo-gies for exchanging data with other devices and systems over the internet. Due to their geographical, socioeconomic, and anatomical characteristics, Dahod (Gujarat), Kohima (Nagaland), Pimpri Chinchwad (Maharashtra), and Rajkot (Gujarat) have Smart Street Lighting and Smart Parking city assets. Leading corporations and system integrators will work with iRAM to complete these projects.

The Smart Parking technology that will be installed by iRAM based on their IoT, includes Smart Occupancy Sensors, Gateways & Repeaters, Parking Management & Guidance Software, Mobile Point of Sale Solution, Citizen Mobile Application & Portals, Sensor Wireless Network (SSWN) In the cities of Pimpri Chinchwad and Rajkot, boom barriers to obstruct the route of oncoming automobiles, parking information displays, and other essentials are required. The cities of Kohima and Dahod shall be graced up with Smart Poles which can be a home to multiple utilities like Street Lighting and Environment Monitoring to examine an environment, evaluate its quality, and develop environmental characteristics to correctly assess the influence of a certain action on the environment. Information Displays and PA System Cameras will cover much larger areas and also can be used in emergencies to address and alert large groups of people over a large area. Panic Alarm Buttons—to be used in any unwanted but panic situation—and Telecom Antennas, among other things have all been developed locally. If we focus on the additional parts of the project, the lat-est Smart Street Lighting Technology will also be implemented in Kohima. When a car or a pedestrian crosses the area, the Intelligent Motion Sensor Street Lighting Control System activates automatically. If there is no activ-ity in the system-defined area, the light will be automatically adjusted to an optimal minimum level. Such a project will be especially beneficial in cities where there is a significant problem with the lack of or poor maintenance of street lighting systems. Even in the most remote sections of Kohima, a solid IT backbone comprised of the Small Sensor Wireless Network (SSWN) and the Central Street Light Management Network will moni-tor and send updates. In addition, the Smart City of Bhubaneswar and its

MSI Partner Honeywell have placed a repeat order with iRAM to automate multi-level car parking facilities there. Elante Mall in Chandigarh and Green Park Metro station in Delhi both have such a feature.

With these recurrent purchases from its customers, iRAM Technologies is gaining confidence in its ability to innovate further. They are erecting a new success fortress and effectively advertising their motto, "Making Urban Living Convenient." This also verifies their product development, engineering, project management, and solution delivery methodology. Dahod and Kohima will install smart poles, which can house numerous entities such as street lights and air quality monitoring equipment, as well as cameras and a panic alarm button system that can alert nearby police stations or hospitals in the event of an emergency. The motion sensor-based street lighting system that both cities are implementing would add to the already in place solar street lighting system in other cities in that it would switch on the lights upon sensing movement of pedestrians or vehicles and turn off when a certain time frame ends. Such initiatives can not only save power but avoid a central switch to turn them on each time. Environment quality monitoring would include air quality in the vicinity along with temperature sensors which can help the local administration relay alerts to the denizens of the locality in times of extreme temperatures. Also, with cameras in place, it can help transmit ground-level situation information in the event of rains.

Pimpri-Chinchwad (PCMC) in Pune and Rajkot in Gujarat on the other hand have taken the initiative to introduce a smart parking technology developed by iRAM. It uses Smart Sensor Wireless Network which can help better manage parking zones and avoid congestion, particularly near malls and other major places of congregation in both cities. In addition, they are inducting parking management and guidance software which uses IoT to upgrade the road transport departments in the city. As it stands, PCMC has also made progress in using IoT-based solutions to solve water wastage under its corporate limits. [24] has noted this in a recent article where it was observed that while the population had gone up, the water consumption under the corporation limits was controlled and wastage reduced by applying smart meters. These meters could be geo tagged to identify authorised as well as unauthorised users of the corporation's water supply and bill them accordingly while preventing waste of water. Hyderabad, which is a major economic hub and also the capital of Telangana, has also started applying IoT albeit at a smaller scale at its international airport. It has done so by deploying an IoT-based baggage trolley system which uses long-range platform technology, to not just track the number of trolleys in use around the airport but to help passengers find an adequate number of trolleys while at departures or arrivals.

This can be further replicated at the corporation level in various ways. One such can be the tracking of garbage trucks and in addition, regular monitoring of garbage yards in colonies so that the waste management system does not fail at any stage. This can be done by putting in smart geo tags for trucks to see how many are out on duty and how many are not; likewise we can know if garbage has been collected from a particular yard or not on that particular day. In addition, such a geo tagging technology, if combined with the smart metering system, can help track pollution levels in lakes in real time along with the water levels during monsoons and alert authorities much before a crisis occurs.

Apart from lakes, it can also include STPs, to reflect how much water is entering the plants to get treated and released for fresh use, and how polluted it is, based on the heat levels and other chemical parameters. This would go a long way in helping authorities involved in water body management to understand the changing water quality and address issues of polluted water mixing with potable water for daily use. Yet another application of IoT-based systems to solve city-level problems includes monitoring the road traffic density and reducing traffic congestion. GoogleMaps already helps track such trends and this can further be replicated in smaller cities. In this manner, a zone-wise waste management grid and similarly, a city grid for lakes and water bodies, can be created to monitor the quality as well as quantity of water present. Such widespread applications will have multiple effects with direct ones being an improvement in efficiency and indirect ones being city-based startups and firms can pitch in further, making it a win-win for the authorities and the citizens as a whole. This would require adequate smart infrastructure to be put in place with control rooms and power supply; private participation has to be encouraged to better address such issues. It also remains to be seen how much of the Rs. 7060 Crore that has been set aside for Smart Cities Mission would be utilized city-wise to develop IoT-based solutions in the coming months and years. Investment in new technology always yields positive benefits for which there should be a proper delegation of powers along with reskilling the workforce responsible for handling it. This brings us to the next section where we highlight the challenges that emerge while implementing IoT-based projects.

12.8   Challenges in IoT-Based Smart City Projects

Broadly, the challenges can be divided into two sections: *Technological* (with respect to security of the systems and privacy) and *Financial-Economic* (with respect to Investment and IoT-based business models).

12.8.1   Technological Challenges

12.8.1.1   Privacy and Security

In a world where data is constantly increasing, security and privacy are major concerns in every development. Since IoT involves having essential city infrastructure on the internet, in smart cities, security, along with privacy, is a major concern. Any hiccup in the city's services can irritate its residents and put human lives and property in jeopardy. In the modern world of the digital revolution, cybercrime is the new tactic in world politics. This somehow makes smart cities vulnerable to malicious attacks. So, data encryption is a must for the transmission and reception process in the IoT network. There could be instances of people's data being used in unwanted ways especially when there is the proliferation of sensor technologies. The participation and cooperation of citizens are crucial in this regard, and solutions will necessitate processes that collect data as per the measured task while ensuring private information confidentially [21].

12.8.1.2   Smart Sensors and Infrastructure Essentials

Smart sensors are the most essential part of the IoT network. These devices are manufactured by a host of vendors, differentiated by sensing abilities, sensing mechanisms, connectivity protocols, data formats, and measurement standards. Any smart city project will be a success if these smart sensors exchange data, allow and perform scheduling of tasks, and aggregate data for final decision-making. The use of open protocols and data formats is one of the solutions to enable communication between all these devices. The use of "standard" access point nodes for IoT systems is another solution (not readily available, however), whereby devices can communicate using several different communication protocols. Some manufacturers have made their products compatible with specific network protocols [22].

12.8.1.3   Networking in IoT Systems

The concept of the network layer is to put the sensed data into action. The quality of service and output in IoT largely depends on the capability of sensing, the transmission and reception abilities of other devices, and the cloud. A huge challenge for us now is to provide networking to these devices to enable constant communication between them. Current networking technologies and routing protocols are inadequate for providing networking services to smart city components. Providing efficient and dynamic routing protocols that can suit IoT requirements and function with both stationary and mobile devices is one answer to this problem (having mobility and throughput requirements that need to be met for acceptable quality of service) [23–27].

12.8.1.4   Big Data Analytics

IoT-connected devices generate massive volumes of data, which is predicted to continue to grow year after year. To make use of this data and continuously improve the services provided in smart cities, the most up-to-date and powerful big data analytics techniques are required. The development of scalable algorithms (so that they may be utilized across a wide range of applications) should take into account the fact that they can work with both structured and unstructured data. New data fusion techniques must also be developed to combine them in meaningful ways and extract inferences and patterns. Deep learning is one of the disciplines that has piqued academics' interest since it can make use of enormous volumes of data to get better results for many applications [25].

12.8.2   Financial - Economic Challenges

As highlighted earlier in this chapter, the attempt to estimate or model IoT's economic value is still at a nascent stage. In addition to that, the economic and financial viability of business models of organizations involved in IoT is evolving and naturally so. Some organizations follow data-driven business models (such as Fitbit Wearables) which while providing helpful data for users, monetize on the same data for the wellness industry, etc. Some others apply the outcome-based business model. This is seen in the bike and bicycle rentals business which enables geotagging of the vehicles. As a consequence, there is no single successful business model at work; rather a combination of approaches needs to be figured out before a firm invests in IoT. On the other hand, the economic viability of using such a technology is subject to the needs of the clients [26–32].

Therefore for firms that are transitioning into the IoT business, the cost of switching will be naturally high due to the size of the investments that are to be made. This implies that the business model the firm decides to opt for makes a lot of difference in its profit function. Given the flexibility involved in the application of IoT, sector-specific, tailor-made IoT solutions are relatively easier to finance and later, sell, rather than a broad umbrella of IoT services. Small is indeed beautiful in the case of IoT business, to borrow the title of E. F. Schumacher's popular book. The other challenge that arises is connecting with the stakeholders involved. The money that is put into developing and further selling IoT products can take time to return (return on investment) but is high. This calls for patience from the business side. Therefore scalability of products must be factored into the business. For firms involved in the purchase of IoT products, while the cost is no doubt high, the priority should be to look at the long-term prospects of higher revenues due to smarter management of operations [32–35].

To conclude, the repeated security concerns of using IoT as enunciated in the previous subsection would result in a secondary investment to be made to strengthen the security apparatus of IoT to prevent hacking or otherwise to prevent malfunctioning of the sensors and other connected devices. This would raise the cost of IoT components for companies. Thus, a foray into the world of IoT presents a million opportunities to help our cities become better while also presenting an equal number of challenges with respect to the business models, the viability of technology at a large and small scale, in addition to aspects of security and database safety.

12.9   Role of Explainable AI

Artificial Intelligence (AI) is one of the disruptive technologies that has a potential to change urban living. Tremendous data-driven decision applications for a smart city such as smart transportation, online education, e-healthcare, smart grid, and public governance, etc., can use AI to reduce cyber vulnerabilities such as threats, attacks, damages, or unauthorized access. To do so, smart cities require smart, which is a combination of SHM and AI algorithms. However, the black-box nature of these algorithms hinders the exploitation of full potential of AI in these smart city practice. XAI is supposed to enhance the transparency, thus the confidence in these algorithms.

12.10   Conclusion and Future Scope

This paper has presented a perspective regarding IoT detailing its fundamentals linking it to technological evolution and further dwells on the nitty-gritty of IoT and the principles that need to be followed along with the technicalities involved. It later looked at how IoT is being implemented in a few Indian cities, as part of the drive to make Indian cities "smart" with the creation of a smart infrastructure which adds in a big way to the overall push to create a Digital India. Finally the paper lays out the concerns that emerge from the use of such technology, in general, highlighting both the technological and financial challenges involved.

In this context, further research can be conducted at a more city-centric level to determine how individual cities are performing on the IoT front. In addition, it would be more interesting to see what business models Indian firms that are in the IoT business adopt. Also, given the policy that has been outlined by MeITY on IoT, it would also be interesting to explore how the public sector is exploring IoT in its various units. More multidisciplinary work can be done exploring the scalability of various types of IoT services and their economic viability along with studying the economic impact of the adoption of IoT at the city and state level using various econometric techniques.

References

1. Indu Bala, Ghanshyam Singh, "Green Communication for Cognitive Cities", In: Ahuja K., Khosla A. (eds.) *Driving the Development, Management, and Sustainability of Cognitive Cities*, IGI Global USA. DOI: 10.4018/978-1-5225-8085-0.
2. T. Sauter, S. Soucek, W. Kastner and D. Dietrich, "The evolution of factory and building automation", *IEEE Ind. Electron. Mag.*, vol. 5, no. 3, pp. 35–48, Mar. 2011.
3. M. Wollschlaeger, T. Sauter and J. Jasperneite, "The Future of Industrial Communication: Automation Networks in the Era of the Internet of Things and Industry 4.0," in *IEEE Industrial Electronics Magazine*, vol. 11, no. 1, pp. 17–27, March 2017, doi: 10.1109/MIE.2017.2649104.
4. K. Chopra, K. Gupta and A. Lambora, "Future Internet: The Internet of Things-A Literature Review," *2019 International Conference on Machine Learning, Big Data, Cloud and Parallel Computing (COMITCon)*, 2019, pp. 135–139, doi: 10.1109/COMITCon.2019.8862269.
5. Nicolescu, R., Huth, M., Radanliev, P., and De Roure, D. (2018b). State of The Art in IoT - Beyond Economic Value. Retrieved from https://iotuk.

org.uk/wp-content/uploads/2018/08/State-of-the-Art-in-IoT---Beyond-EconomicValue2.pdf

6. Pratima Harigunani (2021), https://www.computerweekly.com/feature/India-isbecoming-a-hotspot-for-IoT. March 2021.

7. K. Ota, T. Kumrai, M. Dong, J. Kishigami and M. Guo, "Smart Infrastructure Design for Smart Cities," in *IT Professional*, vol. 19, no. 5, pp. 42–49, 2017, doi: 10.1109/MITP.2017.3680957.

8. S. B. Baker, W. Xiang and I. Atkinson, "Internet of Things for Smart Healthcare: Technologies, Challenges, and Opportunities," in *IEEE Access*, vol. 5, pp. 26521–26544, 2017, doi: 10.1109/ACCESS.2017.2775180.

9. N. M. Kumar, S. Goel and P. K. Mallick, "Smart cities in India: Features, policies, current status, and challenges," *2018 Technologies for Smart-City Energy Security and Power (ICSESP)*, 2018, pp. 1–4, doi: 10.1109/ICSESP.2018.8376669.

10. D. Prochazkova and J. Prochazka, "Smart cities and critical infrastructure," *2018 Smart City Symposium Prague (SCSP)*, 2018, pp. 1–6, doi: 10.1109/SCSP.2018.8402676.

11. Basmi, W., Boulmakoul, A., Karim, L. *et al*. Distributed and scalable platform architecture for smart cities complex events data collection: Covid19 pandemic use case. *J Ambient Intell Human Comput* 12, 75–83 (2021). https://doi.org/10.1007/s12652-020-02852-9

12. Wlodarczak P. (2017) Smart Cities – Enabling Technologies for Future Living. In: Karakitsiou A., Migdalas A., Rassia S., Pardalos P. (eds.) *City Networks. Springer Optimization and Its Applications*, vol. 128. Springer, Cham. https://doi.org/10.1007/978-3-319-65338-9_1

13. Indu Bala, Manjit Singh Bhamrah and Ghanshyam Singh, "Capacity in fading environment based on soft sensing information under spectrum sharing constraints", *Wireless Networks*, vol. 23, no. 2, pp. 519–531, 2017.

14. Vanita Rana, Neelu Jain and Indu Bala, "Resource Allocation Models for cognitive Radio Networks: A Study", *International Journal of Computer Applications*, vol. 91, no.12, pp. 51–55, April 2014.

15. Indu Bala, Kiran Ahuja, "Energy efficient framework for throughput enhancement of cognitive radio network", *International Journal of Communication Systems*, vol. 34, no. 13, 2021.

16. Indu Bala, Manjit Singh Bhamrah and Ghanshyam Singh, "Rate and Power Optimization under Received-Power Constraints for opportunistic Spectrum-Sharing Communication", *Wireless Personal Communications*, vol. 96, no. 4, pp. 5667–5685, 2017.

17. Indu Bala, Manjit Singh Bhamrah and Ghanshyam Singh, "Investigation on Outage Capacity of Spectrum Sharing System using CSI and SSI under Received Power Constraint", *Wireless Networks*, vol. 25, no. 3, pp. 1047–1056, 2019.

18. Indu Bala, Kiran Ahuja, "Energy-efficient framework for throughput enhancement of cognitive radio network by exploiting transmission mode diversity", https://doi.org/10.1007/s12652-021-03428-x, 2021.

19. Indu Bala, Vanita Rana, "Performance analysis of SAC based non-coherent optical CDMA system for OOC with variable data rates under noisy environment", *International Indian Journal of Science and Technology*, vol. 2, no. 8, pp. 49–52, 2009.

20. Laxman Verma, P.S. Mundra and Indu Bala, "Major technical concerns in the practical realization of FO-OCDMA networks", *International Journal of Computer Science & Engineering Technology*, vol. 5, no. 02, Feb. 2014.

21. L. Cui, G. Xie, Y. Qu, L. Gao and Y. Yang, "Security and Privacy in Smart Cities: Challenges and Opportunities," in *IEEE Access*, vol. 6, pp. 46134–46145, 2018, doi: 10.1109/ACCESS.2018.2853985.

22. S. P. Mohanty, H. Thapliyal and R. Bajpai, "Consumer Technologies for Smart Cities to Smart Villages," 2021 *IEEE International Conference on Consumer Electronics (ICCE)*, 2021, pp. 1-1, doi: 10.1109/ICCE50685.2021.9427601.

23. Rubeena Sethi and Indu Bala, "Performance Evaluation of Energy Detector for Cognitive Radio Network, *IOSR Journal of Electronics and Communication Engineering*, vol. 8, no. 5, pp. 46–51, Dec. 2013.

24. Pahuja, R. *Here's how Pune's PCMC is saving 31,000 million litres of water using data and analytics* - ET CIO, 2021.

25. Rubeena Sethi and Indu Bala, "Throughput Enhancement of Cognitive Radio Networks Through Improved Frame Structure", *International Journal of Computer Applications*, vol. 109, no. 14, Jan. 2015.

26. C. F. O. C. Neves, U. F. Moreno and A. Boava, "IoT-Based Distributed Networked Control Systems Architecture," *2018 IEEE 23rd International Conference on Emerging Technologies and Factory Automation (ETFA)*, 2018, pp. 991–998, doi: 10.1109/ETFA.2018.8502500.

27. Kiran Ahuja and Indu Bala, "COVID-19: Creating a Paradigm Shift in Indian Education System", *Emerging Technologies for Battling Covid-19*, Springer, ISBN 978-3-030-60038-9, 2021.

28. Indu Bala, "Fading Channel Capacity of Cognitive Radio Networks", Ch. 16, *Electronic Devices and Circuit Design Challenges and Applications in the Internet of Things*, CRC Press, Taylor & Francis, June 2021, ISBN: 978177188993.

29. B. N. Silva *et al.*, "Exploiting Big Data Analytics for Urban Planning and Smart City Performance Improvement," *2018 12th International Conference on Signal Processing and Communication Systems (ICSPCS)*, 2018, pp. 1–4, doi: 10.1109/ICSPCS.2018.8631726.

30. I. Santos, A. C. B. Nobre, J. C. Ibiapina, P. R. M. Oliveira, Z. V. nia de Carvalho and Á. D. de Oliveira, "Strategies and Methodologies for Civic Engagement and Social Empowerment," *2017 IEEE First Summer School on Smart Cities (S3C)*, 2017, pp. 157–160, doi: 10.1109/S3C.2017.8501396.

31. Ahuja K., Bala I. (2021) Role of Artificial Intelligence and IoT in Next Generation Education System. In: Al-Turjman F., Nayyar A., Devi A., Shukla

P.K. (eds.) *Intelligence of Things: AI-IoT Based Critical-Applications and Innovations.* Springer, Cham. https://doi.org/10.1007/978-3-030-82800-4_8

32. M. Boban and M. Weber, "Internet of Things, legal and regulatory framework in digital transformation from smart to intelligent cities," *2018 41st International Convention on Information and Communication Technology, Electronics and Microelectronics (MIPRO)*, 2018, pp. 1359–1364, doi: 10.23919/MIPRO.2018.8400245.

33. Lata Tripathi, S., and Dwivedi, S. (Eds.). (2022). *Electronic Devices and Circuit Design: Challenges and Applications in the Internet of Things* (1st ed.). Apple Academic Press. https://doi.org/10.1201/9781003145776. ISBN: 9781771889933

34. Sharma, K., Gupta, A., Sharma, B., and Tripathi, S.L. (Eds.). (2021). *Intelligent Communication and Automation Systems* (1st ed.). CRC Press, ISBN: 9781003104599 https://doi.org/10.1201/9781003104599.

35. Thillaiarasu, N., Lata Tripathi, S., and Dhinakaran, V. (Eds.). (2022). *Artificial Intelligence for Internet of Things: Design Principle, Modernization, and Techniques* (1st ed.). CRC Press. https://doi.org/10.1201/9781003335801

Index

Also of Interest

By the same editors

MACHINE LEARNING TECHNIQUES FOR VLSI CHIP DESIGN, Edited by Abhishek Kumar, Suman Lata Tripathi, and K. Srinivasa Rao, ISBN: 9781119910398. This cutting-edge new volume covers the hardware architecture implementation, the software implementation approach, and the efficient hardware of machine learning applications with FPGA or CMOS circuits, and many other aspects and applications of machine learning techniques for VLSI chip design.

INTELLIGENT GREEN TECHNOLOGIES FOR SMART CITIES, Edited by Suman Lata Tripathi, Souvik Ganguli, Abhishek Kumar, and Tengiz Magradze, ISBN: 9781119816065. Presenting the concepts and fundamentals of smart cities and developing "green" technologies, this volume, written and edited by a global team of experts, also goes into the practical applications that can be utilized across multiple disciplines and industries, for both the engineer and the student.

DESIGN AND DEVELOPMENT OF EFFICIENT ENERGY SYSTEMS, edited by Suman Lata Tripathi, Dushyant Kumar Singh, Sanjeevikumar Padmanaban, and P. Raja, ISBN 9781119761631. Covering the concepts and fundamentals of efficient energy systems, this volume, written and edited by a global team of experts, also goes into the practical applications that can be utilized across multiple industries, for both the engineer and the student. *NOW AVAILABLE!*

Electrical and Electronic Devices, Circuits, and Materials: Technical Challenges and Solutions, edited by Suman Lata Tripathi, Parvej Ahmad Alvi, and Umashankar Subramaniam, ISBN 9781119750369. Covering every aspect of the design and improvement needed for solid-state electronic devices and circuit and their reliability issues, this new volume also includes overall system design for all kinds of analog and digital applications and developments in power systems. *NOW AVAILABLE!*

Green Energy: Solar Energy, Photovoltaics, and Smart Cities, edited by Suman Lata Tripathi and Sanjeevikumar Padmanaban, ISBN 9781119760764. Covering the concepts and fundamentals of green energy, this volume, written and edited by a global team of experts, also goes into the practical applications that can be utilized across multiple industries, for both the engineer and the student. *NOW AVAILABLE!*

Check out these other related titles from Scrivener Publishing

CONVERGENCE OF DEEP LEARNING IN CYBER-IOT SYSTEMS AND SECURITY, Edited by Rajdeep Chakraborty, Anupam Ghosh, Jyotsna Kumar Mandal and S. Balamurugan, ISBN: 9781119857211. In-depth analysis of Deep Learning-based cyber-IoT systems and security which will be the industry leader for the next ten years.

MACHINE INTELLIGENCE, BIG DATA ANALYTICS, AND IOT IN IMAGE PROCESSING: Practical Applications, Edited by Ashok Kumar, Megha Bhushan, José A. Galindo, Lalit Garg and Yu-Chen Hu, ISBN: 9781119865049. Discusses both theoretical and practical aspects of how to harness advanced technologies to develop practical applications such as drone-based surveillance, smart transportation, healthcare, farming solutions, and robotics used in automation.

MACHINE LEARNING TECHNIQUES AND ANALYTICS FOR CLOUD SECURITY, Edited by Rajdeep Chakraborty, Anupam Ghosh and Jyotsna Kumar Mandal, ISBN: 9781119762256. This book covers new methods, surveys, case studies, and policy with almost all machine learning techniques and analytics for cloud security solutions.

Printed and bound by CPI Group (UK) Ltd, Croydon, CR0 4YY

27/10/2024

14580470-0001